WHAT OTHERS ARE SA
REFLECTIONS ON RISK III

REFLECTIONS ON RISK

VOLUME III

ASA INSTITUTE FOR RESEARCH AND INNOVATION

ANNIE SEARLE & ASSOCIATES LLC

EDITED BY EMILY OXENFORD

TAUTEGORY PRESS
SEATTLE, WASHINGTON

Printed in the United States of America

First edition: December 2015

Tautegory Press, Seattle, Washington USA

Printing History

All research notes here were previously published as "ASA Research Notes" in ASA Newsletters ©Annie Searle & Associates LLC and at its website www.anniesearle.com, from August 2014 through August 2015.

USA Library of Congress Control Number: 2015960608

ISBN # 978-0-9839347-7-6

Cover design by Jesse Brown

Contents

Forward

Nearly two years ago, the ASA Institute for Risk and Innovation published the second volume in the Reflections on Risk, marking our commitment to publish as more than a one-trick pony. The series of research notes written by multiple authors, all focused generally on key operational risk issues in the public and private sectors, made available first in our newsletter and on our website has exceeded our expectations. The third volume, with 16 different authors, extends the reach of the first two volumes, looking not only at risk-related issues of our time, but also at ethical dimensions of issues such as identity management, culture risk, privacy and security.

Eight of the research notes were written by our last ASA research associate, Divya Yadav (2013-2014). The others are originally papers submitted in graduate courses I teach that generally investigate the effect high risk and financial loss upon organizational outcomes as well as the impact of technology upon ethics, policy and law.

Finally, I would like to thank Emily Oxenford, editor of ASA News & Notes, our monthly newsletter, as well as the designer and production editor of this and the last volume of Reflections on Risk. She has streamlined the production process significantly, by editing the research notes before they first appear in

ASA News & Notes and on the website. She has provided forms of consistency and constancy to authors and to me that make the production of both publications possible.

I am now teaching full time in the MSIM program for the Information School at the University of Washington, and look forward to the next wave of research notes, including ones submitted by risk professionals around the globe. Extending our borders is a high priority for the next volume.

Annie Searle

December 2015

The Contributors

Heather M. Brammer received her Bachelor of Science degree from Texas Tech University, majoring in psychology, French and international marketing. She also attended business school in France and the United Kingdom. Heather is currently employed as the Knowledge Manager and Knowledge Architect for the IT department at The Boeing Company. Her past work experience includes building a knowledge framework for the Ministry of Defence in the United Kingdom, and creating a data library for the City of Seattle's Department of Planning and Development. She received a Master of Science in Information Management degree from the University of Washington in 2015.

Justin Brecese holds a Master of Science in Information Management degree from the University of Washington, and a Master of Liberal Arts from the University of South Florida. Other credentials include academic certificates in information security risk management and digital forensics, as well as a number of industry certifications. His recent research focus has been in computer forensics. His professional experience includes city and federal government work in cybersecurity incident response, forensic analysis, training program development, IT governance and emergency management/disaster response policy; and as a consultant on cybersecurity risk in the aviation and aerospace industry. Currently Justin is a federal employee working in incident response, as well as a network security instructor at a community college.

Brooke Brisbois is a user experience research scientist for the Pacific Northwest National Laboratories, where she researches and develops interesting ways of visualizing information. She is also interested in cybersecurity, cyber-physical infrastructure, and robotics. She recently graduated from the University of Washington with a Master of Science in Information Management degree, where she was a National Science Foundation CyberCorps Scholar. She holds a Bachelor of Fine Arts degree in graphic design and a Bachelor of Arts degree in art history.

John Cann is professional taxonomist with an extensive background in cataloging. He received his Bachelor of Arts degree from the University of California, Irvine in psychology and studio art. After working several years at libraries he decided to pursue his Master's degree in Library and Information Science at San Jose State University. John's career has focused on Digital Asset Management for companies such as DreamWorks and Turner Broadcasting. He is currently on sabbatical from the Master of Science in

Information Management program at the University of Washington.

Matthew Christian received his Bachelor of Science degree in manufacturing and supply chain management from Western Washington University. While working towards his undergraduate degree Matthew completed a six-month manufacturing internship in Guangzhou, China. He received his Master of Science in Information Management degree from the University of Washington in 2015 while working as a demand planning analyst for PACCAR, and continues to work for the same company as an inventory control unit manager. His interests include operations and supply chain management, business intelligence, data visualization, and operational risk management.

Katharine Gallagher holds a Bachelor of Arts degree in business administration with a concentration in information systems, and a Master of Science in Information Management degree from the University of Washington. She currently works for Seattle City Light as a business intelligence analyst and is involved in projects related to data mart development, reporting, and data visualization.

Katherine Hagan graduated from the South Dakota School of Mines and Technology with a Bachelor's of

Science in Interdisciplinary Sciences in 2004. After pursuing a number of different career paths, her work as a multi-site office coordinator at Northrop Grumman inspired her to pursue higher education in the IT field and she completed her Master of Science in Information Management from the University of Washington in 2013. Katherine currently works in Seattle as the Content Manager for Content Harmony. She is involved with the information management of a diverse range of clients, responsible for creation and editing of high-quality web content.

Uma Joshi received her Bachelor of Science in Mechanical Engineering from the University of Maryland, and completed her Master of Science in Information Management from the University of Washington in 2014. She works at The Boeing Company as a systems integration engineer and project manager. Outside of work, she co-owns a software company with her husband which develops communication systems for physicians, and provides consultation on system taxonomy, user interface design and project manages clients. In her free time, she volunteers with Engineers without Borders and is most currently working on an agricultural sustainment design for farmers in Mozambique.

Mike Kelly is a program manager at ExtraHop Networks, where he focuses on information architecture, interaction design, and data visualization. He received his Master of Science in Information Management degree in 2015 and holds a Bachelor of Arts degree in English and Philosophy, both from the University of Washington. He has prior experience doing web development and content management for small businesses.

Kenny Lee is a seasoned technology and risk management professional with over 15 years of experience working with start-ups and Fortune 100 companies. A holder of three certifications: CISSP, CISM, and CEH, he is currently serving as a risk manager with the Enterprise Risk Office at Microsoft advising executives on Strategic, Compliance, and Operational risks. He received his Bachelor of Art from Washington State University majoring in Management Information Systems, and his Master of Science in Information Management from the Information School at University of Washington in 2015.

Andrew Magnusson is an information security professional and received his Master of Science in Information Management degree from the University of Washington iSchool in 2015. He has a Bachelor of Arts degree in philosophy from Clark University, and a Master of Arts degree in philosophy from the University of Connecticut. He has over a decade of experience in aspects of information security ranging from security operations to risk management and has prepared several in-depth security research papers for institutional clients. He is a deployment and integration consultant with Core Security Technologies, Inc.

Kris Tomasovic Nelson is a Senior Vice President of Research at Palisade Capital Management, where she directs equity investments in the consumer sector. During her investment career, Kris has analyzed hundreds of companies across multiple industries, looking for superior business strategies and sustainable competitive advantages. She has a deep interest in data analytics and its effect on business processes and profits. To further that interest and complement her investing experience, she recently received her Master of Science in Information Management from the University of Washington. Kris received her undergraduate degree, a Bachelor of Science in accounting, from Villanova University.

Malavika Ravi received her Bachelor of Science in Computer Science and Engineering with an emphasis in technology management from the University of California – Los Angeles in 2012. She graduated in May 2015 with a Master of Science in Information Management degree, specializing in data science and analytics from the University of Washington, where she received the prestigious Archer Award, conferred for exceptional achievement as a student and as future information management professional. In August 2015, she joined PwC in the IT Advisory group as a consulting associate.

Casey Rodgers received a Master of Science in Information Management from the University of Washington's Information School and holds a Bachelor of Arts in sociology from the same institution. He specializes in information security and risk management focusing on vulnerability assessment, threat analysis, and tabletop exercises. Casey has information security experience working in the U.S. Congress, academia, and the private sector as a consultant.

Carolyn Tweedy holds a Master of Science in Information Management degree from the University of Washington, and a Bachelor of Science in Mathematics from Westminster College. For the last six years, she has worked for Fortune 500 companies, creative agencies, and in the non-profit sector architecting usable technologies for a global audience. She is currently a User Experience Designer at a small creative agency in Denver, Colorado.

Divya Yadav as a risk consultant for PwC, Seattle, and previously worked for three years as a software

developer with multinational corporations like
Mahindra Satyam and HCL Technologies in India.
Her interests lie with risk management, information
architecture and program management. She received
her Master of Science in Information Management
from University of Washington in 2014 and Bachelor
of Science in electronics and communications from
UP Technical University, India.

Emily Oxenford was ASA's research associate for the
academic year of 2010-2011, during her final year in
the Master of Science of Information Management at
the University of Washington. She is a contributing
author to the first volume of Reflections on Risk
published in 2012, and edited the second volume
published in 2014. Emily currently works as a senior
research analyst for Moss Adams LLP, a Seattle-based
accounting and consulting firm, performing a wide
variety of financial and business research services.

Chapter I
Cybersecurity

Not So Smart

Smart Grid and Cybersecurity Challenges of the Department of Energy

Brooke R. Brisbois

August 2014

Abstract: Brooke explores the challenges faced by the Department of Energy with regard to smart grid technology and cybersecurity. In particular, she discusses the policy issues surrounding the problems.

The Department of Energy (DOE) plays a pivotal role in the critical infrastructure of the U.S. It is charged with not only the regulation and generation of the nation's power supply, but the protection of the energy infrastructure as well. Before the rise of the personal computer, Internet, and general digital age, the DOE's focus was on nuclear energy, nuclear attack, and the Cold War. Today, remnants of that era still linger on the DOE's website: the "About Us" page states that they are "working to ensure America's Energy Future, Scientific & Technological Leadership, Nuclear Security and to resolve the environmental legacy of the cold war."[1] Curiously absent from this statement is any mention of cybersecurity or cyberattack. This is remarkable because cybersecurity is arguably the DOE's number one concern, due to the vulnerability of legacy industrial control systems, the widespread implementation of smart grids, and poorly managed cybersecurity practices.

Before the DOE's concerns can be addressed, however, a clear picture of the department itself must be given. As stated on its website, part of the DOE's mission is to "ensure America's security and prosperity by addressing its energy, environmental and nuclear challenges."[2] This mission statement gives a tall order; the department is essentially expected to guarantee America's security and prosperity with regard to any issues in the energy sector. Moreover, the mission statement does not address *how* the department should be doing any of these things, except through "transformative science and technology solutions."[3]

To further demonstrate the sheer size and criticality of their mission, a clearer view of the energy sector landscape in the U.S. must be given. Begin by considering how many types of energy the U.S. is involved with. Oil, natural gas, and electricity are a few. Now delve deeper into one of those areas–try the electric utility sector. According to *Electricity Regulation in the U.S.: A Guide,* the U.S. electric industry "comprises over 3,000 public, private, and cooperative utilities, more than 1,000 independent power generators, three regional synchronized power grids, eight electric reliability councils, about 150 control-area operators, and thousands of separate engineering, economic, environmental, and land-use regulatory authorities."[4] In addition to the variety of different organizations within the industry, there is variety of another kind: industrial control systems, old and new, some state-of-the-art and others woefully old, all needed to monitor the flow of electricity through about 211,000 miles of transmission lines in the U.S.[5] Within these industrial control systems lie the two interconnected problems that currently plague the DOE: smart grids and cybersecurity.

In 2009, the American Recovery and Reinvestment Act was created in order to encourage economic growth. Spurred by this incentive, the DOE invested more than $31 billion toward clean energy projects throughout the U.S., many of which were smart grid-related projects.[6] As explained on the government's Smart Grid website, a smart grid is an electric grid, consisting of not only the technology that has existed since the 1890s (such as transmission lines, substations, and transformers), but the technology of today as well (such as computers, sensors, and automation).[7] Updating legacy systems to include smart grids is a necessity in the digital age; yet doing so brings a host of new problems. Brian Smith of *Smart Grid News* illuminates these issues, explaining,

"The challenge with cybersecurity and smart grid is that there is no finish line...not one that remains constant throughout the life of the system being protected. Adversaries and threats evolve constantly and new vulnerabilities can be discovered at any time."[8] This brand-new technology is ever changing, and so are the cybersecurity threats.

Smart grids are only a part of the DOE's cybersecurity problem. A majority of the 256 incidents that the Industrial Control Systems Cyber Emergency Response Team (ICS-CERT) responded to in 2013 were detected in organizations within the energy sector, some smart grid attacks and others not.[9] Incidents like these are a growing concern within the energy sector due to cyberattacks becoming more sophisticated in nature, as well as originating from increasingly organized (and militarized) sources. In a statement to the Senate Committee on Armed Services, General Keith B. Alexander advocated the importance of cybersecurity, explaining that the energy sector and other elements of critical infrastructure are specifically being targeted by foreign nation-states.[10] *Aljazeera America* reporter Michael Pizzi described the biggest fear associated with cybersecurity as one in which "enemy hackers...could infiltrate the U.S. power grid, shutting down government agencies, crashing planes into buildings, and grinding the economy to a halt."[11] Though nothing of this sort has happened *yet*, Pizzi highlights the opinion of security experts, who say a "large-scale attack on the U.S. power grid that could inflict mass casualties is within the realm of possibility."[12]

The DOE is not only facing challenges due to the mere presence of these threats and vulnerabilities, but also because of the way they are handling them. Though there are numerous standards, documents, and guidelines about smart grids and cybersecurity, there is no single, unifying standard for responding to these challenges. For example, a company that provides electric utilities can look to the National Institute of Standards and Technology (NIST) for cybersecurity guidelines, ICS-CERT or any private cybersecurity vendor for recommendations, the Federal Energy Regulatory Commission (FERC) for regulations, and the Department of Homeland Security (DHS), ICS-CERT, or any number of local or regional organizations for help with attacks. This complex mix of guidelines, agencies, and regulations cannot even be found in one place; the "Standards and Interoperability" section on the government Smart Grid website only mentions NIST, while the DOE's Cybersecurity Risk Management Process site page also mentions NIST as well as the North

American Electric Reliability Corporation (NERC) critical infrastructure cybersecurity standards.[13] Any kind of escalation procedure or need to report and incident to DHS or ICS-CERT is not explicitly mentioned on the DOE's website.[14]

The absence of clear guidelines, explicit communication channels, and a unified incident response procedure makes the issues of cyberattack and cybersecurity an almost insurmountable problem for the DOE. In order to address these issues, an unambiguous plan for cybersecurity must be implemented. The DOE currently has two documents that attempt to do this: the aforementioned *Electricity Subsector Cybersecurity Risk Management Process* and the *Roadmap to Achieve Energy Delivery Systems Cybersecurity*. The issue with both of these documents is that they lack specificity. The first is a risk management framework, and as such is intended to scale to the size of the organization that is implementing it.[15] It is quite coy about mandating actual cybersecurity requirements, and instead only tells the organization how to *determine* its requirements. Conversely, the *Roadmap* has clear goals and milestones with regard to cybersecurity, but again lacks well-defined actions to be executed in order to achieve those goals.

Perhaps to address this lack of clarity, President Obama issued two documents in 2013 that addressed the issue of cybersecurity in critical infrastructure in the U.S., with particular regard to communications and incident reporting. The first document is an executive order entitled "Improving Critical Infrastructure Cybersecurity" and the other is a Presidential Policy Directive/PDD-21 on the subject of "Critical Infrastructure Security and Resilience." Both address the challenges brought forth previously: the need for more coordinated efforts in cybersecurity across critical infrastructure entities. However, neither of these documents are mentioned in the "Cybersecurity Risk Management Process" on the DOE's website.

Additionally, these executive directives read much like the NIST framework; there are orders addressed to specific departments (i.e., DHS, etc.), but these are rather vague statements that qualify *what* but not *how*. For example, the Presidential Policy Directive states, under Strategic Imperative 1) Refine and Clarify Functional Relationships across the Federal Government to Advance the National Unity of Effort to Strengthen Critical Infrastructure Security and Resilience:

As part of this refined structure, there shall be two national critical infrastructure centers operated by

DIIS - one for physical infrastructure and another for cyber infrastructure. They shall function in an integrated manner and serve as focal points for critical infrastructure partners to obtain situational awareness and integrated, actionable information to protect the physical and cyber aspects of critical infrastructure. Just as the physical and cyber elements of critical infrastructure are inextricably linked, so are the vulnerabilities. Accordingly, an integration and analysis function (further developed in Strategic Imperative 3) shall be implemented between these two national centers.[16]

This section outlines what needs to be done (create two national critical infrastructure centers) and what they will do, but does not give any specific direction as to what an "integration and analysis function" that is needed would actually look like.[17] The executive order reads similarly, stating that the Secretary, Attorney General, and Director of National Intelligence should together establish a process that disseminates cybersecurity reports produced.[18] There is no mention of what *kind* of "cyber threat information" should be reported in this process, just that it should be reported.[19] It is also notable that in the Definitions sections of both documents "cybersecurity," "cyberattack," or "cyberwar" are nowhere to be found. Though these presidential directives do give more direction than previous documents on the subject, there is still a substantial lack of the explicit guidance that is much needed in this sector. A recommendation to the DOE would be to clearly define cybersecurity, and cyberattacks and cyberwarfare in particular. It is of the utmost importance that any organization in the energy sector, regardless of its size, know what constitutes a critical cyberattack or an act of cyberwarfare, and when these incidences should be escalated and to whom.

In addition to better cybersecurity and smart grid guidelines, the energy sector needs more personnel versed in cybersecurity. While there are incentive programs, such as the National Science Foundation's CyberCorps, which offers to finance education in return for government service, the numbers are not growing to meet the need fast enough.[20] *Businessweek* writer Dune Lawrence discovered that while there is a big industry demand for cybersecurity, the wages do not typically reflect this, especially in government, where the need for new "cyberwarriors" is arguably the most critical.[21] It is becoming commonplace for government to lose talented cyberprofessionals to government contractors and private companies that can afford to pay more.[22]

However, this problem could be mitigated if government worked more closely with contractors and private companies on a strategically unified cybersecurity plan. This idea is not new to the department, and is specified in the *Roadmap* as a long-term milestone: In eight to ten years, there should be a "significant increase in the number of workers skilled in energy delivery, information systems, and cybersecurity employed by industry."[23] In the same period, the DOE also expects that "private sector investment will surpass Federal investment in developing cybersecurity solutions for energy delivery systems."[24] These two goals can be met if government scholarship programs are changed. Instead of allowing students to work only for government entities, the scholarship should allow students to work for any cybersecurity position within the U.S. energy sector. Scholarships such as these would attract more people to the field through the prospect of the high income that is expected from government contractors and private companies.[25]

The DOE is one of the most critical departments in the U.S., but it also faces some of the most critical challenges, most notably those linked to the country's move into the digital age. Smart grids and cybersecurity are not only pressing issues now, but will continue to be for years to come. If the DOE can improve its incident response and communication strategies, as well as increase cybersecurity manpower, the risks to the nation's critical infrastructure can be significantly reduced, both now and in the future.

---

1 "About Us." U.S. Department of Energy. n.d. Accessed Apr. 2014
    <www.energy.gov>.

2 Ibid.

3 Ibid.

4 *Electricity Regulation in the US: A Guide*. RAP Online. Mar. 2011. Accessed
    Apr. 2014 <www.raponline.org>.

5 *Roadmap to Achieve Energy Delivery Systems Cybersecurity*. Energy Sector
    Control

Systems Working Group. Sep.2011. Accessed Apr. 2014 <www.energy.gov>

6 Ibid.

7 "What is the Smart Grid?" U.S. Department of Energy. n.d. Accessed Apr.

2014 <www.smartgrid.gov>.

8 Smith, Brian. "The 3 kinds of Cybersecurity Every Utility Needs (And A
    Reference

Architecture You Need To Know About)." SmartGridNews.com. 27 Mar. 2014.
    Accessed Apr. 2014 <www.smartgridnews.com>.

9 *ICS-CERT Monitor*. U.S. Department of Homeland Security. Oct-Dec. 2013.

Accessed Apr. 2014 <ics-cert.us-cert.gov>.

10 "Statement of General Keith B. Alexander Commander U.S. Cyber Command
    Before the Senate Committee on Armed Services." U.S. Department of
    Defense. 12 Mar. 2013. Accessed Apr. 2014 <www.defense.gov>.

11 Pizzi, Michael. "Cyberwarfare Greater Threat to U.S. Than Terrorism, Say
    Security

Experts." *Aljazeera America*. Al Jazeera America, LLC. 7 Jan. 2014. Accessed Apr.
    2014 <www.america.aljazeera.com>.

12 Ibid.

13 "Standards and Interoperability" U.S. Department of Energy. n.d. Accessed
    Apr. 2014 <www.smartgrid.gov>.

14 "Cybersecurity Risk Management Process." U.S. Department of Energy. n.d.
    Accessed Apr. 2014 <www.energy.gov>.

15 *Electricity Subsector Cybersecurity Risk Management Process*. U.S. Department
    of Energy. May 2012. Accessed Apr. 2014 <www.energy.gov>.

16 Obama, Barak. "Presidential Policy Directive - Critical Infrastructure Security
    and Resilience."

White House. 12 Feb. 2013. Accessed Apr. 2014 <www.whitehouse.gov>.

17 Ibid.

18 Obama, Barak. "Executive Order: Improving Critical Infrastructure Cybersecurity." White House. 12 Feb. 2013. Accessed Apr. 2014 <www.whitehouse.gov>.

19 Ibid.

20 Lawrence, Dune. "The U.S. Government Wants 6,000 New 'Cyberwarriors' by 2016."

Businessweek. 15 Apr. 2014. Accessed Apr. 2014 <www.businessweek.com>

21 Ibid.

22 Ibid.

23 *Roadmap to Achieve Energy Delivery Systems Cybersecurity.*

24 Ibid.

25 Lawrence, Dune.

Impact of Data Breaches

Divya Yadav

January 2014

Abstract: Data breach has become prevalent across large, mid-size or small business. With the growing emphasis towards big data companies are more than ever securing huge amounts of data that are used for brand segmentation and targeting. But in this process companies forget that they have a bigger responsibility of safeguarding this data from malicious attacks and hacks that exploit user information. This paper reflects on strategies that most organizations can employ to minimize the impact of data breach and pro-actively protect themselves for such breaches and thefts.

Introduction

A data breach is an incident where confidential, private and sensitive financial or personal identifiable information has been compromised by unauthorized access. Data breaches have become a pervasive problem and organizations have a lot at stake. A new study commissioned by Scott & Scott, LLP, a law and technology services firm focusing on data privacy and network security, confirms that the effects of data breaches are far reaching and can be detrimental to a company of any size.[1] While corporations continue to strengthen their firewalls and use security and compliance measures to protect themselves from such vulnerabilities but hackers and cyber criminals always seem to find some way or the other. These attackers are of course outside U.S. which makes it all the more difficult for the authorities to catch these criminals and try them in court. *"In a world where data is everywhere, it has become harder than ever for organizations to protect their confidential information. Complex, heterogeneous IT environments make data protection and threat response very difficult."*[2]

Causes of Data Breach

The most common form of data breach that takes place is a targeted attack by external parties. Protecting this huge amount of data from sophisticated hacking techniques can become quite a challenge.[3] *"These targeted attacks are often automated by using malicious code that can penetrate into an organization undetected and export data to remote hacker sites."*[4]

But attacking an IT system with a malicious code or malware is only the first step, data breach is a result of phased out process and for the data breach to be successful or for hackers to get any meaningful information out the data all the phases of the hack needs to be successful. As a study by Symantec shows that most companies focus on preventing incursions but incursion is only a phase and breach can be stopped at any phase to prevent decryption of the data that has been compromised.

- Incursion: This is definitely the first phase when hackers try to break into the company's system through different types of attacks such as SQL injection, malware, password violation, buffer overflow and so on.[5]
- Discovery: Hackers then try to map out organizational systems to scan for places where confidential data is stored.[6]
- Capture: Data that is stored in not strongly encrypted or unprotected system is immediately captured whereas hackers install components called "root kits" to encrypted network access points to capture confidential data that is part of the organization.[7]
- Exfiltration: Confidential data package is sent back to hackers in its encrypted format and now the hackers have to decrypt this data to get meaningful information out of it.[8]

Therefore if organizations focus on all the four phases it becomes easier for them to protect themselves from such infiltrations. Data breach is just not a one step process and its definitely more than just hacking into a system it is also about where and how organizations store their data, how strongly encrypted it is, what kind of user information they decide to store and so on and focusing on all these minute security points can surely help organizations in securing their data.

Recent Trends and Stats

Recent trends and stats in data breach have been very alarming. The scope of infamous Target data breach is still under investigation and the latest figure suggest that data for around 110 million customers was comprised as opposed to the previously reported 40 million that included personal information such as email, names, addresses and debit and credit information including the PIN's. The magnitude of this breach is enormous and is currently under investigation by the federal government. This breach will not only impact Target's quarterly results and profits but poses for it as a greater brand and reputational risk. To mitigate these losses Target is trying to woo customers by offering them additional discounts, free credit card monitoring and identity theft protection. But is this enough for customers? Certainly not, people have a high level of trust and especially target being a "blue chip" company it would be very hard for customers to trust any provider with their information.

Social Media sites have been hacked often in the past two years, case in point twitter and snapchat. In case of snap chat hackers posted customers personal information such as names, email and phone numbers on a public website. Snapchat apologized for this breach but information has already been compromised and hackers can use this information to pose as frauds to extract more sensitive information such as bank account data and so on.

Sony's PlayStation data breach was another significant event that took place in 2011 where customer's stored information such as credit/debit card details, addresses, email id was compromised. Needless to say this hack damaged Sony's reputation and it didn't help its already plunging market worth. Xbox is a market leader in gaming consoles but there was a time when play station lead in this arena, bust such malicious attacks leave long term impacts on minds of the customers which sometimes makes the path to recovery very difficult of not impossible.

Studies by Symantec have shown that data breach can happen across any sector. Organizations may have installed highest form of encryption methods but most of them get attacked due to a minor unprotected data point. Some of the stats presented below by Symantec point indicate the pervasive nature of these data thefts.

- Most data breach victims fell prey because they were found to possess an (often easily) exploitable weakness rather than because they were pre-identified for attack; 79 percent of victims were targets of opportunity, and 96 percent of attacks were not highly difficult- 2012 Data Breach Investigations Report (DBIR), Verizon Business, April 2012.[9]

- The average cost per record of a healthcare data breach in 2011 was $240, which is 24 percent higher than average. Healthcare data breaches are the fourth highest by industry, behind the financial, pharmaceutical and communications sectors.[10]

For more trends and exact numbers in data theft please refer to this study by Symantec http://www.indefenseofdata.com/data-breach-trends-stats/.

Business Impact

Data Breaches not only cost financial loss for companies but offer a huge reputational loss risk. Organizations build customers trust over a long period of time and this trust can be lost in a matter of minutes and can be very hard for them to regain. Many breaches result in class action lawsuits and litigations which can take years to resolve. Brand Risk is another potential risk companies might suffer where public perception of the brand becomes negative and it may take time to rebuild brand equity.

Prevention

Cost of data breaches can be very high from notification and business loss to tangible ones like brand and customer loyalty. According to a 2010 study by Ponemon total data breach costs have grown every year since 2006, and in 2010, data breaches cost companies an average of $214 per compromised record, up $10 (5 percent) from last year.[11]

But data breach can always be prevented if right measures are taken at every level and policies and processes are in place.

1. Securing more than just IT systems- Organizations sometimes forget to look beyond their IT systems such employee exit policies, remote access, on and off data storage and so on. Policies and procedures for these processes should be in place to fully secure an organization's working environment.[12]

2. A comprehensive breach preparedness plan should be prepared in advance, as it will equip management and employees to make faster decisions when a breach occurs. When a data breach of massive proportions occurs it leaves the entire organization in shock and most people aren't aware what to do. This

readiness plan will help them overcome such paralysis.[13]

3. Employees should be fully aware of the BYOD policies or in case if they are issued office laptops how to safeguard critical information in those systems. In case a system security is compromised they should quickly report it to the higher authorities so that necessary steps can be taken.

4. Data minimization is a good practice since hackers can't get access that is not stored in the systems. Organizations should refrain from collecting information that is not required and clean the system on regular basis of irrelevant data.[14]

5. Continuous risk assessment and audit of internal controls is required to understand if the company is equipped with dealing newer and upcoming risk threats or vulnerabilities.[15] Performing regular penetration and vulnerability testing also helps identify the weaknesses in the system.

6. It is important to be up to date with the latest security patches and updates. These are especially by targeted by hackers and can pose as a severe security flaw in the system.[16]

7. It is important to define security requirements upfront with vendors and organizations should have

access and control of offshore data storage or services at all times.[17]

Conclusion

Data breach can occur in any sector be it retail, healthcare, IT or finance. But integrating security in the long-term risk management[18] and business goals is extremely important for organizations to come out of such targeted attacks. Complex systems make it harder to secure every data point and hackers are on a continuous lookout for an unlocked point through which they can spread their attacks. While it is an enormous task but there shouldn't be any level of complacency when designing the security check points for systems through which transaction of sensitive information takes place. It will forever remain a work in progress and organizations will have to continuous monitor their systems as a single lapse could cost a lot which will make the road to recovery a mammoth task.

---

1 "The Business Impact of Data Breach." Scott & Scott, LLP. N.D. Accessed Jan. 2014 <www.scottandscottllp.com>.

2 *Anatomy of a Data Breach Why Breaches Happen and What to Do About It.* Symantec. Aug. 2011. Accessed Jan. 2014 <www.symantec.com>.

3 Ibid.

4 Ibid.

5 Ibid.

6 Ibid.

7 Ibid.

8 Ibid.

9 *Gartner Top Predictions for 2012: Control Slips Away.* 2011. Accessed Jan. 2014
   <www.indefenseofdata.com>.

10 Ibid.

11 "Data Breach Prevention Tips". Kroll. N.D. Accessed Jan. 2014
   <www.kroll.com>.

12 Ibid.

13 Ibid.

14 Ibid.

15 Ibid.

16 Ibid.

17 Ibid.

18 Bowers, Tom. "Security as Business Risk: How Data Breaches Impact Bottom
   Lines." Experian. Sep. 2011. Accessed Jan. 2014
   <www.annualcreditreport.experian.com>.

Social Media & Terrorism

Kenny Lee

August 2015

Abstract: This paper examines the exploitation of the power of social media by terrorists in disseminating propaganda and recruitment, and explores the implications of the possibility of keeping the terrorists out of social media through the lens of the law and ethic.

Introduction

In October 2009, Colleen LaRose, also known as Jihad Jane, was arrested in Philadelphia International Airport after she returned from Europe allegedly trying to conspire with others to assassinate Lars Viks, the Swedish cartoonist who outraged Muslims around the world for drawing a cartoon of the Prophet Muhammad.[1] What is unique about this case is, before leaving the country, LaRose had converted from a typical hometown American woman into a Muslim Extremist without any direct contact with Islam or other Muslim extremists other than watching the propaganda videos posted on YouTube.[2]

There lies the power of the social media platforms such as YouTube, Facebook and Twitter, which have become the most popular vehicles for terrorists to "blast" its messages to the world's audience, be it for recruitments or propaganda.[3] Most recently, ISIS, by far one of the most violent terrorist organizations in the world, has been leveraging social media to display its blatant brutality by posting videos purporting beheadings of its hostages to make demands or threats against other nations and its adversaries. As of November 16, 2014, there have now been five recorded executions of Westerners.[4] ISIS recently even used social media to "debut" its Hollywood style propaganda video called "Flames of War" that "must have been a very compelling teaser for any young Muslim men looking for excitement and adventure."[5] The immediate reaction for most would be "There has got to be a way to stop this!" This reaction is rational as all of us would be happy to see an end to this so that innocent people, such as LaRose, would not become radicalized and turn against their own country under deceived and misguided circumstance. However, keeping the terrorists from social media in this Internet age proves to be easier said than done. In this paper, I will explore the implications of the possibility of keeping the terrorists out of social media through the lens of the law and ethic.

The Power of Social Media
Social media has seen its phenomenal growth in popularity in recent years. YouTube boasts one billion users in 2014 with 100 hours of video uploaded per

minute and over four billion views per day![6] What is powerful about YouTube is not just a site for storing videos, but the social networking capability that comes with it. Terrorists could monitor conversations of their videos after posting them, could reach out and recruit those who sympathize their cause. With a click of a button, they could monitor the number of times the videos have been viewed, when they are viewed, from which countries, whether they become a subscriber or not, and even the gender of the viewers. The same analytics that give advertisers the ability to gauge the effectiveness of their marketing campaigns benefit the terrorists in the same manner.

Facebook, another hugely successful social media site, has 1.3 billion monthly active users with 640 million minutes spent each month and more than 54 million of Facebook pages, as of June 2014.[7] Similar to YouTube, Facebook provides analytics for pages such as visit count, number of Page Likes, time when a page is viewed, detailed demographic information of the viewers including gender, age, country and language.

Anyone could open an account with YouTube and Facebook with an email address and be able to start publishing contents right away at no cost. It is fast and easy; it is free; and best of all, the users behind the contents can remain anonymous. Indeed, 90 percent of terrorist online activity takes place using social media tools.[8] Social media has become the fertile ground for Islamic extremists and their success has caught many people off-guard including the U.S. government.[9] In a 2008 intelligence report released by the U.S. Army's 304th Military Intelligence Battalion, a chapter titled "Potential for Terrorist Use of Twitter," claimed that Twitter, another social media tool, has been used for both pro and anti-Hezbollah and terrorists could use Twitter to plan and coordinate attacks.[10]

Law

Let us first examine the terrorist use of social media from the law's perspectives. Is posting extremism or violence-promotional videos considered freedom of speech? The First Amendment of the U.S. Constitution protects freedom of speech.[11] Further, the right to freedom of expression is recognized as a human right under Article 19 of the International Covenant on Civil and Political Rights adopted by the United Nations General Assembly.[12] However, freedom of speech does not bestow the right for libel, slander, hate, and incitement among others that are typically determined by using John Stuart Mill's Harm Principle, which is widely, adopted as the "litmus test" for free speech.[13] So the answer is it depends if the posted videos "prevent harm to others" as stated in the Harm Principle. For the videos that incite violence, clearly this is not free speech. In fact, most social media sites have rules against posting such messages, but the effort large depends on end users to take action first by flagging the videos.[14] For those that pass the Harm Principle, social media sites are likely to keep them online since they violate no rules or laws. Indeed, Google fought to defend them even when under pressure from U.S. lawmakers. In 2008, Senator Joseph Lieberman of Connecticut tried to pressure YouTube to remove videos from what he labeled as "Islamist terrorist organizations and their supporters." YouTube removed the ones that promoted hate speech and graphic violence and leave those that meet its guidelines intact. This resulted in an angry letter sent from the Senator to the CEO of Google, Eric Schmidt, demanding the rest of the videos be removed immediately. Nevertheless, the deputy general counsel of Google, Nicole Wong and her colleagues responded by saying, "YouTube encourages free speech and defends everyone's right to express unpopular points of view."[15]

What about passing a law to ban any publication from known terrorist groups regardless of contents? Clearly, this option could potentially save lives. Incidentally, the Senate Committee on Homeland Security and Governmental Affairs led by Senator

Lieberman issued the Violent Islamist Extremism, The Internet and the Homegrown Terrorist Threat in 2008 concluding that "...no cohesive and comprehensive outreach and communications strategy in place to confront this threat...that there is no plan to harness all possible resources including adopting new laws..." Even if a law was crafted, I am doubtful that it would pass constitutionality.[16]

Ethics

From the ethical perspectives, do social media companies have the responsibility to do the right things? While companies removed the contents that are not free speech fairly quickly, should they just shut down all accounts that liken to terrorists and extremists regardless of whether or not their contents violate the Harm Principle? Would this be more proactive in preventing harm to others? What about the media that in some way help amplify the terrorist messages by reporting and rebroadcasting them? When I went to YouTube looking for the ISIS beheading videos, I was not able to find the original, but the edited versions (beheading frames removed) by the media abound.

Most ethical rules call for enhancement of human dignity, peace, happiness, and well-being.[17] Kantianism, a form of deontological ethics, calls for universalizing a maxim that is based on rationality as the ultimate dutifulness. Humanity should be treated not as a means to an end, but always as an end.18 Social media sites are for-profit companies and they need user-generated contents in order to attract other users to come to the sites. One may think that selectively removing contents associated with terrorists and extremists is considered a means to an end. That is to remove non-free speech contents while keeping free speech online so that other people can read them and thus generating more profits for the company through advertising (more people, more money). However, shutting down accounts indiscriminately without consideration of contents could also go against Kantianism because people deserve a universal right to speak up for their concerns. By establishing the "rule of engagement", that is what can and cannot be published, social media companies level the playing field so that everyone has a single set of rules to follow and no one should have special treatments. This places the social media companies in a neutral position, away from political, religious, and other bigotries that for-profit companies would rather eschew.

Consider this hypothetical example of a social media site created by an Islamic minority group in Syria with the goals of exposing the inhumane and brutal treatments of minority by the Bashar al-Assad regime and seeking help for humanitarian aids for their destitute livelihood. They call ISIS and other Islamic militant groups their "brothers" because they share a common enemy, but at no time condone or incite violence as a means to achieve their goals. Should the social media company take down their site? Kantianism would say no because humanity should be well treated universally and rational being would argue that mistreating other people based on their ethnicity is evil. Therefore, providing them a place to voice their plights is ethically acceptable. From this angle, Google had it right when they pushed back on Senator Lieberman's request to remove the contents he did not like.

In contrast with deontology, Utilitarianism is a type of ethics that consider utility, which is the gain or loss of affected parties' values because of the consequences.[19] The principle of utility is that an action is good to the extent that it increases the happiness of the parties in aggregate. Would taking down terrorist and extremist social media sites regardless of contents increase utility, meaning the benefit gained outweighs the drawback? To answer the question, we will need to examine the intents of the contents. For those violent contents that incite fear and promote brutality, they clearly increase the publishers' utility but not the readers. In the context of social media, we can safely assume that the audience is worldwide and thus the utility gained by the publishers would be one-sided.

Let us also look at the same hypothetical example cited above. Taking down such a site would definitely reduce the utility of this Islamic minority group, but it does not necessarily increase or decrease the utility of everyone else. For this reason, Utilitarianism would argue that it is unethical to take this site down because utility is decreased.

What about ethical responsibility of the media? Should they "advertise" the violent videos such as those published by ISIS and help them disseminate their propaganda in the course of reporting the news? It would be irrational to deny the benefits of the media in their societal role to bring about information, facts and stories that are informative and beneficial to readers. After all, the framers of the U.S. Constitution recognized the importance that they put the freedom of the press in the constitution to protect it. However, media could opt for self-censorship by refusing to rebroadcast certain contents such as those posted by ISIS. Recently, Al Jazeera, a Doha based 24-hour news channel, decided not to show any images of ISIS video and suggested other media to do that same, even created a hashtag #ISISmediaBlackout.[20]

A 1994 survey taken by *Times*/Mirror Center for the People and the Press (now the Pew Center) shows 82 percent French, 71 percent British, 68 percent Canadian and 60 percent Americans supported censorship to discourage terrorism.[21] However, as with the First Amendment argument, Terrorists win if we give up our right and freedom. As the late Professor Paul Wilkinson, a world authority in in International Relations and a pioneer of the study of terrorism, said "It is widely recognized that it is important to avoid the mass media being hijacked and manipulated by terrorists, but if the freedom of the media is sacrificed in the name of combating terrorism one has allowed small groups of terrorists to destroy one of the key foundations of a democratic society."[22]

Conclusion

Social media is the cheapest, easiest, yet extremely effective way for terrorist to flaunt their propaganda and will continue to be the case for the foreseeable future. Attempts to quash freedom of speech and freedom of the press in an effort to suppress the terrorist's communication are counterproductive, unjustifiable, and counter to the values of the framers of the U.S. Constitution. If we give up our right, the terrorists win. Cutting off our freedom is never a right answer.

The presence of violent extremists and their propaganda on the Internet actually does provide law enforcement agencies the ability to monitor their online communications to gain intelligence and gather evidence. Homeland Security Project by the Bipartisan Policy Center issued a report in 2012 titled "Countering Online Radicalization in America" shedding light on the importance of monitoring terrorist online communication that "...trying to understand the conversations that happen online and who is involved may be just as important as spying on the terrorist group's leadership..."23 Recognizing the importance of monitoring extremists' online communication, the White House also issued the "Empowering Local Partners to Prevent Violent Extremism in the U.S." calling for investment in intelligence to understand this threat including "closely monitor[ing] the important role the Internet and social networking sites play in advancing violent extremist narratives."24

Government should promote awareness to the public, especially young people, to challenge extremist narratives right in the hotbed of social media and minimize the potentials for radicalization. Although the onslaughts of social media propaganda caught authority by surprise, they are slowly responding to the challenge. Recently, the Department of State created the "Think Again Turn Away" Facebook site[25] and the Twitter account[26] to expose ISIS' crime and urge sympathizers and followers to reject ISIS.

The Homeland Security Project's "Countering Online Radicalization in America" is another example of the government's balanced approach in dealing with this "new frontier" by reducing the supply and demand, and exploiting cyberspace.[27] To reduce supply, the report recommended that government should refrain from engaging wholesale censorship while retaining the capability to aggressively take down websites only if they are foreign-based and when absolutely essential to stop an attack to prevent the loss of life. On reducing demand, the government should invest in partnership with educators, parents, and communities to create awareness about online radicalization and to become more effective and creditable messengers. Finally, exploiting cyberspace requires the increase in cyberspace training for law enforcement agencies so that they are better equipped and ready to respond to online threats. Further, the clarification of legal framework in terms of when and how government is permitted to monitor and collect online communications is needed in addition to periodic review of scope and appropriateness of such actions.

1 Grand Jury. "U.S. of America v. Colleen R. LaRose." U.S. District Court for the Eastern District of Pennsylvania . *NBC Philadelphia*. 4 Mar. 2010. Accessed Nov. 2014 <www.media.nbcphiladelphia.com>.

2 Shiffman, John. "Jane's Jihad: From Abuse to a Chat Room, a Martyr is Made." *Reuters*. 7 Dec. 2012. Accessed Nov. 2014 <www.thomsonreuters.com>.

3 Tadjdeh, Yasmin. "Government, Industry Countering Islamic State's Social Media Campaign." *National Defense Magazine*. Dec. 2014. Accessed Nov. 2014 <www.nationaldefensemagazine.org>.

4 Thompson, Mark. "Peter Kassig's Powerful Silence Before ISIS Beheaded Him." *Time*. 17 Nov. 2014. Accessed Nov. 2014 <www.time.com>.

5 Tapson, Mark. "ISIS Ignites 'Flames of War'." *Frontpage Mag*. 22 Sep. 2014. Accessed Nov. 2014 <www.frontpagemag.com>.

6 Smith, Craig. "By the Numbers: 120+ Amazing YouTube Statistics." DMR. 20 Mar. 2014. Accessed Nov. 2014 <www.expandedramblings.com>.

7"Facebook Statistics." Statistic Brain Research Institute. 1 Jul. 2014. Accessed Mar. 2015 <www.statisticbrain.com>.

8 Noguchi, Yuki. "Tracking Terrorists Online." *The Washington Post*. 19 Apr. 2006. Accessed Nov. 2014 <www.washingtonpost.com>.

9 "CNN -Terrorists Use YouTube." YouTube. 6 Jan. 2010. Accessed Nov. 2014 <www.youtube.com>.

10 304th MI Bn OSINT. *Sample Overview: al Qaida-Like Mobile Discussions & Potential Creative Uses*. Federation of American Scientists. 16 Oct. 2008. Accessed Nov. 2014 <www.fas.org>.

11 "U.S. Constitution, Amendment 1." Cornell University Law School. N.D. Accessed Nov. 2014 <www.law.cornell.edu>.

12 General Assembly of the United Nations. International Covenant on Civil and Political Rights. 19 Dec. 1966. United Nations. Accessed Nov. 2014 <www.treaties.un.org>.

13 van Mill, David, "Freedom of Speech." *The Stanford Encyclopedia of Philosophy, Winter 2012 Edition*. Dec. 2012. Edward N. Zalta (ed.). Accessed Nov. 2014 <www.plato.stanford.edu>.

14 "YouTube Community Guidelines." YouTube. Nov. 2014. Accessed Mar. 2014 <www.youtube.com>.

15 Rosen, Jeffrey, and Wittes, Benjamin. *Constitution 3.0: Freedom and Technological Change*. Washington, D.C.: Brookings Institution Press. 2011.

16 "Violent Islamist Extremism, the Internet, and the Homegrown Terrorist Threat." Council on Foreign Relations. 8 May 2008. Accessed Nov. 2014 <www.cfr.org>.

17 Baase, Sara. *A Gift of Fire: Social, Legal, and Ethical Issues For Computing Technology (4th Edition)*. Upper Saddle River, NJ: Pearson. 2013.

18 Ibid.

19 Moore, Adam D. *Information Ethics: Privacy, Property, and Power (1st ed.).* Seattle: University of Washington Press. 2005.

20 Yan, Holly. "Showing Off Its Crimes: How ISIS Flaunts its Brutality as Propaganda." *CNN.* 4 Sep. 2014. Accessed Nov. 2014 <www.cnn.com>.

21 Silantieva, Okasana. "How Does Media Coverage of a Terrorist Act Depend on the Ethical System Which Media Presents?" MA Multimedia Journalism, Bournemouth University. 2003. Accessed Nov. 2014 <www.academia.edu>

22 Wilkinson, Paul. "The Media and Terrorism: A Reassessment." *Terrorism and Political Violence, Volume 9, Issue 2.* 1997.

23 *ICS-CERT Monitor.*

24 The White House. *Empowering Local Partners to Prevent Violent Extremism in the United States.* The White House. Aug. 2011. Accessed Nov. 2014 <www.whitehouse.gov>.

25 "Think Again Turn Away." (n.d.). Facebook. Accessed Nov. 2014 <www.facebook.com>.

26 @ThinkAgain_DOS. Twitter. Accessed Nov. 2014 <www.twitter.com>.

27 *Countering Online Radicalization in America.* National Security Program, Homeland Security Project. Dec. 2012. Accessed Nov. 2014 <www.bipartisanpolicy.org>.

Chapter II
Economics

Astroturfing: 21st Century False Advertising

Katharine Gallagher

December 2014

Abstract: Astroturfing refers to manufacturing public opinions through anonymous Internet comments, stories or websites that promote misinformation in an attempt to sway consumer opinion or behavior. The concept behind astroturfing is not new. As long as there has been economic competition, people and businesses have sought ways to differentiate themselves from their rivals. The term has found its way into popular press recently thanks to New York Attorney General, Eric T. Schneiderman. In September of 2013, he unveiled the results of a yearlong undercover investigation into the practices of reputation management and online false endorsements. This paper discussed how government policies, the law, and individual ethical decision-making can collectively help to make online review sites more reliable for consumers.

When one hears the term astroturfing, the image that likely comes to mind is that of the green synthetic turf found on many sports fields. AstroTurf ® was invented in 1964 as a substitute for the grass that could not survive in indoor stadiums.[1] In 1985, U.S. Senator Lloyd Bentsen gave the term new meaning when, in response to enormous amounts of mail his office received that promoted the interests of insurance companies he said, "a fellow from Texas can tell the difference between grass roots and Astroturf...this is generated mail."[2] Bentsen used the word astroturf often and is credited with establishing its association with deception, particularly within the political arena. In the age of the World Wide Web, the modified term "astroturfing" refers to manufacturing public opinions through anonymous Internet comments, stories or websites that promote misinformation in an attempt to sway consumer opinion or behavior.[3]

The Internet has "once and forever transformed how information is produced, accessed, and distributed" which has made astroturfing more economical and prolific.[4] With the development of Web 2.0, (the second generation of the Internet which combines concepts and technologies that enable user collaboration and the sharing of user generated content,[5] anyone can participate in the creation and dissemination of information by posting his or her own material.[6] This means that fake information can be posted on the web quickly, inexpensively and on a much grander scale.

The subject of astroturfing has found its way into popular press recently thanks to New York Attorney

General, Eric T. Schneiderman. In September of 2013, he unveiled the results of a yearlong undercover investigation into the practices of astroturfing, reputation management, and online false endorsements. The investigation, called Operation Clean Turf, saw representatives of the Attorney General's office posing as the owner of a yogurt shop located in Brooklyn.[7] They contacted well-known search engine optimization (SEO) companies in New York with requests for assistance in combating negative reviews on websites such as Yelp, Google Local, and Citysearch in order to ascertain how astroturfing practices are conducted. The investigation also highlighted several small businesses - for example, a nightclub, a dental office, and beauty salons - that were engaging in false advertising practices. In the end, 19 companies were assigned fines. These ranged from $2,500 to $100,000, for a total of $350,000 in penalties. In addition, all of the firms entered into an assurance of discontinuance[i] with regard to their illegal behavior.

The concept behind astroturfing is not new. As long as there has been economic competition, people and businesses have sought ways to differentiate themselves from their rivals. Sometimes this creates

---

i An assurance in writing that a person will not engage in the same or in similar conduct in the future.

healthy competition and at other times, it can bring about questionable practices. When comparing businesses on the web, how does one know that the information he or she is reading, or perhaps relying on, is in fact legitimate? Some may say that everything on the Internet should be taken with a grain of salt; however, there is evidence that people, particularly consumers, do in fact make assessments based on information that is gleaned from the Web.

Research indicates that consumers rely on reviews to make decisions about products and services. A 2013 study conducted by BrightLocal found that 85 percent of consumers read online reviews for local businesses. The same study indicates that 67 percent of consumers peruse six or fewer reviews before they feel they can trust a business.[8] In another survey by Cone, results indicated that 87 percent of consumers said that a favorable review cemented the decision to make a purchase while a negative review caused them not to press the buy button.[9] A study by Maritz Research learned that 75 percent of participants (there were 3,404) believed that the information posted on rating sites tends to generally be fair.[10]

In the travel industry, one comes to understand just how much clients rely on consumer review sites. When a client receives a prospective itinerary from a travel agency, that person may compare the recommended accommodations' ratings on sites like TripAdvisor. If a hotel or lodge has recently received unfavorable reviews, the client may ask to be booked at a different property. The places a travel agency might recommend are often based on the personal experience of employees, but when a client wants to stay elsewhere and it is a place that unfamiliar to staff, an agency may defer to the clients wishes, but not before issuing a caveat. Customers go to travel agencies for the professional level of travel and trip planning expertise, but those recommendations are sometimes verified by the opinions of strangers.

Given the data provided in these studies and the ease with which reviews can be accessed, people know that reviews influence the decision making process. This is what makes astroturfing so tempting and the reason why some businesses employ it in marketing plans. Evidence of this practice is found in many countries and almost every industry as well as in both small and large organizations.

In 2010 Orlando Figes, a professor of Russian history, decided to post reviews on amazon.co.uk under the pseudonym, Historian. He praised his own books as "fascinating" and "uplifting"[11] while concurrently posting reviews that criticized the writings of fellow historians. One of his peers, Rachel Polonsky, was a recipient of his critiques.[12] Through her own detective work, she surmised that Figes was the author of these fake reviews, but when she confronted him about it, he accused her of libel. Figes later said that his wife was the architect of the comments before later admitting to being the mastermind behind the entire plan. He then apologized, took sick leave from his teaching job and agreed to pay an undisclosed amount for damages and legal fees to all the authors that Historian had reviewed.

At the beginning of 2013, the South Korean technology company, Samsung, hired students to post comments recommending Samsung phones and asked that they write negative reviews about its biggest rival, HTC. Once the Taiwanese Fair Trade Commission began an investigation into Samsung's marketing practices, the company responded by saying that what happened was "'unfortunate' and that there was 'insufficient understanding' of the 'fundamental principles' of the company's online procedures"[13]. The company claimed that it stopped its activities once the investigation was launched, but in reality Samsung hired more people to write more negative posts.[14] As a result, the Taiwanese Fair Trade Commission fined the company $340,000 and two other companies $100,000 each for their contributions to the marketing sham.

Inherently, people know that this myopic thinking is immoral and unethical, even if they are unaware of the fact that astroturfing is illegal. Since the purpose of this behavior is to deceive, moral reasoning would indicate that this is clearly the wrong action to take.[15] Ethically, this practice is negligent because the voluntary choice of one person can have repercussions that spread mistrust within society. In fact, it goes against the utilitarian ideals that promote acting in a way that increases well-being within a community.[16] Yet when it comes to economic gain or an opportunity to boost one's reputation, some are willing to set aside those morals and ethical principles in an effort to attain greater financial status and prestige.

A 2013 Harvard Business School and Boston University study, which focused on Boston area restaurants and Yelp reviews, found that a one star increase on Yelp could translate into a five to nine percent jump in revenue for a restaurant.[17] Not surprisingly, the study also found that businesses with few reviews are more likely to post a review that boosts their image and companies with dwindling reputations are more likely to post fake positive reviews about their businesses. In another study, Christopher Anderson, an associate professor at Cornell University, researched the impact of social media on hospitality industry sites such as Travelocity, TripAdvisor, STR and Review Pro. His findings indicated three key things: 1) the number of consumers who peruse reviews on TripAdvisor before booking a room has steadily increased over time; 2) data from Travelocity indicate that if a hotel increases its ratings by one star—on a five star scale—a hotel can increase the price of a room by eleven percent and maintain its market share; 3) a one percent increase in the reputation score can bring about a half percent increase in occupancy and about a one and a half percent increase in revenue.[18]

Perhaps the most significant factors in astroturfing behavior are the reach and anonymity that is provided by the Internet. Social media platforms such as Facebook and Twitter, blogs, and consumer review sites enable millions to opine on just about any topic. Behind the guise of an online profile, people enjoy an inconspicuousness that may encourage them to act in such as way or voice an opinion they may not normally reveal in a face-to-face environment. Thus, the combination of online consumer behavior, the hope of fiscal reward and the infrastructure of the Internet present an opportunity that some find too hard to resist.

Once the decision has been made to engage in this behavior, astroturfing campaigns can run the gamut from easily implemented, straightforward modes to highly complex methods, necessitating some type of persona management software. On the small-scale side of the spectrum, a business may instruct its employees to create fake profiles and write reviews for social media or consumer review websites. It may even enlist the assistance of an SEO company to increase the number of reviews on a site or drown out any negative information about the company that is currently present on the Internet. This is the kind of behavior that Schneiderman's investigation discovered. When his office's fake yogurt shop called SEO companies for help, those firms offered to write fake reviews and post the comments on review websites. The SEO firms also hired freelance writers from the Philippines, Bangladesh, and Eastern Europe and paid $1 to $10 per review.[19] In addition, the investigation unearthed solicitations for review writers on websites such as craigslist.com, freelancer.com, and oDesk.com. These advertisements were seeking writers who were familiar with Yelp, could produce content without being flagged, and had multiple IP addresses. All of these requests indicated that the businesses that placed the ads knew the practice involved unethical behavior.

On the other end of the spectrum, larger companies that have funds and an understanding of persona management software can "create armies of virtual astroturfers, complete with fake Internet protocol (IP) addresses, non-political interests and online histories."[20] Each profile has a name, email accounts, web pages, and social media outlets, which are updated automatically through retweets, and RSS feeds.[21] In some cases, the operator's various IP addresses are randomized in such a way as to prevent it from appearing that one person is generating many posts. In other instances, each profile will have a static IP address to give the illusion that a fake persona is coming from the same computer every time.[22] The technology enables a relatively small team of humans to disseminate large amounts of misinformation easily and effectively.

Astroturfing is a widespread problem, one that will not be easy to fight. However, through government policies, the law, and individual ethical decision-making, a concerted effort can be made to make review sites more truthful for consumers.

From a policy standpoint, the Federal Trade Commission (FTC) is the entity in the U.S. that is responsible for consumer protection and regulates advertising, both online and offline. In 2009, the Commission updated its Guide to Endorsements and

Testimonials to establish new rules about social media and word-of-mouth marketing. With the new regulation "'consumer generated media outlets,' such as blogs and other Internet media forms" must provide full disclosure of any "material connections" in association with a review.[23] This means that if anyone is paid for or given free products or services in exchange for the promotion of a business, this fact must be made public. The guidelines do not explain how to go about making this disclosure, but it is clear about the penalties, which may be up to $11,000 per infringement.[24]

For the most part, the FTC takes a hands-off approach and tends to let industry regulate itself.[25] Fines will be issued for noncompliance, but only after a warning has been issued. The FTC will only proclaim a practice unfair if injury to the consumer cannot reasonably be avoided.[26] When the Commission does go after a company, it is usually a larger one, which is why the news of Schneiderman's investigation was most welcome. According to Mary Engel (Associate Director for Advertising Practices at the FTC), "certain cases involving smaller local or regional businesses may be more appropriately resolved by a state attorney general's office."[27]

Legal action against astroturfing is rare and it generally does not generate much press; however,

Schneiderman's investigation may begin to change that. Because the defendants agreed to settle with the State of New York, the case does not set a legal precedent, but it is important for several reasons. First, it uncovered and brought to light the fraud, unfair and deceptive trading practices, and false advertising, of several companies at once. Secondly, the "settlements paint a clear roadmap for private litigation targeting what likely is rampant online fraud" and it may set the stage for "class theories to come into play."[28] This means that private litigators can use the platform and arguments established by the attorney general to go after businesses on behalf of an individual or many individuals. Third, as the momentum for the crackdown on astroturfing builds, it may make it easier for larger businesses to become the focus of an investigation. Lastly, the settlement was made public and it garnered a considerable amount of press. Although the fines that were issued were relatively meager in comparison to the large amount of effort that went into documenting this behavior, it does send the message that this practice will not be tolerated.

From a business perspective, what can be learned from Schneiderman's investigation? For firms that are unaware of astroturfing, this may bring about awareness of a problem that has been on the rise for several years. For companies that engage in this unethical and illegal practice, it lets them know that there can be financial risks in terms of fines and a decline in profits. However, the greatest risk that results from astroturfing, and this is hard to quantify, is the decrease in consumer confidence in one's brand and the diminishing reputation that stems from that. Businesses "build their brands on trust, ethics and personal relationships as opposed to product attributes. A few false reviews for a new product or item may be easily forgotten, whereas the value clients place on peer reviews means that falsifying reviews could damage the firm irreparably."[29]

On an individual level, educating people about astroturfing allows them to be aware of the practice, not only to protect themselves as consumers, but also to serve as a reminder of professional ethics, which encompass the relationships with and the responsibilities they have toward customers, coworkers and employers.[30] At the end of the day it is one's ethics that "govern conduct and illuminate character," therefore understanding how astroturfing affects decision making from a consumer perspective can discourage the practice when that same person is considering how to promote a product or service to the public.[31]

According to Gartner, a technology research firm, ten to 15 percent of social media reviews in 2014 will be fake or paid for by companies.[32] However, the firm believes that increased media exposure of astroturfing and better government regulations will help to restore consumer trust in review and ratings websites. Others feel that public shaming will make astroturfing riskier and may therefore reduce its prevalence.[33] Considering these beliefs, the most significant outcome of Schneiderman's actions is that it has put astroturfing on the radar of other state attorney generals and the general public. Increased action from the states will raise the profile of this unethical behavior on the federal level, which means that it will garner more support from the government. With greater support from the government, regulations that are more robust can be put in place to penalize those who engage in this practice. Schneiderman has raised the bar and set a great example for others to follow. It will be interesting to watch how the law continues to adapt to the practice of astroturfing.

1 "History Timeline." AstroTurf. n.d. Accessed Mar. 2014 <www.astroturf.com>.

2 Sager, Ryan. "Keep Off the Astroturf." The New York Times. 18 Aug. 2009. Accessed Mar. 2014 <www.nytimes.com>.

3 Geigner, Timothy. "Fox News Engaged In Institutionalized Astroturfing Of The Internet." Techdirt. 21 Oct. 2014. Accessed Mar. 2014 <www.techdirt.com>.

4 Morozov, Evgeny. To Save Everything, Click Here: The Folly of Technological Solutionism. Public Affairs. 2013.

5 "Web 2.0." Dictionary.com. n.d. Accessed 12 Mar. 2014.
   <dictionary.reference.com>.

6 Tigner, Ronan. "Online Astroturfing and the European Union's Unfair
   Commercial Practices Directive." Université Libre De Bruxelles. 2010.
   Accessed Mar. 2014 <www.droit-eco-ulb.be>.

7 "Fake Yogurt Shop Snares 'Astroturf' Online Reviewers." BBC News. 24 Sep.
   2013. Accessed Mar. 2014 <www.bbc.com>.

8 Anderson, Myles. "Column: Local Search Column." Search Engine Land. 26
   June 2013. Accessed Mar. 2014 <www.searchengineland.com>.

9 "Game Changer: Cone Survey Finds 4-out-of-5 Consumers Reverse Purchase
   Decisions Based on Negative Online Reviews." Cone. 30 Aug. 2011. Accessed
   Mar. 2014 <www.conecomm.com>.

10 Ensing, David. "Customer Rating and Reviews Site: An Upcoming Crisis of
   Confidence?" Maritz Research, July 2013. Accessed Mar. 2014
   <www.maritzresearch.com>.

11 Lea, Richard and Taylor, Matthew. "Historian Orlando Figes Admits Posting
   Amazon Reviews That Trashed Rivals." The Guardian. 24 Apr. 2010.
   Accessed Mar. 2014 <www.theguardian.com>.

12 Wade, Alex. "Good and Bad Reviews: The Ethical Debate Over 'Astroturfing'".
   The Guardian. 9 Jan. 2011. Accessed Mar. 2014 <www.theguardian.com>.

13 Kerr, Dara. "Samsung Probed for Allegedly Bashing Rival HTC Online."
   CNET News. 15 Apr. 2013. Accessed Mar. 2014 <www.cnet.com>.

14 Neal, Ryan W. "Samsung Caught Astroturfing: Taiwanese FTC Fines Galaxy
   S4 Maker $340,000 For Fake Negative Reviews Of HTC Products."
   International Business Times. 24 Oct. 2013. Accessed Mar. 2014
   <www.ibtimes.com>.

15 Moore, Adam D. Information Ethics: Privacy, Property, and Power.
   University of Washington Press, 2005.

16 Quinn, Michael J. Ethics for the Information Age. Pearson/Addison-Wesley,
   2005.

17 Luca, Michael, and Georgios Zervas. "Fake It Till You Make It: Reputation,
   Competition, and Yelp Review Fraud." Institute for Business Innovation,
   University of Berkeley. 17 Sep. 2013. Accessed Mar. 2014
   <www.businessinnovation.berkeley.edu>.

18 Anderson, Chris. "The Impact of Social Media on Lodging Performance."
   Cornell University School of Hotel Administration. 2012. Accessed Mar. 2014
   <www.hotelschool.cornell.edu>.

19 "A.G. Schneiderman Announces Agreement With 19 Companies To Stop
   Writing Fake Online Reviews And Pay More Than $350,000 In Fines." New
   York Attorney General's Office. 23 Sep. 2013. Accessed Mar. 2014

20 Bienkov, Adam. "Astroturfing: What Is It and Why Does It Matter?" The
   Guardian News. 8 Feb. 2012. Accessed Mar. 2014 <www.theguardian.com>.

21 Rockefeller, Happy. "Updated: The HB Gary Email That Should Concern Us
   All." Daily Kos. 16 Feb. 2011. Accessed Mar. 2014 <www.dailykos.com>.

22 Webster, Stephen. "Revealed: Air Force Ordered Software to Manage Army of
   Fake Virtual People." The Raw Story. 18 Feb. 2011. Accessed Mar. 2014
   <www.rawstory.com>.

23 "Internet Law — Advertising and Consumer Protection — FTC Extends
   Endorsement And Testimonial Guides To Cover Bloggers." Harvard Law
   Review. 15 Oct. 2009. Accessed Mar. 2014 <www.harvardlawreview.org>

24 Bangeman, Eric. "More Transparency Coming to Blog Reviews Under New
   FTC Rules." ArsTechnica. 5 Oct. 2009. Accessed Mar. 2014.
   <www.arstechnica.com>.

25 Haynes, A W. "Online Privacy Policies: Contracting Away Control Over
   Personal Information?" Penn State Law Review. 2007.

26 Nehf, James P. "Shopping for Privacy Online: Consumer Decision-Making
   Strategies and the Emerging Market for Information Privacy." University of
   Illinois Journal of Law, Technology & Policy. 2005.

27 Steinmetz, Katy. "The Audacity of Hype Feds States Fight Fake Etail Reviews
   Comments." Time. 24 Sep. 2013. Accessed Mar. 2014
   <www.swampland.time.com>.

28 Brush, Pete. "NY 'Astroturfing' Cases Mark Fertile Ground for Civil Suits."
   Law360. 13 Sep. 2013. Accessed Mar. 2014 <www.law360.com>.

29 Wade, Alex. "Good and Bad Reviews: The Ethical Debate over 'astroturfing'".
   The Guardian. 9 Jan. 2011. Accessed Mar. 2014 <www.theguardian.com>.

30 Baase, Sara. A Gift of Fire: Social, Legal, and Ethical Issues for Computing
   Technology. Pearson. 2013.

31 Searle, Annie. "Ethical Misconduct: Is It Your Biggest Risk?" The Risk
   Universe. Nov. 2012.

32 "Gartner Says By 2014, 10-15 Percent of Social Media Reviews to Be Fake,
   Paid for By Companies." Gartner. 17 Sep. 2013. Accessed Mar. 2014
   <www.gartner.com>.

33 Streitfeld, David. "Buy Reviews on Yelp, Get Black Mark." The New York
   Times. 17 Oct. 2012. Accessed Mar. 2014 <www.nytimes.com>.

Bottling Trouble Waters
John Cann
July 2014

Abstract: This reports discusses the vital role water and wastewater infrastructure plays in any society, and the relationship between public and private sectors in the role of managing water-related resources. The report examines how the two sectors relate to water, and the key roles of water and wastewater infrastructure, external threats, and management.

"Multinational companies now run water systems for 7 percent of the world's population, and analysts say that figure could grow to 17 percent by 2015. Private water management is estimated to be a $200 billion business, and the World Bank, which has encouraged governments to sell off their utilities to reduce public debt, projects it could be worth $1 trillion by 2021. The potential for profits is staggering: in May 2000 Fortune magazine predicted that water is about to become 'one of the world's great business opportunities', and that 'it promises to be to the 21st century what oil was to the 20th.'" —John Louma, "Water Thieves," The Ecologist, March 2004

The simple connection of two hydrogen atoms to one oxygen atom forms the chemical compound of the molecule known as water. Water covers approximately 71 percent of the surface of the earth, and is found in the air, the ground, and in every living thing. Comprising nearly 60 percent of the body mass of all living species, water is the basis for life. Water is not only the basis for life; it is the basis of civilization. And ensuring that clean water is easily and cheaply available to the population of any civilization is of vital importance to the state.

The U.S. Department of Homeland Security identifies Water and Wastewater Systems as one of the 17 critical infrastructures that support our country. In conjunction with private agencies, the U.S. government maintains over 150,000 public water systems across the country to provide safe and clean water to the population, and to remove wastewater and excess water from natural events. This report will focus on how the public and private sectors are dealing with the following challenges:

- Infrastructure – maintaining and developing water and wastewater systems that serve an exponentially growing population of 300 million

- External Threats – ensuring the safety of water and wastewater systems from contamination, bioterrorism, sabotage and natural events

- Management – the growing struggle between government control and the privatization of water resources, including water as a commodity (bottled water)

Infrastructure of Water and Wastewater Systems

Before the 1800s in the U.S., there was no real infrastructure of water and wastewater systems worth mentioning. Water inside the American home came from a well or was carried from a nearby river or lake. It was not until the mid-1800s that America saw its first comprehensive sewage system in Chicago.[1] The idea of water and wastewater systems began to catch on in U.S and spread to other major cities. According to the U.S. Census Bureau, the population in 1850 increased from 23 million to 76 million by 1900. And during this time is when most metropolises in the U.S. began to install water and wastewater systems, many of which were privatized operations. All of these systems used different materials, such as wood or lead, to create the water pipes leading to a complete lack of consistency between all the competing agencies.[2]

The late 1800s and early 1900s also showed great advances in medicine. The greatest advance being in microbiology and the spread of communicable diseases. John Snow discovered in London that cholera was being passed through the water supply.[3]

Robert Koch isolated the bacteria for tuberculosis and its possibility of spreading through the water supply.[4] Other medical research began to investigate the detrimental effects of lead on human physiology. At the turn of the century now, the idea was introduced that lead pipes bringing in the water supply were responsible for the drop in infant mortality in places like New Hampshire.[5]

Lead pipes may quite possibly be the greatest threat to the infrastructure of water systems in the U.S. Private institutions recognized that these pipes which were laid by at the turn of the century would propose an astronomical cost for replacing with safer materials. Rather than assume any risk of such a problem, and before government regulation, these water systems were transferred into the hands of government institutions.

It was not until the 1970's that the government passed the Safe Drinking Water Act.[6] By this point, the demand for water now answers to a population of over 200 million people. The infrastructure has been overloaded with such strain that government agencies cannot keep up with the cost of repairing the old systems in place and the demand to construct new systems for a population that reached 300 million in 2007.

External Threats to Water and Wastewater Systems

Perhaps the most damaging and debilitating threat to the water and wastewater systems of our country is the desecration of water quality. Clean, safe, and drinkable water is an inalienable right to all living species, which is threatened on all sides by the inequities of our civilization. External threats to our water supply are wide and varied. Contamination by pollution and careless dumping. Bioterrorism and sabotage of facilities. While most of these threats are imbued by human activity, there remain unpredictable natural events. Many civilizations throughout history have been lost due to all of these external threats. Whether the poisoning of wells and waterways as the agenda of military conquest, or awesome natural catastrophe, the imminent and debilitating threats to our water systems are external.

Contamination of our water systems is bestowed on us in a variety of insidious methods. Pollution caused by human activity has affected the quality of our freshwater resources to the point that more than half are too contaminated to sustain aquatic life.[7] Industrial dumping in water resources is most likely the main culprit in this pollution. Avoiding the cost and time it takes to properly dispose of chemical waste, corporations often dump this is the water supply. The amount of waste produced and dumped each year far exceeds any possibility of a homeostatic natural recovery. While the ecosystem can sustain a certain amount of pollution and recover, the amount of chemicals dumped far exceeds what the ecosystem can handle.

Pollution in the water does not always result from direct dumping. A significant portion of the pollution is collected from runoff water as it moves through the environment. Running down streets and hills, rainwater collects all of the pollutants and contaminants along the way. Even if the water is not collected by runoff, chemical pollutants saturate into the ground and eventually reach the ground water supply.[8] Most of these chemicals and pollutants are the direct result of oil from the automotive industry. Automobiles, busses, boats, and airplanes are the culprit in disseminating oil-based pollutions into the air and on the ground – all of which end up in the water system. Treating this water is a complex process that is expensive and does not always work. The *New York Times* reports that only 91 contaminants are regulated in drinking water – which is 0.0015 percent of the identifiable contaminants found in the water.[9]

Another major contaminant in the water supply is the increasing amount of drugs found from the pharmaceutical industry. The prevalent use and administration of drugs such as amoxicillin, doxycycline, acetaminophen, and fluoxetine are now regularly found in our water supply.[10] Since they are reaching measurable amounts, there is no precedent for determining their effect. Up here in the Pacific Northwest, the local addiction to coffee has caused unprecedented amounts of caffeine in the water.[11] While caffeine may seem to be relatively harmless substance to humans, in the marine world it can cause significant stress.

While most of the contamination discussed so far is unintentional, special consideration must be given to intentional contamination – more specifically, bioterrorism. Bioterrorism is the intentional poisoning of a water supply using a biological agent such as bacteria, virus, or other toxins. These biological agents are released in the water supply with the intention of causing illness or death. While these agents are often already found in the water supply, bioterrorism seeks to unnaturally add these agents. Well poisoning has long been a military technique to deliver a debilitating blow to the enemy. Bioterrorism is usually thought to be part of external campaign, but nonetheless there are domestic enemies who would seek this method first. Poisoning the water of a city or a large arena seems to be the prime targets of foreign terrorists. However, there are a handful of U.S. citizens who would use bioterrorism to curb illegal immigration. California has long fought domestic terrorists who leave poisoned water supplies for illegal immigrants under the guise of compassionate aid.[12] This method often backfires when random hikers or children find the water and drink it.

Lastly, and probably the most devastating external threat to the water and wastewater threats, is natural events. Any naturally occurring phenomenon can have a debilitating and devastating effect on the water supply. Large magnitude earthquakes can completely disrupt the flow of water. Earthquakes can alter the flow of a river, which would either completely wipe a population out or deprive an area of its water supply. Any water system that uses outdated, or even modern, technology can be obliterated and rendered useless. In addition to altering the water system itself, an earthquake can cause the devastation of a chemical or nuclear plant causing all of contained contaminants to enter the water supply. And what does not immediately enter the water supply, eventually enters the groundwater supply.

Flooding can be equally damaging. As climate change takes its toll on the environment, excessive rain and flooding are becoming a more common occurrence and not just a threat. Flooding can overfill storm drains causing backup in the wastewater system. Now instead of the wastewater flowing to its destination, it simply spreads everywhere – including raw sewage. Flooding also picks up a large amount of debris including chemical contaminants that now float freely in the water supply and eventually seep into the groundwater.

Drought inevitably takes its toll too. When an area becomes impoverished of water, painstaking efforts are sought to reroute water back to the area. Southern California has long fought this problem with the aqueduct – which has been a long and heated political debate. Drought causes massive crop loss and without rerouting water supply, there is little chance of recovery. Rerouting water supply is often a major political debate between public sectors and private sectors because of the fiscal cost in rerouting and the environmental damage caused in the area from where the water was routed. Who owns the water?

Management of Water and Wastewater Systems
As talked about earlier in this report, the management of the water and wastewater systems has had an uneven balance between the public and private sector. Now that we are faced with the imperative dilemma of upgrading the infrastructure, while protecting against contamination, bioterrorism, and natural phenomenon, and recognizing that we live in an exponentially increasing population. The question emerges: who should be in charge of it? Public

institutions have failed us due to poor management. Private institutions have bailed out on us when the going got tough. As a critical infrastructure, the problem must be addressed now.

As it is, a public service, our water and wastewater systems are failing us. They are unstaffed and underfunded, forced to work with yesterday's technology. The continued management of water as a public resource means little progress and our problems will get bigger. Lost in political debate, corporations will continue to contaminate the water with an underfunded government institution trying to fight back. However, public management of the water ensures the most efficient management. Keeping water as a public utility ensures that corporations will not gouge the price and effectively kill off those who cannot afford to be a consumer. Public agencies can work with other public agencies to ensure the safety of the methods in practice.

Privatizing the water systems seems to be a step in the wrong direction. Private industries answer to investors and must continue to turn a profit – usually at the expense of the consumer. While we know this to be true, profiting off the most essential resource to sustain life seems to ensure natural selection – at the expense of the poor who cannot afford it. Privatizing water has the advantage of ensuring (perceived) better management, void of political backlash. Also, with a steady stream of increased profit there would be room for research and technology to enter the scene and strive for efficiency.

The question becomes, do we pay for our water in private profits or public taxes? Neither seems to be a favorable answer. Water systems currently owned by private sectors have risen to the challenge by selling bottled water. Ounce for ounce, bottled water is worth more than gasoline.[13] Public institutions do not have the option of selling off excess water for profit. There is a shaky balance now, neither of which really seems to benefit the public. Working together on this solution seems to be the optimal answer. However, such an agreement would imply an endorsement of a particular institution. Causing unfair competition would probably lead to lawsuits that would completely strangle everyone and everything involved instead of progressing toward an answer.

Conclusion

The inception of water and wastewater systems in the U.S. has had an extraordinary history and prevalence. Shared water systems began to develop as the result of urbanization. Recognizing the demand for a supply private institutions began to take control of water systems as did public institutions. Who should be providing the service has always been a question.

Regardless, water and wastewater systems are a critical infrastructure to our nation and need to be protected as vital elements of the state.

The current state of the infrastructure of the 150,000 water and wastewater systems in the nation lacks fluidity. Our current systems are based on technology that developed at the end of the 1800s. Since then, our population has more than tripled and the areas we service have grown just as much. Serving this demand is a daunting task that requires an overhaul of not just the infrastructure's physical components, but also its management.

Protecting the water and wastewater systems from external threats is vital to our safety. Water is the target of contamination from outside sources. Chemical contaminants are regularly dumped in our water system and infect not only the water supply, but also the ground itself. The other major source of contamination is runoff water that collects oil from the street and pesticides from our yards. Bioterrorism is also a major concern to the well being of our water systems. There are those that would poison our wells and rivers with agents of destruction that cause illness and death. All of these factors are compounded by the imminent threat of natural phenomenon. Earthquakes, flood, and drought all equally have the potential to devastate our water systems. Protecting against these external threats is astronomical, in terms of management and cost.

The final challenge to our water system is management. The argument between water systems being a public or private institution has been prevalent since the inception of water systems. Public institutions are often underfunded and mismanaged by government resources. Although they seek to provide service to all, this widespread action is costly and inefficient. Private institutions proffer glamorous ideas of efficiency, technology, and profit – but at whose expense. Private institutions also have the options of selling off water resources for a profit. This could easily lead to the destruction of a natural resource. The argument may forever ebb and tide.

Forging an alliance between the public and private sectors to protect our critical infrastructure resource seems to be like mixing oil and water. Infrastructure, external threats, and management of the water and wastewater systems need to come together in a manner that satisfies the public. Privatization of water may seem like a good answer in the short run, but it also transfers the power out of the people's hands. Ideally, the two institutions will work together, but paying taxes and profits on the lifeblood of life seems inane. Ensuring that water is available to everyone without destroying our environment is on the hands of government. The technology to do this will emanate from the private sector. The real work is piecing these two together – just as the old pipes used to build the initial infrastructure. Eventually we must make it work together, and it will flow like the river.

---

1 "History of Wastewater Treatment in the United States." Macalester College. Apr. 2006. Accessed Jun. 2014 <www.macalester.edu>

2 "Environmental Fact Sheet." New Hampshire Department of Environmental Services. 1999. Accessed Jun. 2014 <www.des.nh.gov>

3 Hempel, Sandra. The Strange Case of the Broad Street Pump: John Snow and the Mystery of Cholera. Berkeley: University of California Press. 2007.

4 Gradmann, Christopher. "Robert Koch and The White Death: From Tuberculosis to Tuberculin." Microbes Infect. Jan. 2006.

5 Troesken, Werner. "Lead Water Pipes and Infant Mortality at the Turn of the Twentieth Century." Journal of Human Resources. 2008. Accessed Jun. 2014 <www.nber.org>.

6 "An Environmental Law: Highlights of the Safe Drinking Water Act of 1974." U.S. Environmental Protection Agency. 1976. Accessed Jun. 2014 <www.epa.gov>.

7 EPA: Most U.S. Waters Polluted." United Press International. 27 Mar. 2013. Accessed Jun. 2014

<www.upi.com>.

8 "Surface Waters Contamination." U.S. Environmental Protection Agency. n.d. Accessed Jun. 2014 <www.epa.gov>.

9 Duhigg, Charles. "That Tap Water Is Legal but May Be Unhealthy." New York Times. 16 Dec. 2009. Accessed Jun. 2014 <www.nytimes.com>.

10 "Pharmaceuticals in Water." BeCause Water. n.d. Accessed Jun. 2014 <www.becausewater.org>

11 Handwerk, Brian. "Caffeinated Seas Found off U.S. Pacific Northwest." National Geographic. 30 Jul. 2012. Accessed Jun. 2014 <www.news.nationalgeographic.com>.

12 Raferty, Miriam. "Dying to Come to America." East County Magazine. Sep. 2008. Accessed Jun. 2014 <www.eastcountymagazine.org>.

13 Owen, James. "Bottled Water Isn't Healthier Than Tap, Report Reveals." National Geographic. 24 Feb. 2006. Accessed Jun. 2014. <www.nationalgeographic.com>.

Managing Third Party Risks

Divya Yadav

November 2013

Abstract: Third Party contracts have become the norm in today's competitive business environment which essentially means handling of an organization's business processes by an external service provider. This form of operational arrangement can sometimes result in loss of accountability and ownership, non-compliance to regulations, and data breaches that can cause financial and reputational risks. This research note highlights some key points that can help organizations manage their third party vendors and contractors and mitigate potential risks.

Introduction

Third Party vendors and contractors exist across all vertical markets, be it manufacturing, finance, retail, IT or healthcare. The term Third Party essentially means that organizations hand over some of their operational functions or products and services to an external party. A term that became synonymous with third party vendors a decade ago was "outsourcing," where companies contract their functions or line of business to third parties that can otherwise be performed in house.1

Third party contracts and Vendor Management is a complex issue that needs to be dealt with care as organizations are not only trusting external parties with their sensitive data but are also relying on them to deliver on time, hence making it a complex equation of fulfillment of each criteria. Growing competition has compelled companies to give control of their core processes to external providers, which has potential risks and therefore a need for risk framework that protects proprietary data and intellectual property cannot be emphasized enough. An important question that arises is how do organizations go about selecting contractors and what strategy do they have in place to hire contractors on which they can rely completely to effectively perform their tasks and protect the company data. The aim of this research note is to learn more about the potential risks across industry verticals, and how these risks can be mitigated.

Risks Arising from Third Party Contracts

Much has been read and written about Edward Snowden who was a SharePoint contractor for NSA and how he managed to leak sensitive information that caused much of embarrassment to the US government and other countries as well. What caused the information to travel from NSA premises to media outlets may very well have been the lack of contractual compliance, ineffective third party governance and security policies. Another very different form of third party risk is the healthare.gov website. Much of the development for the site was led by contractors that were in compliance with federal norms and regulations but still were not able to deliver for the government on time. Here the reasons are slightly different: ineffective vendor management or lack of co-ordination between government and vendors. In another instance, Boeing outsourced much of its manufacturing of components as well as the some of the design to outside contractors that made it look susceptible to financial risks.2

Why? Outsourcing design to contractors with weak business implementation and requirement plans can cause a gap between what actually needs to be done. Such contractors don't have the vision or big picture in mind, and it is the job of the business owner to know about the end-to-end process. Similarly, managing contractors for construction and infrastructure management is a huge challenge and requires maximum scrutiny in order to avoid any substandard materials and procedures being used to build roads, bridges and buildings. These examples from different verticals point out that third party risks are prevalent in each sector and they differ from one another depending on the line of service outsourced.

Perhaps the most popular is IT outsourcing and almost every vertical market engages in this form of contractual arrangement. Companies are more than ever facing scrutiny to be able to protect customer data and sensitive information and create norms and regulations for third party vendors to handle this information discretely. Data security breaches have taken place in the past that comprises not only financial risk but reputational risk as well. Cloud computing and software as a services are examples of emerging risk areas that are privy to sensitive information and require strong regulatory environments.3

Coordinating with vendors is a huge task and needs effective vendor project management. While contracting to vendors seems lucrative for driving decreased costs and increased revenues, an inherent understanding of what a complex ecosystem a company is venturing into should be apparent.4 A strategy complete with risk and gap analysis as well as integration plan should be in place to begin with or else the project can be a huge failure.

Third Party Risk Management and Compliance

The landscape for risk and compliance continues to evolve5 and not all risks are equal, a fact that a flexible framework should be able to take into account. Companies have contracts with multiple contractors and vendors, and to manage this comprehensive list should be the first step toward building a sustainable framework. Process mapping and accountability of work for each contractor can be managed and keeps the company aware of what's going on at each stage. Secondly, identification of core processes that are outsourced and whether the data or information can be comprised, as well as what impact it will have on the organization, is a useful matrix. If created, such a matrix can help in the monitoring and evaluation of risks that have the highest impact.

Prioritization of processes and risks is important as not all risks are equal and this will impact their handling and treatment. Cloud providers, helpdesk processes, outsourced financial processes, and medical claims processes are examples of critical processes that organizations outsource. Assigning risk ratings to these processes can make the audit and risk management process more streamlined. A dedicated team to handle and manage third party should be in place as well as identification of Key Risk Indicators also assist in managing risk. Internal controls are created as part of risk management framework for each process that should be accounted in Services Organizations Reports (SOC) as part of the audit and assurance practice.6

Vendor Management

Vendor Management is a cross functional process schema that integrates IT, Compliance, Risk assurance and business owners to manage the risk portfolios of vendors.7 It brings together all the individual business units and helps manage their third party processes to mitigate gaps and unify process framework. The heart of vendor management is managing and retaining ownership from a key or senior leader of the organization. The leader will oversee regulations, internal controls and standards to ensure that they are being followed, and to institute penalties for violations from the vendors.

Vendor training and assessment should be a part of vendor management and these trainings should be organized on annual or bi- annual basis depending on the need or criticality of the processes.

Dedicated curriculum designers should hired to make the content relevant and effective.

Hiring Right Contractors

Hiring third party contractors and vendors is unavoidable due to the increased revenues, decreased cost of production and competitive advantage that make it so compelling. Companies must understand that hiring the right contractors that get the work done and pose minimum risks is the most optimum strategy. Besides the risk, governance and compliance that comes into effect when contracting work to third parties a key point to note is that a failure to align with business requirements can compromise the line of business being contracted and will result in a failed product or service. A detailed and comprehensive business plan that covers the scale of the project and business requirements should be prepared. An evaluation team that has a vested interest in selecting vendors should be formed as it ensures strong participation and less margin for errors. Define vendor requirements clearly and search for vendors that fulfill these requirement criteria. Evaluate proposals from vendors based on an already formed list of business requirements along with priority and importance for each requirement. This methodology will help assign scores to each vendors and display how their proposal aligns with the company's needs and requirements.8

Conclusion

While third party contracts are here to stay if effective strategies, frameworks, trainings and process plans are in place companies get reap in more benefits rather than fighting it. Risk monitoring and assessment is the key in managing vendors and contractors.

Identifying processes and hiring contractors based on the requirements is a complex process and specialized people should be assigned to effectively manage third party contactors. Companies should build guidelines and strategies to not only manage contractors, but to be constantly aware of the potential risks that might ensue and to mitigate them adequately.

1 *FDIC Compliance Examination Manual — January 2014.* Federal Deposit Insurance Corporation. Jan. 2014. Accessed Nov. 2013 <www.fdic.gov>.

2 Harrison, Denise. "Lessons Learned from Boeing's Stumble: Risk Assessment is Key to a Successful Strategy." Center for Simplified Strategic Planning, N.D. Accessed Nov. 2013 <www.cssp.com>.

3 *Keeping Third-Party Risk in Check.* Grant Thornton. Oct. 2012. Accessed Nov. 2013 <www.grantthornton.com>.

4 "Third Party & Vendor Management." Astea. N.D. Accessed Nov. 2013 <www.astea.com>.

5 Krivin, Dmitry, et. al. "Managing Third-Party Risk in a Changing Regulatory Environment." McKinsey & Company. May 2013. Accessed Nov. 2013 <www.mckinsey.com>.

6 Grant Thornton, 2012.

7 Katz, David. "Contracting in a World of Data Breaches and Insecurity: Managing Third-Party Vendor Engagements." Nelson Mullins. 15 May 2013. Accessed Nov. 2013 <www.nelsonmullins.com>.

8 Bucki, James. "The Successful Vendor Selection Process." *About.com.* N.D. Accessed Nov. 2013 <www.operationstech.about.com>.

Money From Nothing

The Socioeconomic Implications of "Cyber-Currencies"

Justine Brecese
August 2013

Abstract: This research note holistically examines the phenomena of "cyber-currencies" by delineating the primary types currently in circulation, identifying the risks associated with each, and ultimately providing a high-level risk assessment of the overall landscape. While "crypto-currency" such as Bitcoin tends to dominate the news, myriad other forms of "cyber" or "digital" currencies exist, each posing their own risks. For this reason, I argue that it is important to establish the differences between these currencies and to understand the scope and implications of each.

Introduction

"Virtual currency" has recently been gaining a notable amount of attention from the media, the federal government, and private investors. But what is it exactly? The U.S. Department of the Treasury Financial Crimes Enforcement Network (FinCEN) states that virtual currency is: "a medium of exchange that operates like a currency in some environments, but does not have all the attributes of real currency. In particular, virtual currency does not have legal tender status in any jurisdiction."1 Even though this type of currency lacks any "legal tender status"—i.e. official government backing—a large draw towards certain versions of cyber-currency is their promise of anonymity in an increasingly surveilled world. Privacy is the primary attribute surrounding much of the more prominent digital currencies, such as Bitcoin, lending to their increasing popularity. Specifically, currencies like Bitcoin can be understood as "peer-to-peer" systems which, "endeavor to re-establish both privacy and autonomy by avoiding the banking and government middlemen."2 The key is that these currencies are decentralized, unsupported by any government, anonymous, and entirely immaterial; all attributes which make them potentially disruptive to economies across the globe, via the risks they bear for citizens, institutions and governments.

These definitions are fairly broad and overarching, however, and a distinction should be made between the different types of "cyber-currencies" in order to garner a holistic understanding of their functionality and implications. As with most relatively new technology - based issues there are many terms floating around the media and public discourse, often used interchangeably - much to the detriment of properly understanding crucial nuances or differences between particular concepts. FinCEN's recent paper briefly describes the differences between several types of virtual currencies, but only does so to describe the basic mechanics of each for regulatory purposes.3

There are currently at least four terms that tend to be used interchangeably in the discourse on this subject: virtual currency, digital currency, crypto-currency and electronic money (or e-money). To establish a comprehensive examination of these four separate-but- similar concepts, this research note will use the moniker "cyber- currency" as an umbrella term for all types of currency discussed herein. More specifically, crypto-currencies will be examined as a subset of digital currencies, which should not be confused with virtual currencies—all three of which differ from e-money. It should also be noted that all forms of cyber-currency are linked to "real world" economics—some just more overtly than others. This paper will break the issue of cyber-currency down into its components, examining each sub-type with the intent of constructing a "wide angle" view of the issue along with identifying the primary risks involved. Finally, following these delineations and risk identifications will be a high-level risk assessment of the current cyber-economic milieu using the three-step process outlined by the COSO internal controls framework.4

Virtual Currency

The term "virtual currency" is linked to virtual economies that develop within (and rely upon) the context of specific virtual environments or worlds, such as those found in massively multi-player online role-playing games (MMORPGs) such as World of Warcraft, or simulations like Second Life.5 Virtual currencies are largely restricted to their respective virtual environments, with no direct ties to the physical economy. That said, one obvious overlap can be seen in the fact that items and money from virtual worlds do sell for "real world money"— whether going against the policies of game companies and selling virtual items through online commerce websites such as Ebay, or participating in sanctioned in-game "micro-transactions."6 One critical distinction between this form of virtual economics and others, however, is the fact that no "real" goods or services are delivered as a result of a virtual economic exchange. Even in instances where actual currency is exchanged for virtual goods or services, the goods or services that are delivered are non-existent outside of their respective virtual context.

So with virtual currency being tethered to virtual worlds, it seems as though there might not really be any significant risks involved. This is a false notion, however. While certainly less risky than other forms of cyber-currency, there are still several issues that arise from these "virtual economies." For one, as with real economies, black markets and crime tends to spring up within bustling virtual economies—and such crime can have effects that reach the "real world" economy. For example, in 2006 there was a large-scale "virtual banking" incident in a game titled Eve Online wherein one of the in-game virtual bank executives essentially ripped off thousands of players, selling their bank deposits and collateral on the in-game black market for a real cash payout of $120,000.7

It does not take a stretch of the imagination to see the mimesis in activity such as this with the rash of similar real-world corporate scandals in recent years. Other scenarios arise in virtual economies where virtual "crime syndicates" steal from other players within the virtual worlds to ultimately turn a real cash profit from their stolen items and pilfered virtual currency.8 Another particular incident that hit the media involved a profitable brothel being run within a game called The Sims. In this incident, one player was banned from the game because he discovered that the in-game brothel's madam was actually a 17-year-old boy and exposed his identity.9 This incident not only raised questions of "virtual crime" and selling the in-game virtual currency for real money but also issues of censorship, anonymity online, and the exposure of children to inappropriate scenarios were raised. Two of these issues, censorship and online anonymity, are central to other forms of cyber-currency, the implications of which will be expanded upon later in this research note. Other risks with virtual currency include the potential for addiction and resultant over--spending.10 Gaming in itself has a tendency to be addicting which, coupled with the engrossing, vicarious living experience provided by MMORPGs and (aptly titled) "life simulators," makes it even easier to "hook" players. Overall though, virtual currencies and their risks remain somewhat contained due to their largely restricted nature. Other cyber--currencies, conversely, are free of this limitation.

E-Currency

As with "virtual currency," the term "digital currency" has a tendency to be loosely used in reference to any form of cyber-currency and/or electronic commerce (e-commerce). Perhaps most importantly, a differentiation must be made between the concept of e-currency (or e-money) and other types of digital currencies since their functionality and risks can vary quite drastically. "E-currency" is defined as "a type of currency in electronic form that is designed especially for paying for goods and services bought on the Internet."11 Again, this is a very broad definition. The distinguishing factor is that e-money is directly linked to legal tender - i.e. centralized currency that is backed by governments and central banks existing in the physical world. It should essentially be understood as electronic payments or money transfers that are used for purchasing "real" goods online. In a nutshell, e-money is a traceable electronic transfer of legal tender from one person or entity to another, through a regulated third party, typically in exchange for real goods or services. Direct deposits, electronic funds transfers (EFTs), payment processors, and electronic "wallets" are some examples of e-money systems.

Risks surrounding these forms of electronic payment and e-money are primarily embedded in information security issues. Since this type of currency is directly linked to legal tender, it does not generate quite as many risks as other forms of cyber-currency. Concerns with e-money transactions lie primarily in fraud, identity theft, data breaches, and other cyber-attacks on individuals or financial institutions, which result in loss of availability for the institution(s) or loss of confidentiality for personal financial credentials.12 Of course fraud, identity theft and theft in general have long been concerns in the "real world" banking and finance sector, which have spread to the "virtual world" of the e- transactions and e-banking as many other crimes have.

Digital Gold

Beyond this type of e-money, other digital currencies have evolved that are not directly tied to legal tender. A relative to the above-described forms of e-money are digital gold currencies (DGCs) such as e-gold, OS-Gold, and e-Bullion—two of which are now defunct. As the name implies, digital gold currencies are based on precious metals (typically gold bullion) and are privately backed as opposed to nationally-controlled legal tender.13 DGCs pose more substantial risks to their investors than e-money largely because of their private backing. This means, among other things, a higher risk of volatility in the market. There is also the issue of DGCs functioning as international currencies. Because they are backed by precious metals, rather than national legal tender, they allow for easy trade and transactions across borders without going through "official" channels. This notion generates new risks, as DGCs can easily be used towards nefarious ends such as illicit purchases, money laundering, and funding terrorist groups or other criminal organizations. It does so though the fact that many exchanges only require minimal sign-up credentials, meaning transactions in DGC can not only cross borders easily, but they can do so with relative anonymity.14 That said, crypto-currency, the final type of cyber-currency that will be discussed, has taken this ability much further by basing itself entirely upon anonymity.

Introduction to Crypto--Currency

Crypto-currencies emerged following Satoshi Nakamoto's 2008 paper detailing the (then only theoretical) Bitcoin protocol.15 This type of cyber-currency has recently become fairly popular worldwide, garnering widespread media attention and notable investors—such as the Winklevoss twins of Facebook-related "fame" who own millions of dollars' worth of Bitcoins.16 What differentiates crypto-currencies from the other forms of cyber-currency discussed thus far is also what makes them far more risky—they are de-centralized, anonymous, and highly volatile as a result.[i] But even with the risks involved, these currencies have been gaining a lot of attention this year. This is likely because the very factors that make it so risky are also what make it

---

[i] For more information on how digital currency works, see: Klimas, Liz. "Confused By Digital Currency? This Three Minute Video Has the Basics of What You Need to Know About 'Bitcoins'." The Blaze. 10 Apr. 2013. <www.theblaze.com>.

For information on the Bitcoin mining process, see: Seaver, Jesse. "Mining for Digital Gold - New Digital Crypto-Currencies Bitcoin, LiteCoin, PPCoin and Other." The Huffington Post. 26 Apr. 2013. <www.huffingtonpost.com>.

attractive—that is, the resistance to any form of censorship or tracking/monitoring of transactions by governments or institutions. In a sense, crypto-currency is "pure" currency; it is the essence of the economic concept. Put simply, because it is decentralized and unregulated by any third party, it can only exist if people accept and circulate it as a medium of exchange and its exchange rate is purely based upon its circulation.

Political Motivation

Because of their foundation in online privacy and anonymity, crypto-currencies are inherently politically charged. This fact alone makes them a more significant threat to existing economic systems and institutions than other forms of privately-backed digital currencies. They carry with them the weight of a specific movement advocating resistance to surveillance and the lack of privacy in the digital age that dates (at least) as far back as the 1980s when Timothy May began distributing The Crypto Anarchist Manifesto. In other words, crypto-currency is absolutely not just another digital currency, it is symbolic of a particular counter-culture and belief system. Indeed, activists which identify themselves as Crypto Anarchists and/or Cypherpunks are largely responsible for the foundational concepts embodied by crypto- currencies.[ii] This anonymity-as-a lifestyle or political statement is reflected in the very fact that the name "Satoshi Nakamoto," creator of Bitcoin, is a pseudonym. The identity of the original creator is unknown, and there is even uncertainty over whether or not it is one person or multiple. The pseudonym, "Satoshi Nakamoto," is theorized as being a reference to William Gibson's Japanese-inspired cyberpunk culture of the 1980s, meaning there is no evidence that the writer is actually even Japanese.17 Today, crypto-currencies are relied upon for anonymous transactions across the globe - many of which, of course, are not legal.

The Breadth of Crypto-currencies and Associated Risks

While Bitcoin is the most well-known and widely circulated crypto-currency, it is not the only one. Many others exist (roughly 40+), some notable ones being: Litecoin, PPCoin, and Namecoin, which are all either minor variations of, or at least highly inspired by, the Bitcoin protocol developed by Nakamoto.18 To get an idea of how large crypto- currency has gotten in recent years, there are currently almost 11.25 million Bitcoins in circulation, which by the exchange rate at the time of this writing is roughly

---

[ii] For more information, Tim May's Crypto Anarchist Manifesto can be read at activism.net.

1.386 billion U.S. dollars' worth.19 With this much already in circulation, and such a volatile exchange rate—spiking to above $260 and falling below $100 within a span of one month—the continually growing amount of crypto-currency being globally circulated demands attention.20 This form of decentralized currency is risky to both investors and established institutions. Its inherently IT-based nature further interweaves the finance and IT critical infrastructure sectors, exposing both to the risks imposed by a globally-traded ethereal form of digital currency which has zero ties to any third party institutions (public or private).

Along with the economic risks imposed on investors due to market volatility and unreliability, there is a long list of other risks generated by anonymous, decentralized currencies. For instance, with crypto-currencies there is a lack of consumer protection, dispute resolution mechanisms and deposit insurance, leaving consumers fairly vulnerable to losses.21 Beyond consumer vulnerability, these currencies also allow for circumventing laws and committing crimes such as: tax evasion, potential violations of securities laws, money laundering, terrorism funding, and the sale and purchase of any type of illegal goods imaginable (as seen on "underground" websites like the infamous Silk

Road).[iii] The fact of the matter is that using these currencies means supporting an "underground economy," so whether or not a consumer using crypto-currency is breaking any laws, he/she is still propagating a system which works to subvert existing government- backed economic systems.

Risk Analysis of Cyber--Currencies

Now, with each type of cyber-currency defined and contextualized, the next step is to further assess the risks that have been identified. The following table (Figure 1) outlines the list of risks identified thus far and maps them accordingly to each of the cyber-currency types. It shows the general areas of impact as well as measures of risk on a four-point scale. Measures of risk magnitude were determined based on a correlation of the significance of each risk and their respective likelihood or frequency of occurrence—following the first two steps of the COSO three-step risk assessment process.22 It must be noted, however, that these are merely

---

[iii] The "Silk Road" is an 'underground' black market website which uses the Tor network for anonymity. A wide array of goods are sold on the site, with a focus on illegal narcotics and drug paraphernalia. Everything on the site is bought and sold for Bitcoins. The website cannot be reached unless the user is operating on a Tor browser. For more information on the Silk Road, see: Chen, Adrian. "The Underground Website Where You Can Buy Any Drug Imaginable." Gawker. 1 Jun. 2011. <www.gawker.com>.
For more information on Tor, see <www.torproject.org>.

approximations based on qualitative research of secondary sources and should therefore not be taken at face value. The risk magnitude scale for Figure 1 should be interpreted as such:

- **N/A** = That particular risk is not really applicable to that particular cyber-currency; its likelihood or frequency is close to zero
- **Low** = That particular risk would not have a strong impact and/or is unlikely to occur
- **Medium** = That particular risk could have a moderate impact and might occur
- **High** = That particular risk could have a large impact and it is likely to occur

			Notable Risks	Cyber-Currencies			
				E-Money	Virtual Currency	Digital Gold	Crypto-Currency
			Market Volatility	Low	High	Medium	High
			Lack of Consumer Protections / Insurance	N/A	Medium	High	High
			Addiction/Over Spending	N/A	Medium	N/A	N/A
			Anonymity	N/A	Medium	High	High
			Data Breaches	Medium	Medium	Medium	Low
			Cyber "Attacks"	Medium	Medium	Medium	Low
			Theft	Medium	High	Medium	Low
			Fraud/Identity Theft	Medium	Medium	High	High
			Unmediated International Trade	N/A	Low	High	High
			Lack of Regulation	Low	Low	High	High
			Black Markets	N/A	High	High	High
			Securities Law Violations	Low	N/A	High	High
			Tax Evasion	Low	Medium	High	High
			Money Laundering	Low	Medium	High	High
			Terrorism Funding	Low	N/A	High	High

Figure 1: (Approximated) Risk Assessment Table for Cyber-Currencies

Regulations (or Lack Thereof)

Currently there is little regulation on most of these currencies and it is difficult to pin them to existing financial laws since they operate independently of government-backed legal tender. Of course, with crypto-currencies being such a controversial topic, the U.S. Government has not turned a blind eye—even though they do not consider "virtual currencies" such as Bitcoin to be the same as money.23 FinCEN's recently issued guidelines outline how the various types of cyber--currencies shall be regulated, including the application of "money- laundering rules" to what they call "convertible virtual currency."24 What distinguishes FinCEN's definition of "convertible virtual currency" from other virtual currencies is that it "has an equivalent value in real currency or [it] acts as a substitute for real currency."25 One factor of this enforcement worth noting is that it functions alongside the Bank Secrecy Act and only applies to "money transmission service[s]," rather than individual users of convertible virtual currency.26 This means that cyber-currency exchanges, and financial institutions which conduct business with said exchanges, are the entities susceptible to these rules put forth by FinCEN.

In the wake of these guidelines, government agencies have already made large moves against Bitcoin exchanges. Charges have been brought against Liberty Reserve, a Costa Rican exchange, with accusations of having laundered billions of dollars.27 The U.S. Treasury Department is also proposing rules to "prohibit regulated financial institutions from doing business with anyone who processes Liberty Reserve transactions."28 Similarly, some U.S. accounts of Mt. Gox, the largest of all Bitcoin exchanges, were also frozen, and the Department of Homeland Security has ordered services not to do business with Mt. Gox.32 Mt. Gox processes roughly 75 percent of all Bitcoin transactions, so halting their U.S. activity is not insignificant.29

Moving Forward

With the future of these crypto-currencies being so uncertain, and the government beginning to take actions towards mitigating some of the risks involved, there are mixed reactions and opinions surrounding what will happen next and what should be done (if anything). The fact that many digital currencies, such as e-bullion, have fallen in the past due to illegal activities, aids in the wealth of public speculation that it is only a matter of time until the government takes down the current heavy-hitter—Bitcoin.30 Others believe the IRS is likely to follow FinCEN and issue tax-reporting rules for Bitcoin users and exchanges.31 Also, as expected, many existing businesses built on digital currencies are now trying to quickly ensure their compliance with the recent FinCEN rules so as to avoid a similar fate to what Liberty Reserve now faces.32 All the while, the debate over whether or not these currencies should be regulated still rages on as well.

In the end, if these currencies continue to grow, their associated risks will grow with them. Some of the risks involved may even out, such as their volatility and other consumer-centered risks, but the larger risks to governments and regulated financial institutions will only grow with the popularity of crypto-currencies. The intrinsically political nature of this currency cannot be ignored as it intentionally flies in the face of government-regulated money. Put simply, a decentralized and entirely anonymous currency will always harbor the risk of allowing for serious illegal activities such as tax evasion, black market dealings, money laundering and terrorist funding (to name a few). So regardless of whether one stands for restoring privacy in the electronic age, the risks that must be weighed against our desire for anonymity in transactions are heavy. Unfortunately, with the issue of crypto- currencies we stand on a cusp, upon which there can only be room for either privacy or security, not both. So which one wins in the end? The impossible nature of having to make such a decision is the very reason such currency will never truly flourish.

1 "Application of FinCEN's Regulations to Persons Administering, Exchanging, or Using Virtual Currencies." Financial Crimes Enforcement Network, U.S. Department of Treasury. Mar. 2013. Accessed Jun. 2013 <www.fincen.gov>.

2 Reitman, Rainey. "Bitcoin – a Step Toward Censorship-Resistant Digital Currency." 20 Jan. 2011. Electronic Frontier Foundation. Accessed Jun. 2013. <www.eff.org>.

3 "Application of FinCEN's Regulations", 2013.

4 Moeller, Robert. *COSO Enterprise Risk Management: Establishing Effective Governance, Risk, and Compliance Processes, Second Edition.* 20 Dec. 2011.

5 Castronova, Edward. "On Virtual Economies." *Game Sudies.* Dec. 2013. Accessed Jun. 2013 <www.gamestudies.org>.

6 Halliday, Simon. "The Future of Virtual Economies and MMORPGs." *Digital Gameplay.* 15 Jun. 2007. Accessed Jun. 2013 <www.invertlook.com>.

7 Halliday, 2007.

8 Schaefer, Jim. "Sex and the Simulated City: Virtual World Raises Issues in the Real One." 27 Jan. 2004. *Detroit Free Press.* Accessed Jun. 2013 <www.archive.org>.

9 Ibid.

10 "Wiki: Virtual Currency." *Internet Safety Project.* N.D. Accessed Jun. 2013 <www.internetsafetyproject.org>.

11 "E-Currency." Cambridge Dictionaries Online. N.D. Accessed Jun. 2013 <www.dictionary.cambridge.org>.

12 "E-Banking Risks." FFIEC IT Examination Handbook InfoBase. N.D. Accessed Jun. 2013 <www.ithandbook.ffiec.gov>.

13 "Digital Gold Currency – DGC." *Investopedia.* N.D. Accessed Jun. 2013 <www.investopedia.com>.

14 Kosich, Dorothy. "Regulators Worry About Digital Gold Currency's Potential As Tool for Criminal Activity." *International Business Times.* 28 May 2008. Accessed Jun. 2013 <www.ibtimes.com>.

15 Nakamoto, Satoshi. "Bitcoin: A Peer-to-Peer Electronic Cash System." *Bitcoin.* 2009. Accessed Jun. 2013 <www.bitcoin.org>.

16 Cowley, Stacy. "The Winklevoss Twins and Bitcoin Bulls." *CNN.* 18 May 2013. Accessed Jun. 2013 <www.cnn.com>.

17 Worstall, Tim. "Ted Nelson Says that Bitcoin's Satoshi Nakamoto is Shinichi Mochizuki." *Forbes.* 19 May 2013. Accessed Jun. 2013 <www.forbes.com>.

18 Siluk, Shirley. "What Other Digital Currencies Are There?" *CoinDesk.* 2013. Accessed Jun. 2013 <www.coindesk.com>.

xorxor. "List of All Cryptocoins." Bitcoin Forum. 01 Jan. 2013. Accessed Jun. 2013 <www.bitcointalk.org>.

19 "Total Bitcoins in Circulation." *Blockchain*. N.D. Accessed Jun. 2013
   <www.blockchain.info>.
   "Simple Bitcoin Converter." Preev. Accessed Jun. 2013 <www.preev.com>.
20 Fowlkes, Michael. "Bitcoin Volatility Spikes Again as Silk Road Website
   Crashes." *Market Intelligence Center*. 2 May 2013. Accessed Jun. 2013
   <www.marketintelligencecenter.com>.
21 Duhaime, Christine. "The Dangers of Bitcoin – The Legal Risks It Poses To
   Consumers and The Particular Risks It Poses In Combatting Terrorist
   Financing and Money Laundering." Duhaime Law. 21 Apr. 2013. Accessed
   Jun. 2013 <www.duhaimelaw.com>.
22 Moeller, 2011.
23 Fuchs, Erin. "Why the Feds Aren't Shutting Down Bitcoin – At Least Not
   Yet." *Business Insider*. Apr. 2013. Accessed Jun. 2013
   <www.businessinsider.com>.
24 Lamm, Jim. "Convertible Virtual Currency (Like Bitcoin) is Subject to U.S.
   Money-Laundering Rules." Digital Passing. 22 Mar. 2013. Accessed Jun. 2013
   <www.digitalpassing.com>
25 Ibid.
26 Ibid.
27 Albergotti, Reed and Jeffrey Sparshott. "U.S. Says Firm Laundered Billions."
   The Wall Street Journal. 28 May 2013. Accessed Jun. 2013 <www.wsj.com>.
28 Santora, Marc, Rashbaum, William K. and Perolroth, Nicole. "Online
   Currency Exchange Accused of Laundering $6 Billion." *The New York Times*.
   29 May 2013. Accessed Jun. 2013 <www.nytimes.com>.
29 Penenberg, Adam. "U.S. Authorities Launch Their First Attack on BitCoin."
   Radio Pando. 15 May 2013. Accessed Jun. 2013 <www.pandodaily.com>.
30 Hernandez, Raul. "Millions to be Repaid to Victims of e-Bullion.com, Feds
   Say." *Ventura County Star*. Aug. 2012. Accessed Jun. 2013
   <www.venturacountystart.com>.
   Cohan, Peter. "After Liberty Reserve Shut Down, Is Bitcoin Next?" *Forbes*. 29
   May 2013. Accessed Jun. 2013 <www.forbes.com>.
31 Wood, Robert W. "IRS Takes a Bite out of Bitcoin." *Forbes*. 2 May 2013.
   Accessed Jun. 2013 <www.forbes.com>.
32 Flitter, Emily. "Digital Currency Firms Rush to Adopt Anit-Money
   Laundering Rules." *Fox Business*. 31 May 2013. Accessed Jun. 2013
   <www.foxbusiness.com>.

Open Source Policies for Commercial Software Companies

Mike Kelly

July 2015

Abstract: Creating software is a collaborative process, relying not only on the efforts of one team, but also on those of a community. Open source software explicitly allows sharing and reuse, while proprietary software, or closed source software, disallows sharing or modification by anyone but the copyright holder. In consideration of the collaborative process of making software, which often mixes open and closed source software, this paper argues that private companies should have an open source software policy in place if they are using free third-party software to produce their own proprietary software for sale or as part of a paid service. This policy should specify what open source software may be used for which purposes, per license, and set ethical guidelines for the company to give back to the communities on whose work they rely.

Introduction

A piece of computer software is a creative work. Like painting or architecture, software draws from and builds on prior work. This is true for any art or craft. The body of accumulated knowledge, patterns, and practices in a given field are continuously shared, mixed, reused, and improved upon by its practitioners from one generation to the next. Jack Balkin argues that, in the digital age, our most cherished right, free speech and expression, should entail the right to interact with and appropriate information objects freely to protect a democratic culture in which everyone can participate in the production and distribution of culture, each person building on the what others did before her.[1] Even if particular information objects are not always free, we might say that ideas are free: no one can lay claim to exclusive use of an idea. Ideas themselves are not copyrightable, but expressions of ideas are. Copyright protects the intellectual property of creative work, from poetry to software, granting exclusive rights to its owners. Under copyright law in the U.S., all software is copyright protected. Software licenses, which fall under contract law, are used by copyright holders to grant rights or impose restrictions on how users may use the software.

Software copyrights and licenses fill a vast arena of law and philosophy. This paper focuses on ethical use of third-party open source code by businesses building proprietary software and urges businesses facing this issue to institute an open source policy that specifies what type of open source software may be used, to what end, how external software sources are to be tracked, and how the company and its employees should contribute back to the communities whose work it appropriates. To do so we will begin with a definition of open source and proprietary software and the philosophical differences between these licensing models. Then we will look at news of the U.S. government implementing an open source policy and how a similar policy is beneficial to private organizations. After diving into some ethical considerations of how software is produced and used, we will suggest discuss what belongs in an open source policy and how it benefits employees as well as the larger community of developers and users.

Open Source and Proprietary Software

Software consists of code and we distinguish between two kinds: source code and object code. There is further nuance to the distinction, but suffice it to say that source code is human-readable code, written by and for programmers, while object code is the machine executable code, opaque to human readers, which results from compiling or interpreting source code. It is therefore possible to release software that is either open (with source code) or closed (without source code).

The motivation to release closed source software is to protect intellectual property by hiding underlying functionality and design.[2] The motivation to release open source software, on the other hand, is typically a social or ethical one: a desire to share with others, collaborate with or receive contributions from others, to gain skill or reputation, or simply produce something of use to the community.

Open source software is based on an ethical principle, put forward by computer ethics pioneer Norbert Wiener in 1948, that technology should be used to promote human freedom and creativity. In Weiner's words, justice requires that we grant "the liberty of each human being to develop in his freedom the full measure of the human possibilities embodied in him."[3] By this way of thought, to limit a person's ability to use software freely is to stifle a human right. Open source software, which is roughly synonymous with free software, is not a matter of price. "Free as in free speech, not as in free beer" is the common refrain. Lawyers know this as the libre vs. gratis distinction. Free and open source software ("FOSS") allows users to use, copy, and modify it without restriction.[4] Proprietary software may or may not be gratis, but is, by definition, not libre.

Proprietary Software Licenses

Proprietary software licenses preserve ownership of software solely to its publisher and grant limited rights to using copies of the software to end-users. Any company selling software products or services will already have an end-user license agreement in place for its customers.

Open Source Software Licenses

There are dozens of open source licenses. Broadly speaking, they all grant freedom to use, share, and modify the software, but beyond that, there are important differences from one license to another.[5] Due to what may be considered a philosophical divide, open source software licenses are split into two broad categories. There are permissive licenses, such as the MIT license and BSD licenses, which have minimal requirements on how software may be redistributed, and there are copyleft licenses, such as GNU (an operating system), which ensure redistributions of modified software have the same freedoms (i.e. the same copyleft license) as the original distribution.

Copyleft licenses, popularized by Richard Stallman's GNU General Public License, maintain four freedoms, which cannily start from zero:

- Freedom 0 – the freedom to use the work,
- Freedom 1 – the freedom to study the work,
- Freedom 2 – the freedom to copy and share the work with others,

- Freedom 3 – the freedom to modify the work, and the freedom to distribute modified and therefore derivative works.[6]

These are freedoms of the user, not the original software publisher. Freedom 0 allows the user to use the program in ways different than the publisher intended. Freedom 2 lets the user distribute copies of the software (either for free or for a fee!) without having to ask permission. Freedom 3, as it is interpreted by GNU Free Software Foundation, is the strongest freedom and the one that sets copyleft licenses apart from permissive licenses because this freedom requires that derivative works, if distributed, be distributed with open source code. Only by ensuring that derivative works preserve the same four freedoms as the original work does software stay free as it is used, modified, and shared from person to person. In other words, strong copyleft licenses only allow derivative work to be distributed only under equally strong copyleft licenses. Copyleft treats owner and user the same. It is a controversial license, which its detractors pejoratively call "viral licensing."

Permissive licenses generally share the same four freedoms but without the requirement that derivative work preserve those freedoms. In turn, copyleft supporters are quick to point out that—freedom being a right—any "freedom" that can be revoked at whim is not a true freedom.

The divide between these two camps of open source software is due as much to ethics as to practicality. Copyleft licenses empower users to use software freely as long as they, in turn, maintain those freedoms for others. Permissive licenses give permission to "do as you please" with the software with fewer strings attached. The implications for businesses making proprietary software are important. There are legal restrictions to how software may be used and which licenses are compatible with proprietary software, as well as ethical considerations to make for those whose work has been used.

U.S. Government Announces Open Source Policy

The federal government is giving open source software its own stamp of approval. In September 2014, at the U.N. General Assembly, President Obama promised to produce an open source policy for the federal government by the end of 2015.[7] This policy is part of the Open Government commitment "to promote transparency, fight corruption, energize civic engagement, and leverage new technologies to open up governments worldwide".[8] The administration claims that it will use and contribute back to open source software as a way of spurring innovation and cutting costs.

Although details of the policy are unknown, the tenets of the initiative are already established. 18F is a new digital services agency that resembles a Silicon Valley startup, but is actually run by the federal government. Created in the wake up the Healthcare.gov debacle in effort to reform citizen-facing government technology, 18F embraces lean software development practices and releases open source code. Anyone can view their code repositories online and track project updates from their webpage. Its Open Source Policy specifies the benefits and uses of FOSS, its commitment to community involvement, and the software licenses under which their own code is released.[9]

Ethical Considerations

An open source policy is not just for the public sector. Private companies should give equal concern to how they draw from and give back to the wide community of open source software developers. By its nature, software is creative work that builds on work before it. One program is built on others, which, in turn, may become a building block for yet another. The desire to preserve intellectual property should be balanced by ethical considerations.

Returning to Weiner, the great principles of ethics concerning information technology are freedom for human development, equality of positions, benevolence towards all, and minimal infringement of freedom by the community and state.[10] FOSS embodies the principles of freedom, equality, and minimal infringement quite well. Lawrence Lessig, Stanford Law professor, has claimed, "open code is a constraint on state power."[11] To that one might add corporate power. Indeed, Stallman, for whom free software is a moral imperative, considers proprietary software unethical: "I cannot in good conscience sign a NDA or a software license agreement."[12] Copyleft licenses prevent any one owner from taking away freedoms from others.

Is selling proprietary software unethical? Can Weiner's principles be reconciled with proprietary software, which uses copyright to limit free use and distribution, withholds source code that others could benefit from, and holds the rights of the owner above those of the user? Contra Stallman, I suggest that it is not. Open source and closed source software projects can coexist as peacefully as public libraries and private bookstores, or, more to the point, nonprofit organizations and for-profit businesses. Information is a public good as well as a traded good. Selling some information (e.g. object code) while withholding other information (e.g. source code) may not be morally commendable, but is morally permissible.

In order for software businesses and makers of proprietary software to be socially responsible, they should recognize that they have benefitted directly or indirectly from free information and free software and give back accordingly. For example, a proprietary software project that draws heavily on the work of third-party software under an MIT license has legal right to sell its product for profit without permission from or payment to the third-party developer. Nevertheless, the company has an ethical duty to support that developer or her community in some way, such as contributing open source work back to the original project or publically sharing related research. This is how open source and proprietary software can coexist and benefit from each other. An open source policy sets the conditions and boundaries for employees to do the right thing, with company support.

Creating an Open Source Policy

The details of an open source policy will differ from company to company. A company that only creates internal IT software that is not sold or widely distributed will have different considerations and concerns than a software publisher. So, too, will the software license for a company's product affect how it deals with using outside code under various open source licenses.

As a rule, proprietary software is incompatible with strong copyleft software licenses such as GPL. This means that GPL-licensed code cannot be used in production code for proprietary software, but GPL-licensed software may be used for developer tools in support of producing that software. It is good practice for engineering teams to record and track all open-source contributions and dependencies in their code base and for management to audit this list regularly. Practical guidelines such as these should be laid out in the policy for developers to follow when pulling bits of code or programs from the Internet.

In addition, the policy should set ethical guidelines for community engagement and socially good practices. It is common for developers to modify open-source projects to fit their needs. In many cases, these modifications would be of benefit to the community. The open source policy should establish a procedure for internally reviewing code and approving it for release back into the wild (i.e. open-source project). The policy may also specify whether this is to be done through a developer's personal account or through a company account. Regular contribution to an open-source community is not only socially responsible but also improves the public reputation of the company.

Just as the federal government is using the open source policy to improve transparency by doing its work in the open, a commercial company can use the policy to ensure copyright law is followed internally and the guiding principles of information technology are well respected.

Conclusion

After three decades of development, the open source movement has become mainstream. For over a decade, Linux, a FOSS alternative to proprietary operating systems like Windows or Mac, has seen widespread use in production servers. Today open source is gaining ground in cloud stacks, software networks, and big data platforms.[13] From operating systems to applications to single-purpose programs to snippets of code, open source software is everywhere. Any business that creates its own software will use third-party open source software: as a platform, as a development or operations tool, as a dependency for one's own software, as code directly integrated into one's own software, or all of the above. Developers working on a software product must know how this mixture of external (shared as open source) and internal work (released as closed source) should be handled. The policy should establish when and how open source software may be used in accordance with license agreements and upholding ethical obligations towards the community.

---

1 Balkin, Jack M. *Digital Speech and Democratic Culture: a Theory of Freedom of Expression for the Information Society.* New York University Law Review, Vol. 79, No. 1, 2004.

2 Lessig, Lawrence. *Code: And Other Laws of Cyberspace, Version 2.0.* Basic Books. Dec. 2006.

3 Bynum, Terrell. "Computer and Information Ethics." *The Stanford Encyclopedia of Philosophy.* 2011. Accessed Dec. 2014 <plato.stanford.edu>.

4 Baase, Sara. *A Gift of Fire: Social, Legal, and Ethical Issues for Computing Technology – 4th Revised Edition.* Pearson Education Limited. 2012.

5 "Open Source Licenses by Category." Open Source Initiative. 4 Dec. 2014. Accessed Dec. 2014 <opensource.org>.

6 "What Is Free Software?" GNU Project - Free Software Foundation. 5 Aug. 2014. Accessed Dec. 2014 <www.gnu.org>.

7 Clozel, Lalita. "U.S. to Craft Open Source Policy by Next Year." *Technical.ly.* 29 Sep. 2014. Accessed Dec. 2014 <www.technical.ly>

8 "Announcing New U.S. Open Government Commitments on the Third Anniversary of the Open Government Partnership." The White House. 24 Sep. 2014. Accessed Dec. 2014 <www.whitehouse.gov>.

9 "18F/open-source-policy." *GitHub.* 18F. 20 Nov. 2014. Accessed Dec. 2014 <github.com>.

10 Bynum.

11 Lessig.

12 Marko, Kurt. "Open Source Vs. Proprietary: Time For A New Manifesto - Network Computing." Network Computing. 20 Nov. 2014. Accessed Dec. 2014 <www.networkcomputing.com>.

13 Ibid.

The Future of Bitcoin

Divya Yadav

March 2014

Abstract: Bitcoin is a form of digital currency that has gained popularity since its inception. While Bitcoin seems to be facing tough times with the shutdown of the Mt. Gox exchange, this research note discusses its history and its future.

Introduction

Bitcoin has been in the news lately, having gained momentum over the last few years. Bitcoin is a peer-to-peer payment system and digital currency introduced as open source software in 2009 by developer Satoshi Nakamoto.[1] A Bitcoin in itself is an encrypted string of data, or a hash, encoded to signify one unit of currency.[2] Bitcoin has value just like gold or silver but it is mined from code.[3] Bitcoin is also an online financial network that is similar to conventional payment networks like Visa or PayPal, except that it is a decentralized payment system. Its peer-to-peer structure has with hundreds of computers all over the Internet working together to process Bitcoin transactions.[4]

What makes Bitcoin so appealing? To create a new financial service one needs to collaborate with a financial institution but Bitcoin has no such restrictions. Currently, people do not need permission to create a Bitcoin Financial Service. This low barrier to entry may allow the creation of a new generation of innovative financial services, in much the same way that the Internet's open architecture led to innovative new online services.[5] Bitcoin appeals to people who believe it represents the spirit of libertarianism-- free, unfettered, and uncontrolled.[6] However, this uncontrolled and free of government regulations environment also offers a safe haven for criminal activities to flourish.

Transactions with Bitcoins

Nakamoto wanted people to be able to exchange money electronically and securely without the need for a third party, such as a bank or a company like PayPal. He based Bitcoin on cryptographic techniques that allow one to be sure the money received is genuine, even if you do not trust the sender.[7] Bitcoin client software needs to be installed by users in order to make transactions with Bitcoins. Once the software is downloaded, it connects over the Internet to the decentralized network of all Bitcoin users and also generates a pair of unique, mathematically linked keys, which a user will need to exchange Bitcoins with any other client. One key is private and the other is public, and a version of it called a Bitcoin address is given to other people so they can send you Bitcoins.

Crucially, it is practically impossible—even with the most powerful supercomputer—to work out someone's private key from their public key, which in theory (and until recently) prevents anyone from impersonating the users. When users perform a transaction, their Bitcoin software performs a mathematical operation to combine the other party's public key and their own private key with the amount of Bitcoins that the user wants to transfer. The result of that operation is then sent out across the distributed Bitcoin network so the transaction can be verified by Bitcoin software clients not involved in the transfer. This process ensures at least theoretically the safety of the users and validates that the transaction is happening between two real users.[8]

The nature of the mathematics ensures that it is computationally easy to verify a transaction but practically impossible to generate fake transactions and spend Bitcoins that users do not own. Since there is a public log for each transaction, it also serves as a deterrent for money laundering and provides an additional layer of security to Bitcoin transaction system.[9]

How to Secure Bitcoins
Bitcoins can be bought and exchanged in different currencies from exchange servers like Mt. Gox. To store this digital currency all users need is an account

for Bitcoin wallet which essentially is just a website or a program and stores the digital codes for Bitcoins and provides an easy interface to monitor the transactions.

This all seems fast and easy, but the bottom line is all the money is being saved online and this makes it vulnerable to hackers who can go at great lengths to secure these codes and a user be virtually without any money in a matter of seconds. This poses a huge security risk for Bitcoin and will very likely prevent users from relying on models such as this. If a user wants to deal with Bitcoin he or she needs to be computer savvy, and at this point it is risky for computer novices. One of the ways to secure Bitcoins on a personal computer is to add a layer of encryption and not only by just means of a strong password because hackers can still track keystrokes. A good idea would be to store all the information offline with the help what is called cold storage wallets. Cold storage wallets store private Bitcoin keys offline, so that they cannot be stolen by someone else on the Internet.[10]

Impact on Economy

Now we know how Bitcoin works and the mechanisms that make the transactions and store the currency. However, we still need to know if Bitcoin or virtual currency in general is here to stay and, if it is, how it will affect the economy. Interestingly enough,

Bitcoin is not the first digital currency to have come out in the market but is definitely the first one to survive because it is "the first crypto-currency with the deep structure, wide adoption, and trading momentum to achieve escape velocity."[11]

Timothy Carmody says that:

"Bitcoin is backed by no government, and its value is not rooted in precious metals. Instead, it is distributed across the entire network of users, its roots in complex digital mathematics. Bitcoin supporters say that this makes the currency immune to manipulation by politicians or oligarchs seeking to move its value up or down for politics or profit."[12]

Some researchers and investors note that Bitcoin could be a permanent solution to a fluctuating economy. Carmody suggests further that, with governments' financial and credit troubles causing major problems for their currencies, global investors are looking for something firmer than the promise of a central bank. He suggests that, like gold or other precious metals used as currencies Bitcoins are scarce. However, their scarcity is algorithmic, as opposed to natural or accidental. Additionally, according to Carmody, "Bitcoin mining guarantees a fixed rate of inflation (relative to itself)."[13]

Bitcoin can be especially helpful in countries that still do not deal in credit and debit cards. It will provide a way for people to make transfers without having to worry about fraud. Carmody says

"money has become data, especially when you view money as a transactional unit that needs to be transferred and delivered from one platform to another. Digital currency offers that and with much more security especially the world we live in today where ever transaction happens online. Though it will never replace financial institutions' current systems, Carmody believes that Bitcoin has the capability to set up an "international payment system."[14]

He suggests that "if Bitcoin becomes widespread, respected, and legitimate, that pressures everyone - all the central banks and banking companies—to bring down those costs in order to stay competitive."[15]

Regulation

Regulation on Bitcoin differs in each country. While it is legal to complete transactions in Bitcoins in the U.S. and Germany, Russia on the other hand has branded it illegal because it views a substitute for money.[16] Government has no centralized control over Bitcoins like they do have at traditional financial institutions, which makes it particularly hard to regulate Bitcoin. Nevertheless, in the wake of recent failures of Mt. Gox and the breakup of Silk Road, the U.S. is planning to impose some regulation.

Benjamin Lawsky, New York's financial services superintendent, said he will issue "BitLicenses" to companies dealing with Bitcoins. That would mark the most significant step thus far in the U.S. to regulate the digital currency.[17] These "Bitcoin exchanges should have to warn their customers virtual transactions are irreversible, Bitcoin values are volatile and they should carefully guard their digital wallet keys."[18] Bitcoin exchanges might also be forced to adopt the same "know-your- customer" requirements, which currently force financial institutions to keep an eye on customer behavior and report suspicious activity to law enforcement. Regulation will only add credibility to the digital currency and provide a trusted and safe platform for customers to make transactions.[19]

Ethical Considerations and Recent Cases

While the idea of Bitcoin and digital currency seems appealing and very scientific, there are still many ethical considerations. Criminal activity involving Bitcoin has largely centered on theft of the currency, money laundering, the use of botnets for mining, and the use of Bitcoins in exchange for illegal items or services.

Bitcoin's decentralized network is being put to test in wake of recent incidents that test the lack of regulations. The most fundamental threat was a bug in some basic software that determines how Bitcoins are moved between digital accounts. That forced several of the largest Bitcoin exchanges to shut down for most of last week and raised questions about the sturdiness of the programming underlying the currency.[20] But the biggest shock came from the shutdown of Mt. Gox, a Bitcoin exchange that handled almost 70 percent of Bitcoin transactions.[21] "It announced that around 850,000 Bitcoins belonging to customers and the company were missing and likely stolen, an amount valued at more than $450 million at the time."[22] This incident seriously challenges the credibility and future of Bitcoin. While people may view regulations a way for government to interfere, a lack of regulation has a way of attracting criminals and a ground to conduct illegal activities.

Silk Road was a marketplace that dealt in drug related transactions made through Bitcoin. In October 2013, the U.S. Federal Bureau of Investigation shut the marketplace down. Shortly thereafter, however, tech savvy outlaws started Silk Road 2.0.[23] It is primarily used to buy and sell drugs. Bitcoins are the only kind of currency accepted on the site, because they are traded electronically and are difficult to trace to individuals. However, Bitcoin accounts also lack protections that most bank accounts have, including government-backed insurance. That means the Bitcoins stolen from the Silk Road users are gone forever. The hackers took advantage of the same the glitch that impacted Mt. Gox and stole worth $2.7 million from customers. [24] This incident serves as a reminder that regulations and laws are necessary to keep harmful entities at bay and in order for a novel concept like Bitcoin to boom.

Conclusion

Public reception of Bitcoin has largely been mixed and most people are not even aware such a mode of money exists. People generally are very careful with money and want it secured by credible institutions that are protected by the government. Banks succeed because people have confidence in them, and because their deposits are insured. Bitcoin might not succeed but the idea of digital currency will live and flourish. Bitcoin has already made history and has provided an outlet in the times of a very fluctuating economy.

1 Davis, Joshua. "The Crypto-Currency." *The New Yorker*. 10 Oct. 2011. Accessed Mar. 2014 <www.newyorker.com>.
2 "Bitcoin 101- The Digital Currency Revolution". *Online Accounting Degree Guide*. N.D. Accessed Mar. 2014 <www.online- accounting-degrees.net>.
3 Ibid.

4 Lee, Timothy B. "12 Questions about Bitcoin You Were Too Embarrassed to Ask." *The Washington Post*. 19 Nov. 2013. Accessed Mar. 2014 <www.washingtonpost.com>.

5 Ibid.

6 Krigsman, Michael. "Is Bitcoin the Future of Money? Not a Chance." *ZDNet*. 11 Oct. 2013. Accessed Mar. 2014 <www.zdnet.com>.

7 Simonite, Tom. "What Bitcoin Is, and Why It Matters." *MIT Technology Review*. 25 Mar. 2011. Accessed Mar. 2014 <www.technologyreview.com>.

8 Ibid.

9 Ibid.

10 "How to Store Your Bitcoins." *CoinDesk*. 20 Feb. 2014. Accessed Mar. 2014 <www.coindesk.com>.

11 Carmody, Timothy. "Money 3.0: How Bitcoins May Change the Global Economy." *National Geographic*. 13 Oct. 2013. Accessed Mar. 2014 <www.nationalgeographic.com>

12 Ibid.

13 Ibid.

14 Ibid.

15 Ibid.

16 "Regulation of Bitcoin in Selected Jurisdictions." The Law Library of Congress. Jan. 2014. Accessed Mar. 2014 <www.loc.gov>.

17 Pagliery, Jose. "Bitcoin Regulations Coming This Year." *CNN Money*. 12 Feb. 2014. Accessed Mar. 2014 <www.money.cnn.com>.

18 Ibid.

19 Ibid.

20 Poper, Nathanial. "Regulators and Hackers Put Bitcoin to the Test." *The New York Times*. 17 Feb. 2014. Accessed Mar. 2014 <www.nytimes.com>.

21 Vigna, Paul. "5 Things About Mt. Gox's Crisis." *The Wall Street Journal*. 25 Feb. 2014. Accessed Mar. 2014 <www.wsj.com>.

22 Abrams, Rachel and Nathaniel Popper. "Trading Side Failure Stirs Ire and Hope for Bitcoin." *The New York Times*. 25 Feb. 2014. Accessed Mar. 2014 <www.nytimes.com>.

23 Pagliery, Jose. "Drug Site Silk Road Wiped Out By Bitcoin." *CNN Money*. 14 Feb. 2014. Accessed Mar. 2014 <www.money.cnn.com>.

24 Ibid.

The Olympics - Impact on Security, Economy & Culture

Divya Yadav

February 2014

Abstract: Hosting the Olympics is a matter of pride and glory for any country but the current landscape has introduced so many factors that not every city or country can claim this prized possession. Security has been at the forefront with the ongoing Sochi Winter Olympics. Security is always a challenge with mega sporting events like the Olympics but countries are willing to do anything to overcome the fear and grab that chance of hosting the Olympics. This paper explores different aspects of hosting the Olympics and the tradeoffs that make them so appealing.

Introduction

The Winter Olympics of 2014 were hosted by Sochi, Russia, and garnered attention for a variety of reasons, including its proximity to a volatile region marred by violence, human rights issues, terrorist threats, and the fact that the region does not naturally produce much snow. Russia marketed itself well seven years ago to win the bid for the 2014 Winter Olympics. Russia's president, Vladimir Putin, lobbied the International Olympic committee and made helped ensure that his country won the right to host the Olympics – a triumph, since the last time Moscow hosted the Olympics in 1980 it was marred with controversy over Russia's invasion of Afghanistan and the subsequent withdrawal of 65 nations, including the U.S. The Olympics have been seen as Putin's pet project, where he can display Russia as a force to reckoned with, and promote himself a great leader. However, this Olympics is not just about Russia, it is about terrorist threats and the fundamental security of the venue, the athletes, and their families. Many athletes have decided to leave their families back home. The U.S. specifically asked its participants not to wear clothing that identifies them as Americans in public; and the U.S. government has prepared a naval escape route through the Black Sea in the event of a terrorist attack.[1]

The 2014 Winter Olympics is widely viewed as the most expensive games ever, with an estimated \$50 billion in spending on venue and infrastructure.[2] Hosting the Olympics is a big task and has social, economic, and political implications. Almost all the Olympics venues in the modern era are scrutinized by the global community, particularly regarding security, and responsibility of a government to host a secure Olympics has become even more challenging.

Criteria for Selecting Olympic Venues

Winning the bid to the host the Olympics is a long and rigorous process that involves getting through different phases. Cities bid for a chance to host the Olympics and the application fee alone is significant, with the fee for hosting the 2012 Olympics totaling $150,000.[3] This is meant to help filter out cities that are not up the task of committing to the extensive and expensive undertaking that is hosting the Olympics. The International Olympic Committee (IOC) investigates each city on several points that include the size of the city, its ability to host the events, and its ability to accommodate number of athletes, journalists, tourists, and politicians from different nations that will come for the games. They must have adequate hotels and commit build new stadiums and venues for the games if necessary. Cities also need to show that they have or will build a good mass transit system for transportation within the city. The new infrastructure comes under what is called building an "Olympic Village." This requires a large investment in infrastructure and the city needs to be able to prove that this investment is in the best interest of economic and social empowerment for the city. Each city needs to convince the committee how the local residents are going to benefit from the games and if it will help in job creation and similar economic interests5.

When it was announced Sochi was going to host the Winter Olympics for 2014, it came as a surprise to many. Sochi is primarily a summer resort town situated on the east side of Black Sea. The temperatures rarely drop below 37 degrees Fahrenheit, and the city barely had one ski track and ski lift. The astonishing cost for this particular Olympics is because the entire ski resort had to essentially be built from the ground up. This venue selection also points toward the fact that political and economic power also plays an important role in the selection process, as well. Hosting the Olympics brings a sense of pride for the nation, keeps it in the spotlight for two complete weeks, and provides an opportunity to boost tourism in the city.[4] The Russian government and particularly Putin pulled many strings to win the bid, but it is still to be seen if the $50 billion investment will pay off in the long run for Russia or not. As we saw in the opening ceremonies, Russia took the opportunity to highlight certain parts of its history to the stadium audience and billions around the world.

Security at Olympics

The Olympic committee also determines if the city is secure enough to host the games and if it will be able step up the security if necessary, as the Olympics can be a very prominent target for terrorist organizations.

The current winter Olympics at Sochi have proved this point beyond doubt. Around 100,000 security guards are deployed in the zone and the venue is also protected by mass surveillance technology.[5]

The Russian government has received numerous threats from insurgents groups that have vowed to disturb the Olympics. The question on everyone minds is why was Sochi ever selected to host the games? In these times security is the single most important point of consideration when venues are decided for hosting the Olympics. How did the committee fail to see the terrorist volatility of Sochi? The 2012 London Summer Olympics in had to take extreme security precautions. However, due to several terrorist attacks and threats since 2000, London's security in all forms (air, naval, IT and physical assets) was already strengthened. London is a major city and has multiple evacuation routes, if anything were to happen to the city. It might be hard for extremists to disrupt a city as big as London, but in Sochi, it is an entirely different story.

A NBC reported claimed that his cellphone and laptop were immediately hacked in Sochi once he connected to the Wi-Fi.[6] Recent cases of data breaches and personal identity thefts connected to major U.S. retail stores have left the people wondering if they really should be logged in with their personal devices.

Providing IT security has become so important now given the fact most people have smartphones, laptops, tablets and will use them especially in a place unknown to them but at the same risking all the personal and financial information stored in those devices.

The parameters and scope of providing security at Olympics has changed a lot in recent years. It will be interesting to see how this unfolds in the years to come and Sochi will serve as a good reminder to the Olympic Committee about mistakes not to be made in the future, when selecting a venue.

Impact of Hosting the Olympics

Hosting the Olympics is widely perceived to have a huge social, cultural, and economic impact on the country. The results have been mixed: some host cities and countries had to settle for net losses whereas some cities actually benefitted in the end. The fact of the matter is these are just estimates and best guess and cannot serve as a predictor for future events. It is all about timely planning and building infrastructures that could be used once the games are over. Most countries have to do with structures that cannot be used for any practical purpose, so building the structure becomes a waste of money. While most cities recover a major amount of their investments from broadcast rights around the world, the infrastructure costs are particularly difficult. A smart workaround to tackle these costs is to use existing structure and build only that which is required in terms of sporting venues and arenas. This strategy does not only compensate for the losses but ends up to be quite profitable.

Santo and Gildner say "cities pursue the Olympic Games for three important reasons: tourism, image, and regeneration."[7] The Olympics bring the world's attention to the host city, which people will remember for years to come, as well as having a huge impact on country's tourism prospects. The fact that people are willing to travel and spend so much on "mega" sporting events such as Olympics is a good sign for the global economy. In 2005, for example, the Travel Industry Association of America (2006) reported that domestic and international travel added $650 billion to the U.S. economy, generating 8 million jobs, $171 billion in payroll income, and $105 billion in federal, state, and local tax revenues.[8]

In addition to boosting tourism, city officials and government market the venues for investment opportunities to large corporations, promising future job growth for the area. "At the city level, policy makers attempt to attract travelers through the branding of places and by focusing regeneration strategies to attract investment funds and human

capital."[9] London successfully hosted the Summer
Olympics in 2012, and has since then seen a boost in
its economic growth based on its Olympics
investment.[10]

Conclusion

Hosting the Olympics is definitely a matter of pride
and joy for most nations and so many of them dream
of being able to host it one day. Benefits aside, it is a
chance for nations not only to put themselves in
spotlight but showcase to the world their culture,
heritage, history and how they have adopted modern
technology and have transitioned into the future.
There is more to it than just establishing world
supremacy - it is so much a matter of pride that the
world will remember the events for years to come.
One can argue it is the most expensive sporting event
to host, thus countries have to be realistic when it
comes to hosting and should look beyond mere glory
and pride. Hosting also requires smart and strategic
administration for planning in a way that its citizens
can benefit in the end. With security being the new
focus, countries now more than ever will have to be
open about its military and other associate defense
capabilities and do a realistic evaluation if they can
provide a safe environment for athletes and all the
people attending the event. A time may come in the
future where every country and city will be able to

attain it with ease but for now there are many considerations to be made.

---

1 Vandiver, John. "EUCOM Commander: U.S. Troops Ready if Called to Assist in Sochi." *Stars & Stripes*. 1 Feb. 2014. Accessed Feb. 2014 <www.stripes.com>.

2 Rosenberg, Steve. "Putin's Hopes to Burnish Russia's Image with Sochi 2014." *BBC News*. 6 Feb. 2014. Accessed Feb. 2014 <www.bbc.com>.

3 "How the Olympic Locations Are Chosen." *Scholastic*. N.D. Accessed Feb. 2014 <www.teacher.scholastic.com>.

4 Ibid.

5 "Sochi 2014: A Security Challenge." *Forbes*. 9 Jan. 2014. Accessed Feb. 2014 <www.forbes.com>.

6 Cosman, Ben. "Hackers Run Rampant in Sochi as Journalists Pour In." *The Wire*. 5 Feb. 2014. Accessed Feb. 2014 <www.thewire.com>.

7 Santo, Charles A. and Cerard C.S. Mildner. "Political Economy and the Olympic Games." *Sports and Public Policy*. 2010.

8 Ibid.

9 Ibid.

10 "Olympic Games Legacy Boosts Economy by Billions." UK Department for Culture, Media & Sport. 19 Jul. 2013. Accessed Feb. 2014 <www.gov.uk>.

Chapter III
Privacy

The Law: The Right to be Forgotten
Heather M. Brammer
February 2015

Abstract: While online privacy is a concern for all, there is no international standard for users to limit personal information that has been either intentionally or inadvertently released to the public. The Right To Be Forgotten is a law enacted recently in the European Union. The law requires search engines to limit content about citizens that they themselves deem inadequate, irrelevant, or outdated. The new legislation has thrown the global online community into an uproar due to its broad and vague nature. Questions regarding free speech, censorship and legality abound. Similar laws exist and continue to evolve in other countries as well. There are very few federal laws in the U.S. to protect users at this time.

Introduction

On a Friday night in early November, Vinita Hegwood posted a few thoughts to her Twitter account, as she did on most evenings. However one particular tweet was so racially charged that it went viral and swiftly led to Ms. Hegwood's dismissal from her teaching position at Duncanville High School the following Monday[1]. Annmarie Chiarini, a college English professor, was traumatized after a former lover posted nude images of her, along with her name and place of employment, on several websites from 2010 to 2012.[2] John and Jessica Kier have been dogged by multiple online images of their mug shots from an arrest for a minor crime of which they were later found Not Guilty. Mrs. Kier believes that she has been turned down for multiple jobs due to these images that appear when searching for her name on Google.[3]

Countless individuals make conscious decisions to post personal and often damaging information on the Internet on a daily basis. People around the world are reporting loss of employment, rejection from universities and other repercussions from social media postings. Others are the victims of "revenge porn," and may have private photographs and other personal details about them released to the public without their consent. Still more have criminal records that are available for anyone to find simply by typing in their name. These damaging stories and images may now be forever linked with these ordinary citizens, and are available to anyone who performs an Internet search on their names in the future.

Some might argue that people should have the right to expunge this negative personal information from the Internet. Others feel that to do so would be a dangerous and slippery play on free speech rights. Scholars and historians might object to what is perceived as a whitewashing of history. There are even more who would argue for victims who did not willingly volunteer any of their personal data or images. Legislation currently exists in the US to protect some victims of Internet harassment, but these laws do not exist across all fifty states, and are often difficult to prosecute and enforce.

The European Union has recently instituted a legal avenue for erasing Internet content, but it has yet to be truly tested and faces extreme criticism both domestically and abroad. It remains to be seen what new laws and regulations might arise due to unflattering Internet content, and how they will be applied in a global context.

The Right to Be Forgotten – European Union

In response to recent lawsuits in the European Union, the EU has recently passed "The Right To Be Forgotten", an addendum to the European Data Protection Directive.[4] The European Court of Justice (ECJ) issued this ruling on May 13, 2014, following the outcome of a court case brought by a Spanish citizen[5]. Mario Consteja Gonzales brought the case to trial through the Spanish Data Protection agency after several national news outlets printed reports of his financial insolvency in 1998. Gonzales, a businessman, felt that although he had rectified his financial problems, the continued availability of this information would hurt his business prospects in the future. He petitioned to have this information removed from Google search results and from the newspaper articles themselves. While the Spanish agency was not successful in having the references from the actual articles removed, the ECJ ruled that Google bore the responsibility to remove the search engines' capability to register and display these references.[6]

Paragraph 93 of the ruling states

> *"that even initially lawful processing of accurate data may, in the course of time, become incompatible with the directive where those data are no longer necessary... That is so in particular where they appear to be inadequate, irrelevant or no longer relevant, or excessive in relation to those purposes and in the light of the time that has elapsed."*[7]

This language directly correlates the difference between the European definitions of privacy versus the American definition. Certain European rights dictate that convicted criminals, once they have served time for their crime, may petition to have their criminal records obscured,[8] while in America these facts are considered to be a matter of public record. However this new ruling does not pertain only to criminals or those with negative publicity. Under this law, all citizens of the European Union have the right to request that pertinent information about themselves be hidden from Internet searches.

While this law is directed at all search engines, it primarily affects Google, Inc., as the company has over 90 percent of the market share in the European Union.[9] The law requires that search engines such as Google remove links to content as requested by the individual. It does not require that the original reporting agency remove the information. Therefore, while the information is still available on the Internet, it will now be much more difficult to locate.[10] In response to the ruling, Google set up a page to receive and process requests from members of the 28 countries in the European Union and also Iceland, Lichtenstein, Norway, and Switzerland. Google makes it clear that their team will consider all requests to limit certain search results, but that not all requests may be granted, based upon the nature of the content:

"When evaluating your request, we will look at whether the results include outdated information about you, as well as whether there's a public interest in the information — for example, we may decline to remove certain information about financial scams, professional malpractice, criminal convictions, or public conduct of government officials."[11]

To date, Google has processed over 175,000 requests, and has removed hundreds of thousands of links to content[12]. These requests have come from child predators, politicians, and celebrities, among other private citizens.[13] The BBC recently reported that over half of the requests from the UK were from criminals seeking to have their information concealed.[14]

Criticisms

The most obvious criticism to the EU's new Right To Be Forgotten is censorship. It is easy to question why a citizen should be able to simply erase items from the public record that they deem to be negative. There are several arguments both for and against this practice. Obviously, not many would argue against the right to have libelous or slanderous content removed from the Internet. Incorrect information would certainly qualify as something that could easily be remedied by limiting search results. However, the argument against targeting search engines like Google is that the content remains on the internet, and is just a little more difficult to recover, not gone completely. In cases of libel or slander, it would be more effective to petition the actual publishers of the content and to have the information truly removed, not simply obscured. The European court's opinion of this line of thinking is "that the results of a Google search often matter more than the information on any individual Web site."[15]

While it does make sense to limit the availability of libelous or slanderous information that was posted erroneously or without the consent of an individual, it is unclear why a law would be written in such a way to allow for the obliteration of content an individual willingly posted in a public forum. If such a law was to exist in the U.S., persons like Vinita Hegwood could simply petition to have all evidence of their politically incorrect musings removed from search results, potentially giving the impression that she was an upstanding educator who valued diversity, or at least, had never publicly issued discriminatory sentiments. We cannot simply have a "do-over" in this new paradigm of over-sharing. While it is one thing to regret posting a photograph of oneself while intoxicated, it is quite another to post a series of hateful rants and then ask the world to pretend that it never happened. The Internet could quickly devolve into an environment in which evidence of any egregious act can simply be washed away in an instant. Users should bear some responsibility for their actions. In the face of an environment in which everything we write and post is public, people should simply be more vigilant about how, where and of whom they speak. The House of Lords in the United

Kingdom has vociferously spoken out against the
Right To Be Forgotten for this very reason:

"We do not believe that individuals should be able to
have links to accurate and lawfully available
information about them removed, simply because
they do not like what is said."[i]

Another criticism of this new ruling is that the
language is too vague, and leaves a lot of room for
interpretation on behalf of the data provider. As it is
written, the law allows for deletion of data deemed no
longer relevant, or for information pertaining to an
event that occurred a reasonable amount of time in
the past. This new law did not provide for a governing
body to preside over these requests, it placed the onus
directly on the data provider. Thus, Google had to
quickly develop a system of criteria for making
decisions about these requests, including assembling a
group of lawyers and other professionals to weigh in
on individual issues. Microsoft Bing, Facebook,
Wikipedia and Yahoo also have subsidiaries in
Europe and are currently devising their own
guidelines for complying with the new regulation[16].
While Google and these other large companies have
large teams of legal professionals to help make these

---

i House of Lords EU Home Affairs, Health and Education Sub-Committee, "'Right to Be Forgotten'
    Is Misguided in Principle and Unworkable in Practice, Say Lords."

determinations, smaller search engine companies may not have those resources available to them and would have no choice but to indiscriminately grant these requests or face financial ruin.[17] The UK House of Lords also voiced these objections:

"We believe that the judgment of the Court is unworkable. It does not take into account the effect the ruling will have on smaller search engines which, unlike Google, are unlikely to have the resources to process the thousands of removal requests they are likely to receive...We also believe that it is wrong in principle to leave search engines themselves the task of deciding whether to delete information or not, based on vague, ambiguous and unhelpful criteria, and we heard from witnesses how uncomfortable they are with the idea of a commercial company sitting in judgment on issues like that."[18]

A task force has been set up to assist with definition of the regulation, in the interest of the public, but spokespersons have admitted that the team is still in the learning phase.[19]

Lastly, the current assumption is that link removal only occurs in the country of which the requestor resides. For example, if a user in Belgium requests that content about them is removed, one supposition is that Google is only responsible for removing those content links from Google.be. However it is unclear as to whether the removal requests should be applied across all of the Google European subsidiary search engines, or strictly for the country in which the citizen currently inhabits.[20]

A case has already been tried in France that challenges these boundaries. The plaintiff first sued Google in August 2013 to have falsely reported information removed from search indexes. The French court ordered Google to remove the links to the erroneous content. Google complied with the order, but now more recently been accused of removing links only on the Google France site. The French court is now demanding that Google remove the information across all of its subsidiary sites, including the Google site in the U.S.[21] A precedent such as this could quickly lead to chaos on the Internet, with radically different information being available in each country.

The Right to Be Forgotten in Other Countries

The European Union is not the first community to institute Right to Be Forgotten laws. The majority of Latin American countries have some form of data protection laws, most notably in Argentina. An Argentinian law was created in 2000 (Ley 25.326), stating "that data be destroyed when it ceases to be necessary or relevant for the purposes for which they were collected" and also decrees that databases are required to remove such data when it is deemed no longer relevant.[22]   Most notably, this law has been applied in situations where female performers are finding their images associated with pornographic sites or sites promoting illegal activity, the most famous being Da Cunha v. Yahoo and Google. The initial lawsuit did not allege any wrongdoing on behalf of the search engines that link to this content, but did demand that the search engines remove the links to the content associated with the actress' name.[23] Later appeals on behalf of Yahoo and Google saw this ruling overturned, a decision hailed by some as a successful win against censorship.[24] Even in the wake of this decision, still more Argentinian celebrities have been waging battle with the Internet to have damaging content removed.

Australia has recently been investigating a reform to their data privacy laws. According to a report by the Australian Law Reform Commission, Australia does not currently have any laws in place for invasion of privacy, and has been growing increasingly concerned in the digital era.[25] Australia's proposed new regulation differs from the EU in that it only makes provisions for content that was placed on the Internet by the individuals themselves.[26] This is contradictory to a 2012 lawsuit in Melbourne in which an Australian citizen successfully sued Google for defamation after his name repeatedly appeared in Google search results in relation to Melbourne's Most Wanted, even though he had never been associated with any crimes.[27] The problem with this proposed legislation is that it does not appear to allow for victims of revenge or libel to clear their names.

A plaintiff in Tokyo recently won a suit against Google for similar issues involving wrongful accusation, however Japan has made this a one-time ruling and has not decreed any changes to Japanese law.[28]

U.S. Internet Privacy Laws

No legislation like the European Union's Right To Be Forgotten law exists in the U.S.. U.S. Internet users can make a request to Google to have certain information removed from search results. Google has stated that the search engine will remove Personally Identifiable Information such as bank account and credit card numbers,[29] but makes it clear that this service is very limited. Google also allows for removal of illegal information, primarily copyright violations.[30]

Citizens who speak indelicately on social media run the risk of having their indiscretions be permanently accessible to all. Those who are lucky enough to have their behavior picked up by major news outlets, such as Ms. Hegwood will face real difficulty when attempting to hide their past. There are currently no US laws in place protecting employees from being terminated based upon social media activity. Online services (such as Reputation.com) exist to assist users in cleaning up their online image, by flooding the Internet with alternate information, the intent being to obscure the damaging data. Other companies (CleanSearch.com, ClearMyRecord.com) claim that they can have information such as arrest records and online mug shot images removed, for a fee.

Only a handful of US states have enacted legislation to assist victims of revenge porn, by prohibiting the transmission of sexually explicit images of someone without their consent[31]. These laws can help victims when requesting removal of their personal images and data, but only within these thirteen states. No federal laws of this nature exist. In most states, it is not a crime to post sexually explicit images of an individual without their consent. Therefore it is most often the responsibility of the victim, like Ms. Chiarini who must pursue these sites for the removal of images and data, but they are often unsuccessful and have no legal recourse. Even ordinary users who have a clean criminal history but who want to remove some or all of their online presence face an almost impossible set of tasks that would take days to accomplish.[32] Simply deleting a Facebook account takes fourteen days, and the company still reserves the right to keep some of your images and data.[33]

Conclusion

Many Internet users are guilty of self-publishing damning information on social media outlets that they later regret. Others face having their private mistakes reported in multiple news outlets across the world. While some citizens feel that they have ownership over their public image and of content that pertains to them, there is no global standard for how, when and if this information should be obscured from the public. The legal understanding in Europe and Latin America is that private citizens should and do have control over their public image, and should have the ability to make adjustments to Internet content they feel is unflattering, including criminal records. The U.S. steadfast dedication to the First Amendment right to Freedom of Speech directly opposes this type of censorship.

The European Union has recently enacted legislation to enable users to erase online content from search engine results. While this new functionality has already been heavily used, the new law has been met with much criticism. It is important that people have an avenue to resolve incorrect or slanderous information, but some critics feel that the law was passed in haste and is deeply flawed. Private enterprise has been left to interpret and enforce a public law without much regulation. Much concern has been voiced about the obfuscation of criminal history, while others are worried that this law sets a dangerous precedent in that it could be used to erase major historical events.

Obviously, more discussion and research is needed. While the laws of countries may not always align, usage of the Internet is global. Perhaps an International summit is needed to come to a more cohesive solution to this issue. If regulations vary wildly from country to country, we will soon have a lack of transparency and trust in our global neighborhood, which may lead to disastrous consequences.

---

1 Young, Stephen. "A Duncanville Teacher Tweeted That 'Dumb Duck Ass Crackers' Should Kill Themselves." *Unfair Park*. 10 Nov. 2014. Accessed Dec. 2014 <www.blogs.dallasobserver.com>.

2 Chiarini, Annmarie. "I Was a Victim of Revenge Porn. I Don't Want Anyone Else to Face This." *The Guardian*. 19 Nov. 2013. Accessed Dec. 2014 <www.theguardian.com>.

3 Fields, Gary, and John R. Emshwiller. "As Arrest Records Rise, Americans Find Consequences Can Last a Lifetime." *The Wall Street Journal*. 19 Aug. 2014. Accessed Dec. 2014 <www.wsj.com>.

4 European Commission. "Fact Sheet on the 'Right To Be Forgotten' Ruling (C-131/12)." European Commission. 13 May 2014. Accessed Dec. 2014 <www.ec.europa.eu>.

5 Neal, Ryan W. "Google Search Removal Requests: European Criminals, Politicians and Pedophiles Exercising 'Right To Be Forgotten.'" *International Business Times.* 30 May 2014. Accessed Dec. 2014 <www.ibtimes.com>.

6 Toobin, Jeffrey. "Google and the Right to Be Forgotten." *The New Yorker.* 22 Sep. 2014. Accessed Dec. 2014 <www.newyorker.com>.

7 Court of Justice of the European Union, *Directive 95/46/EC — Articles 2, 4, 12 and 14.* 13 May 2014. Accessed Dec. 2014 <www.curia.europa.edu>.

8 Stefanou, Constantin, and Helen Xanthaki. *Towards a European Criminal Record.* Cambridge University Press. 2008. Accessed Dec. 2014 <www.books.google.com>.

9 Goldman, Eric. "Primer on European Union's Right to Be Forgotten." *Technology & Marketing Law Blog.* Aug. 2014. Accessed Dec. 2014 <www.blog.ericgoldman.org>.

10 Ibid.

11 Google.com. "Legal Help: Search Removal Request under Data Protection Law in Europe." Google.com. N.D. Accessed Dec. 2014 <www.support.google.com>.

12 Preece, Caroline, and Rosie Clark. "Google 'Right to Be Forgotten': Everything You Need to Know." *IT PRO.* 2 Dec. 2014. Accessed Dec. 2014 <www.itpro.co.uk>.

13 Neal, Ryan W.

14 Lee, Dave. "Google Offers 'Right to Forget' Form." *BBC News.* 30 May 2014. Accessed Dec. 2014 <www.bbc.com>

15 Toobin, Jeffrey.

16 Preece and Clark.

17 Rosen, Jeffrey.

18 Vincent, James. "House of Lords Criticises Right-to-Be-Forgotten Laws as 'Unworkable and Wrong in Principle.'" *The Independent.* Accessed Dec. 2014 <www.independent.co.uk>.

19 Preece and Clark.

20 Toobin, Jeffrey.

21 Vaas, Lisa. "Google Fined for Not Taking down 'Right to Be Forgotten' Links Worldwide." *Naked Security.* Accessed Dec. 2014 <nakedsecurity.sophos.com>.

22 Carter, Edward L. "Argentina's Right to Be Forgotten." Emory
   University School of Law. 2013. Accessed Dec. 2014
   <law.emory.edu>.

23 Condon, Stephanie. "Argentine Judge: Google, Yahoo Must Censor
   Searches." *CNET*. 12 Nov. 2008. Accessed Dec. 2014
   <www.cnet.com>.

24 Whitney, Lance. "Google, Yahoo Win Argentine Celebrity Search
   Case." *CNET*. 20 Aug. 2010. Accessed Dec. 2014 <www.cnet.com>

25 Australian Law Reform Commission. *Serious Invasions of Privacy in
   the Digital Era (ALRC 123 Summary)*. Australian Law Reform
   Commission. 9 Mar. 2014. Accessed Dec. 2014 <www.alrc.gov.au>.

26 Australian Law Reform Commission. *A New Privacy Principle for
   Deletion of Personal Information*. Australian Law Reform
   Commission. 31 Mar. 2014. Accessed Dec. 2014 <www.alrc.gov.au>.

27 Khalid, Amrita. "Google Loses Lawsuit in Australia Over Defamatory
   Search Results." *Slate*. 12 Nov. 2012. Accessed Dec. 2014 <
   www.slate.com>.

28 "Japan Court Orders Google to Delete Data." *Yahoo News*. 10 Oct.
   2014. Accessed Dec. 2014 <www.news.yahoo.com>.

29 Google.com, "Removal Policies - Search Help." Google.com. N.D.
   Accessed Dec. 2014 <www.support.google.com>.

30 Google.com, "Removing Content From Google - Legal Help."
   Google.com. N.D. Accessed Dec. 2014 <www.support.google.com>.

31 "State 'Revenge Porn' Legislation." National Conference of State
   Legislatures. 19 Nov. 2014. Accessed Dec. 2014 <www.ncsl.org>.

32 Pinola, Melanie. "This Infographic Shows You How to Delete
   Yourself from the Internet." *Lifehacker*. 5 Mar. 2014. Accessed Dec.
   2014 <www.lifehacker.com>

33 Gibbs, Samuel. "How to Delete Your Facebook Account." *The
   Guardian*. 4 Feb. 2014. Accessed Dec. 2014
   <www.theguardian.com>.

Privacy Policies and Public Awareness in the Healthcare Industry

Katharine Gallagher

October 2014

Abstract: Technology has become a popular and convenient mode for delivering healthcare services. Self-service tools allow people to assess and proactively act upon certain aspects of their personal health and providers have learned that it is good business to reach out to patients when and where it is convenient for patients. However, some providers of these self-service tools do not always make it clear to people how their personal information is being stored, used, or if it will be passed on to a third party. There is no federal mandate that requires a business to have a privacy policy, but studies show that consumers are increasingly anxious about protecting their personal data.

Technology has become a popular and convenient mode for delivering healthcare services. Self-service tools allow people to assess and proactively act upon certain aspects of their personal health. Providers have learned that it is good business to reach out to patients when and where it is convenient for patients.[1] Today that could be through a smart phone application or at a grocery store, not just the doctor's office. The feedback from consumers with regard to these technologies has been positive and there are many businesses that are responding to this demand.

SoloHealth was founded in 2007 with the goal of providing free and convenient health information to the masses. Its principle product is a self-service kiosk that checks blood pressure, tests vision, measures body mass index, and delivers health risk assessments. The machine's user interface shows a person in a white coat with a stethoscope indicating the presence of a doctor, but the machine is not actually connected to a live doctor. The user is asked questions about personal and family medical history, diet, and mental health. The average user spends about 4.5 minutes at the kiosk and collectively these stations serve approximately 130,000 people each day for an average of 10 million customers each quarter.[2] The company has over 3,500 stations in popular stores such as Wal-Mart, Safeway, and Sam's Club.[3] All of the stations are strategically located to be within driving distance of 79 percent of the U.S. population.[4] In addition to providing the user with vital health information, the system also collects personal information such as names, email addresses, weight, age and ethnicity.[5]

When SoloHealth first started, it raised revenue by selling ad space for pharmacy items that were displayed in close proximity to the kiosks. However, as the business grew and the number of people using this product increased, the company soon realized that its most valuable asset was the health and personal data it collected from its customers. This wealth of information is attractive to businesses within the health industry, particularly insurance companies.

In 2014, *National Public Radio* (NPR) in conjunction with *Kaiser Health News*, ran a story about SoloHealth claiming that it was not being forthright with consumers about the data it collects, stores, and sells. According to NPR, until recently SoloHealth's comprehensive privacy policy was not available at any of the stations; it was only obtainable on its website.[6] The company provided its website address at the kiosk, but since the stations do not have internet access, there is no way for anyone to actually read the policy prior to using the machine. SoloHealth claims that it did not provide access to its privacy policy because it would be burdensome for consumers to read the information on the kiosk's small computer screen. NPR says the company only sells "names, email addresses, and phone numbers to insurers who want to market health plans directly to consumers."[7] However, *Kaiser Health News* asserts in a separate article "all information, except the email addresses, is aggregated and shared with SoloHealth sponsors without personal identifiers."[8] The conflicting reports lead one to question how patience information is actually being handled and whether personal data is truly being separated from health data.

Some doctors' groups and privacy advocates wonder how the health data collected by these tools could be used, or rather misused, in the future. Many people consider their health information to be private. Something as sensitive as this should be protected and there should be control over who gets to see it and what aspects can be disclosed. When a person visits a doctor, it is common knowledge that he or she is protected by a patient physician confidentiality agreement. The Health Insurance Portability and Accountability Act (HIPAA) ensures that people are able to keep individual health information private. Under its notice of privacy practices, it is stated that a person's health information cannot be used for purposes not directly related to his or her care without permission. It also states that one may ask that health information not be shared with other individuals or companies.[9] SoloHealth is not considered a covered entity under HIPAA law, but its practices are questionable and should be reviewed by a regulatory agency.[10] Users of SoloHealth's product may be under the impression that information conveyed at the kiosk is just as secure as it is in a doctor's office due to the personal nature of the questions they answer, but that is not the case. This reinforces why it is vital for consumers to have the right to know who else may be privy to their data.

In mid-December of last year, SoloHealth finally made its comprehensive privacy policy available at its kiosks. This was an effort to be more transparent. Bart Foster, SoloHealth's CEO, said, "we work with retail partners, our attorneys and our corporate sponsors to make sure that we're totally buttoned up."[11] That begs the questions: Is the privacy policy designed to protect the consumer or the business? Is it the responsibility of the business to be more transparent? Or is the onus on the consumer to understand that any or all of the information provided may be passed along to a third party?

A privacy policy explains what data is collected by a business, how it is stored, used, and distributed. Many companies with an online presence have them, but there is no federal mandate that requires a business to have one. In fact, privacy policies can be considered part of a company's marketing strategy, a public relations move to make a consumer feel that his or her search and personal data are protected. They give the impression of security; however, often times, when the policy is actually read there is very little protection being promised.[12] The Federal Trade

Commission only steps in to regulate if a company does not conform to the mandates that are outlined in its policy, otherwise the world of privacy policies is self-regulating.

From a behavioral economics perspective, many studies indicate that consumers are becoming increasingly anxious about protecting their personal data. However, despite this, many people are still not likely to read online privacy policies, or even understand them.[13] In addition, the presence of a privacy policy may be interpreted as protection even if the information disclosed in the policy indicates otherwise.[14] Given the outcome of these studies, businesses know that they still have the upper hand. Privacy policies provide a level of protection for companies; they can lay out exactly how consumer data is collected and used, knowing that most people won't even bother to read about it. This leaves companies with an ethical duty to explain in a clear and concise manner how a consumer's data is collected, stored, and distributed. This information should also be easily accessible, not buried at the bottom of a website.

In a situation where a service is provided free, such as with SoloHealth, the notion of caveat emptor certainly applies. Health information is paid for through the exchange of personal information. When people voluntarily provide information, there is no guarantee of privacy protection. Although a customer may find it acceptable to trade this information with a business, he or she should absolutely be notified about the fact that this information may not be entirely private before the exchange occurs. In a world where so much personal data is stored in databases or in the cloud, consumers need to be educated on the ramifications of big data in a manner that is easy to understand. There is, without a doubt, great benefit from collecting and analyzing personal data; it simplifies a person's life and provides fast and individualized assessments. In contrast, the massive amounts of data that can be easily obtained about an individual are unsettling. A balance must be found between the risk and the reward. In this age many would not give up the everyday conveniences provided by technology, but in the campaign to promote privacy awareness, the best hope is to inform people how data is being used and present people with the choice of whether to participate.[15] This is best facilitated by the entity that is asking for the information.

The concept of privacy is a gray area. Disagreements over its scope and meaning make it difficult to establish a definition that everyone can agree upon. The notion of privacy will vary depending on how and where a person grew up and is shaped by personal experience. There is, however, one aspect of this subject that should be black and white and that is upfront and full disclosure in a "simplified and human-friendly manner" of how a person's data is shared with other parties.[16] Through this practice, people can be educated on how businesses use data to understand their customers. Consumers can then decide for themselves what their level of comfort is on the privacy spectrum and be empowered to proceed in the manner they deem best.

---

1 Dowling, Jim. "A Convenient Truth: Self-Service Works in Healthcare." *Healthcare IT News.* 31 Oct. 2013. Accessed Feb. 2014 <www.healthcareitnews.com>.

2 "SoloHealth Station Surpasses the 40-Million Mark for Consumer Engagements; Now in More Than 3,500 Retail Locations Nationwide." *PR Web.* 20 Dec. 2013. Accessed Feb. 2014 <www.prweb.com>.

3 Ibid.

4 Dearment, Alaric. "About 130,000 People Use SoloHealth Stations Per Day, Company Says." *Drug Store News.* 20 Dec. 2013. Accessed Feb. 2014 <www.drugstorenews.com>.

5 Dembosky, April. "After Checking Blood Pressure, Kiosks Give Sales Leads To Insurers." *National Public Radio.* 15 Jan. 2013. Accessed Feb. 2014 <www.npr.org>.

6 Ibid.

7 Ibid.

8 Appleby, Julie. "Health Care Without the Doctors Coming to a Wal-Mart Near You." *PBS Newshour.* 20 Dec. 2013. Accessed Feb. 2014 <www.pbs.org>.

9 "Your Health Information Privacy Rights." U.S. Department of Health and Human Services. n.d. Accessed Feb. 2014 <www.hhs.gov>.

10 Appleby, Julie.

11 Dembosky, April.

12 Nehf, James P. "Shopping for Privacy Online: Consumer Decision-Making Strategies and the Emerging Market for Information Privacy." *University of*

Illinois Journal of Law, Technology & Policy. Jan. 2005. Accessed Feb. 2014
<www.illinoisjltp.com/journal>.

13 Haynes, Allyson W. "Online Privacy Policies: Contracting Away Control Over
Personal Information?" *Penn State Law Review*. 1 Jan. 2007. Accessed Feb.
2014 <www.pennstatelaw.psu.edu >.

14 Acquisti, Alessandro., et al. *Digital Privacy: Theory, Technologies, and
Practices*. Auerbach Publications. 2007.

15 Sengupta, Somini. "Letting Down Our Guard with Web Privacy." *New York
Times*. 30 March 2013. Accessed Feb. 2014. <www.nytimes.com>.

16 Steinberg, Joseph. "This Flashlight Android App Has Been Secretly And
Illegally Sharing Your Personal Data With Advertisers." *Forbes*. 16 Dec. 2013.
Accessed Feb. 2014 <www.forbes.com>.

Anonymity on the Internet: A Tool for Tyranny?

Kristine Tomasovic Nelson

March 2015

Abstract: Anonymity has been a precept of free speech and democracy since the establishment of the U.S., and courts and citizens recognize its role in facilitating dissent and debate. In the internet age, however, anonymity enables tyrannical and stifling behaviors. The hosts and moderators of internet forums have struggled to protect both the principle of anonymity and its victims.

"Anonymity is a shield from the tyranny of the majority," wrote Justice John Paul Stevens of the U.S. Supreme Court in *McIntyre v. Ohio Elections Commission* (1995). It is a relatively recent quote, but anonymity has been a precept of free speech and democracy since the establishment of this country, and since then, numerous Supreme Court decisions have recognized both the right to free speech and the principle of anonymity. Many of these decisions – and *McIntyre* in particular -- present a one-dimensional view of anonymity and fail to comprehend its negative consequences. The *McIntyre* court went on to say, "…we also believe that keeping authorship anonymous moves the focus of discussion to the content of speech and away from the speaker- as it should be." On the internet, this is not always the case. The Supreme Court wrote the McIntyre opinion less than ten years ago, in full view of the digital era emerging, but it failed to anticipate the real harms made possible by internet anonymity. In fact, anonymity and the internet in combination have been used to engender the very tyranny "we the people" abhor.

That is not to say anonymity is incompatible with the internet. In the digital era, anonymity is no less important because technology is both an enabler of democracy and a tool of repression. On one hand, the internet lowers barriers for free speech. Protestors, whistleblowers, and dissidents today rely on the internet instead of the printing press. It lowers the cost of copying and distributing information and enables that information to cross cultural and geographic boundaries more easily. Similarly, content can reach audiences directly, bypassing the mass media gatekeepers of the past.[1] Finally, content can be forwarded and amplified, building to a digital rallying cry. In the last five years, digital and social media networks played an important role in democratic uprisings and protests in Iran, Egypt, Tunisia, Venezuela, and most recently, Hong Kong. On the other hand, the internet gives governments and other entities exponential power to track and trace individual activities. For people living under repressive regimes, anonymity is particularly important. In 2010, following the "Green Revolution", the Iranian authorities began to investigate those who protested or supported the protestors. Authorities easily identified many protestors via social media accounts that used real names, and those accounts became life-threatening liabilities.[2]

However, while anonymity can enable free speech, others have used it to stifle and silence debate. It may be time for our legal or regulatory system to formally recognize the ills of unbridled and unaccountable internet speech. Recent news presents a stark example: the treatment of Anita Sarkeesian and other (mainly female) internet journalists and gaming-industry notables in an internet blow-up dubbed "GamerGate." The complicated personal and professional dramas that spawned "GamerGate" are too lengthy to recount in this account, but it hinged on one (mainly female) side decrying gaming-culture misogyny, and the other side alleging a lack of journalistic integrity. Many of the female individuals involved, including Sarkeesian, received anonymous death threats, were spammed with child pornography, and were "doxed."[3] Doxxing is the collection and publication of an individual's personal information, usually with the intent to harass, threaten or harm said person digitally and/or in real life.[4] Ironically, doxxing done anonymously with the goal of intimidating someone holding a contrary position into silence. In other words, anonymity becomes a shield for tyranny. Indeed, well-known actor and gamer Felicia Day wrote in a blog post about GamerGate about her experience with this.

"I have been terrified of inviting a deluge of abusive and condescending tweets into my timeline. I did one simple @ reply to one of the main victims several weeks back, and got a flood of things I simply couldn't stand to read directed at me. I had to log offline for a few days until it went away."[5]

Day was too frightened to exercise her right to speak[6]. And while "GamerGate" is an extreme example of online terrorizing that made national headlines, abusive speech and cyberbullying large and small happens daily.

In contrast to the view contained in McIntyre, GamerGate demonstrates that anonymity on the Internet does not always keep the focus on the message and not the messenger. Why is this the case? The first amendment does not protect threats or the right to incite actions that would harm others, but on the Internet, relative anonymity, decentralized distribution, and multiple points of access all make it difficult to control speech or action online.[7] The perpetrator often remains undetected. Cultural norms cannot be brought to bear because public censure is impossible. Is there a solution to this? How can we protect the anonymity necessary to free speech and democracy while protecting the individual from anonymous ad hominem attacks? Technological or legal remedies are certainly possible, but either have not proven adequate or have not been fully explored.

In the absence of legal, regulatory or technological solutions, Internet entities have been experimenting with various forms of self-regulation. One approach is to ban anonymity. Facebook, for example, requires real identities (with a notable exception for drag queens). This may encourage greater civility, but for many Facebook is simply a place for sunny status updates and a like (but no equivalent dislike) button, not a go-to forum for debate. Moreover, personalization efforts at Facebook may be narrowing our view away from a diversity of opinions. In a TED Talk, author Eli Pariser described how Facebook's personalization algorithms edited out the news feeds of friends on whose content Eli clicked less frequently. Eli noted that these friends generally held political or other views he did not agree with, but he believes those opinions are valuable to him nonetheless and he wanted to see them.[8] In essence, the algorithms were filtering opportunities for discussion and debate. Finally, as discussed, real identities can be a liability when agitating for political freedoms in societies where Internet speech is monitored and censored.

Another possible solution is the elimination of online gathering points such as comment boards. This is not a violation of free speech; a media platform is private property, and its owner is not required to host a debate any more than the owner of a store is required to let you and your friend hang out and conduct a loud and heated debate. The shop owner would show you out or call the police. However, eliminating venues for debate is a heavy-handed approach for an issue caused by a minority of users. Moreover, discouraging or eliminating discussion is counterproductive for democracy and democratic societies, so perhaps society should not widely practice or encourage this approach.

As an alternative or a complement to other tactics, many websites employ moderators to scrub their user-contributed content. It is no small task. Recent estimates say that there are as many as 100,000 workers worldwide viewing and censoring hundreds of images per day, eliminating offensive material such as pornography, gore, minors, sexual solicitation, sexual body parts/images, and racism.[9] Nevertheless, moderating has a financial cost and even a human one: viewing the imagery repeatedly has a psychological impact on the moderators, some of whom end up in counseling. Moreover, while much of the population would be grateful for this policing if they knew of it, it is in fact censorship of a sort. Another question arises: who is moderating the moderators?

Other websites enlist the users themselves to act as moderators. Reddit, an entertainment, news and social networking site allows registered members to submit content and vote site submissions up or down. These votes organize the posts and determine their position on the page. Unpopular, irrelevant, or offensive speech should settle to the bottom. Users do not have to share their real names. The site declares itself an "open platform and free speech place" and has a lengthy list of values called "Reddiquette"[10] but very few rules. The first "Reddiquette" listed is "Remember the human", a plea for users to keep in mind that online communications should retain the civility we would afford a face-to-face conversation. If users were to comply, Reddit might, indeed, be a shining example of constructive free speech, but despite the site's policies – or perhaps because of them – Reddit has generated a sizable list of controversies. These include the infamous misidentification of an innocent student as one of the Boston Marathon bombing perpetrators and even a "hate speech problem". Journalist Jason Abbruzzese writes that:

"A persistent, organized and particularly hateful strain of racism has emerged on the site. Enabled by Reddit is system and permitted thanks to its fervent stance against any censorship, it has proven capable of overwhelming the site's volunteer moderators and rendering entire subreddits unusable. Moderators have pled with Reddit for help, but little has come."[11]

The subreddit prominently featured is called /r/blackladies, but a letter of protest to Reddit is organizers was co-signed by the moderators of more than 60 other subreddits, hinting at the breadth of the problem. On Reddit, community-based moderators were unable to turn back the tyranny of a racist minority.

While not perfect, each of these self-regulatory solutions offer small-sized experiments for how we should govern ourselves online, and each can have some positive effect against misuse of anonymity. However, despite these efforts, the internet allows free speech to go too far. There is no easy answer, but it is clear that society must examine the current modes of governance for online anonymity and free speech across the legal, regulatory and self-regulatory landscape.

1 Balkin, J.M. "Commentaries - Digital Speech and Democratic Culture: A Theory of Freedom of Expression for the Information Society". *New York University Law Review*. Jan. 2004. Accessed Oct. 2014 <www.yale.edu>.

2 Butcher, Mike. "The Future for Anonymity Apps: Defamations and Revolutions." *TechCrunch*. 16 Mar. 2014. Accessed Oct. 2014 <www.techcrunnch.com>.

3 Hathaway, Jay. "What is GamerGate, and Why? An Explainer for Non-Geeks." *Gawker*. 10 Oct. 2014. Accessed Oct. 2014 <www.gawker.com>.

4 Pelisek, Christine., "Doxxing: It is like Hacking but Legal." *The Daily Beast*. 13 Mar. 2013. Accessed Oct. 2014 <www.thedailybeast.com>.

5 Day, Felicity. "The Only Thing I Have to Say about GamerGate." Tumblr: This Felicity Day. 22 Oct. 2014. Accessed Oct. 2014 <www. thisfeliciaday.tumblr.com>.

6 Hamilton, Kirk. "Felicia Day And Gamergate: This Is What Happens Now." *Kotaku*. 24 Oct. 2014. Accessed Oct. 2014 <kotaku.com>.

7 Lessig, Lawrence. "Free Speech." *Code: And Other Laws of Cyberspace Version 2.0*. 5 Dec. 2006. Accessed Oct. 2014 <http://codev2.cc>.

8 Pariser, Eli. "Beware Online 'Filter Bubbles.'" *Ted.com*. May 2011. Accessed Oct. 2014 <www.ted.com>.

9 Chen, Adrian. "The Laborers Who Keep Dick Pics and Beheadings Out of Your Facebook Feed." *Wired*. 23 Oct. 2014. Accessed Oct. 2014 <www.wired.com>.

10 "Reddiquette". Reddit.com. N.D. Accessed Oct. 2014 <www.reddit.com>.

11 Abbruzzese, Jason. "Hate Speech Is Drowning Reddit and No One Can Stop It." *Mashable*. 26 Oct. 2014. Accessed Oct. 2014 <www.mashable.com>.

Who Needs ID: DNA-fication in the Modern World

Malavika Ravi

April 2015

Abstract: It is hard to find an industry that does not rely heavily on technology to run the operational, strategic, and tactical aspects of business. The most interesting aspect of information technology, to me, is its potential to revolutionize healthcare. One of my many undergraduate courses was bioinformatics, the intersection of informatics and biology, which focuses on utilizing computer analysis on genomic data. Each organism has a genome, a complete set of DNA, which contains the information needed to build and maintain that organism.[1] In humans, the genome is three billion DNA base pairs long. Scientists sequence and analyze the genomes of humans in order to help identify diseases that are caused by genetic mutations, or variances found when individuals inherit genes from their parents or are exposed to environmental factors. I had the opportunity to mimic scientists and analyze public genomes stored in computer databases using software I created. It opened my eyes to how easy it was for those with no research experience to extract important personally identifiably information. Just like other industries that rely on information technology, there is a catch-22 that is inherent when software and personally identifiably information meet: "new technology [poses] new risks."[2] Scientists, lawmakers, and even the public must weigh the potential for these databases to cause undue harm to the DNA donors against the potential for these databases to help the collective. This decision must be made as soon as possible as some scientific communities have begun to reject privacy all together.

In March 2014, the European Molecular Biology Laboratory (EMBL) in Heidlberg, Germany committed a serious blunder. One of the foremost research organizations in the world allowed Lars Steinmetz and his team of researchers to publish the genome sequence for one of the most famous cell lines in the world, HeLa, extracted from Henrietta Lacks. The scientific community was outraged. On one hand, this genetic blueprint provides data to the much needed field of genomics. Scientists are able to use advanced tools to extract information from the genomes that will help diagnose, treat, and sometimes prevent diseases.[3] On the other hand, the very tools which are used to benefit humans can be used to identify the participants who are tied to the genomic profile. The EMBL denied that this double edge sword existed claiming that the sequence published did not reveal anything about the Lacks family or even about Henrietta, herself. Yaniv Erlich, known as "the

Genome Hacker" believed otherwise tweeting "Nice lie EMBL!"[4] In fact, a few scientists decided to prove Erlich right. They uploaded the published genome to a site called SNPedia, a Wikipedia site used for translating genetic data. Within minutes, the site produced a report that contained personally identifiably information (PII) about Lacks and her family.[5] The EMBL were forced to admit their folly; it was possible to garner information about the Lacks family from the genome. They quickly pulled the genome from their public database. However, Erlich believes this move was fruitless. He states, "People don't realize it is impossible to hide genetic information once it is out there."[6] Erlich would know, his study published in January 2014 proved exactly that.

The ability to link a genome profile in an anonymous database to a real-world donor was not supposed to be possible. Yaniv Erlich and his team from the Whitehead Institute for Biomedical Research at M.I.T. were able to uncover the names of fifty people whose anonymous genome profiles were available online in a free-access database known as the 1000 Genomes Project.[7] The 1000 Genomes Project was created to help researchers find genes associated with different human diseases.[8] The creators of the 1000 Genomes Project never imagined that an ingenious team would develop an algorithm to connect donor profiles to surnames. Erlich and his team created an algorithm which focused on extracting genetic markers from the Y chromosome. The short tandem repeats (STRs) on the Y chromosome (Y-STRs) are passed from father to son with very little mutational change from one generation to the next.[9] The team used the Y-STR along with the age and location metadata attached to each genome profile in the database to help refine the search of possible DNA matches. They were left with a potential pool of ten thousand men who matched the age metadata and lived in Utah at the time of the DNA donation. The team then used free genealogy sites, Ysearch and SMGF, to connect the Y-STR markers to the surnames. Erlich and his team published their findings to much furor. In response, the 1000 Genomes Project has made small strides to increase donor anonymity such as stripping the age metadata attached to the genome profiles. However, teams inspired by Erlich have begun decoding genomes to detect DNA variants that identify characteristics such as hair, eye color, and facial features. They plan to use this data to filter through public databases that contains these identifiers to reveal the identity of the donors. This study highlights how fast technology has evolved and how scientists are struggling with these new advancements.

The first human genome was sequenced roughly eleven years ago, with the help of over two hundred scientists, costing the U.S. government approximately three billion dollars.[10] Sponsored by National Human Genome Research Institute (NHGRI), the Human Genome Project was able to publish all three billion base pairs that comprise the human genome. After the end of the Human Genome Project, the cost of genome sequencing declined exponentially roughly following Moore's law. When next generation sequencing entered the market seven years ago, the cost to sequence the whole human genome dropped dramatically. Today, a full genome profile hovers around five thousand dollars.[11] Since then, sequencing costs have dropped dramatically and it was estimated to cost approximately five thousand dollars to sequence the whole human genome one year ago. The NHGRI has launched the new Advanced Sequence Technology award to spur innovators to create a thousand dollar sequencer. Illumina claims to have reached this goal and supplies these fast machines to research centers, pharmaceutical companies, academic intuitions, and biotechnology companies. With cheap but powerful technology, doctors around the world now have the ability to quickly sequence genomes to save lives.

The Children's Mercy Hospital in Kansas City is saving the lives of newborns one genome sequence at a time. A two month year old boy has spent his entire life in their neonatal intensive care unit (NICU) at the brink of death. Doctors were mystified and could not determine the cause of his abnormalities.[12] They warned his parents that his life may be cut short. Refusing to accept that as an answer, geneticist Stephen Kingsmore and his team used rapid sequencing technology to quickly identify differences between the genomes of the boy and his parents. They were able to find a rare mutation that was linked to a disease that results in an overactive immune system which damages the liver and spleen.[13] This diagnosis helped the doctors tailor a remedy which helped lower the boy's immune response. The boy is now at home and is expected to live a long and healthy life. This rapid genome sequencing technology has been used by experts to successfully help diagnose and treat forty-four sick infants. The team is now faced with determining what to do with the extra information they gleaned that is unrelated to the diagnosis. This information could potentially shed light on diseases that may help other children. So while this story highlights the benefits of genome analysis, it raises the question: should individuals have an expectation of privacy when it comes to their genetic material and is it considered property?

Genome privacy revolves around the fundamental concepts of ownership and authorized use. Traditionally speaking, a person has property rights or ownership of his/her body. This is why donors must consent before any or all parts of their body are given away. However, if the individual is in anyway involved with a criminal investigation, he/she can expect no privacy. DNA evidence found at a crime scene or DNA extracted in the context of a criminal prosecution does not violate the Fourth Amendment. Once convicted, the U.S. Federal Bureau of Investigation has a database of all "samples from convicted offenders, crime scenes, victims of crime, and unidentified human remains".[14] The court believes that defendants have no expectation of privacy. But what happens when an individual is not a felon? The consensual donation of genetic matter for the purposes of research either for academic or commercial applications raises multiple issues and with genomic policies still in a nascent stage, subjects are at risk.[15] For the past few years, the media has been in an uproar about database breaches that contain social security numbers, credit card information, and other personally identifiable information. It is time for the public to be as concerned about the privacy and security of human genomic data.

There are a myriad of potentials way to abuse the information collected from genetic materials and without privacy laws, this is difficult to stop. Baase defines privacy as having three key aspects: "freedom from intrusion…control of information about oneself, [and the] free from surveillance…"[16] Genomic information falls under the second category of privacy. Individuals are concerned that their genetic information will be used to screen potential employees or even used to deny, limit, or cancel insurance policies.[17] Though the U.S. government contends this is a small concern since only a limited number of cases have been brought to their attention.[18] They do admit that this may be due to the fact that it is difficult to uncover and document the discriminatory use of data. The federal government has attempted to prevent genomic discrimination with the Genetic Information Nondiscrimination Act of 2008 (GINA). GINA supplements the Privacy Act of the Health Insurance Portability and Accountability Act (HIPAA) and the Americans with Disabilities Act (ADA). GINA and HIPAA state that health insurance companies cannot use the genetic data for their own testing in either the capacity of providing samples to researchers or sponsoring researchers to test samples.[19] They can however use the genome to define life insurance policies and long-term disability care.[20] GINA and the ADA state that employers cannot ask prospective employees for genetic information (medical examination) during the pre-employment stage. However, at the pre-placement state, the employer can require a medical examination to be conducted. The employee has no right to be told what they are getting screened for, how the test will be used, or what the test results are. Furthermore, if the employer decides to withdraw an offer of employment, the employee will not be told why. It is against ADA policy to withdraw a conditional offer based on medical reasons but if the company fails to disclose a reason for unemployment, it is difficult to take up legal action. At the state level, approximately half the states have legislation that prohibits genetic discrimination in the workplace.[21] Each state has its own spin regarding genetic testing and many of them fail to adequately define the what, how, and when genetic material can be used. The need for proper federal regulations is increasing especially as government, medical, and research organizations begin to work together to create large databases that can be breached with genome profiles stolen and sold to the highest bidder.

Last year, seventy leading medical and research organizations spanning forty one countries, including the NIH, has declared their intent to form an alliance that will build a shared database of genomic and clinical data. They hope that this huge database will uncover genetic links that have so far proven to be elusive.[22] The gene variants will help pinpoint diseases such as cancer and diabetes and will usher the advent of a new type of personal medicine; one where physicians use each patient's genome sequence to prevent diseases and to help customize treatment plans. The most troubling aspect is that the alliance has no plan for how to protect the privacy of genetic donors. If this database is breached, the genome can be used not only against the donor but also against their relatives who have not consented to the study. This is not the only database individuals should be concerned about.

23andMe is marketed as a personal genome service that allows their customers to learn more about their health. The company stores all the genomic data in a database that contains metadata that volunteers submit about themselves. Their current privacy policy states that they only share aggregate information about user's genomes to third parties and not personal genetic information.[23] However, just like any corporation they protect themselves by having "a broad use of the [user's] personal information."[24] In this case, 23andMe reserves the right to use their customers' personal information, which includes their genome, to try to sell them products and services. As a private corporation they have the ability to change their privacy policies on a whim which gives them the ability to sell their customer's DNA to the highest bidder. If that is not ominous enough their website warns, "Genetic information that you share with others could be used against your interest."[25] 23andMe state that they only use the information for their own research purposes of finding genetic anomalies. The extremes between privacy and access have forced scientists to rethink which side they lean towards.

The biggest challenge with genome data is the balancing act between access and privacy. On one hand, researchers want to make sure the data is widely available without restrictions. On the other hand, researchers understand that restricting how the data will be used and increasing privacy and confidentiality will draw more donors to the study.[26] Jeffrey Khan, a professor of bioethics and public policy at Johns Hopkins Berman Institute of Bioethics, believes that "[i]f privacy can't be guaranteed, then the focus should be shifted to mitigating data misusage."[27] It is not enough for researchers to simply inform people that there is a risk of re-identification. Many individuals who sign up for genome based research studies will have a hard time fully grasping how their data might be used in the future especially when researchers themselves are still finding out. Informed consent is no longer sufficient enough to cover the potential repercussions to donors. Lawmakers along with scientists, both in public and private organizations, need to focus on way to minimize the risk to individuals who are willing to share their genetic material.

The first task lawmakers can focus on is determining if genetic material is considered uniquely private or if it should be lumped together with other sensitive information in individual's medical records. If genetic material is considered to be to be common medial information, then the existing confidentiality laws with HIPAA and ADA should suffice and the only amendment needed would be to explicitly state this within those acts. However, the best course of action would be for the federal government to support genetic exceptionalism, or the idea that genetic material is unique, because of its distinct abilities.[28] Genetic material is the source of all medical information and similar to a personal medical record, can be stored and accessed without the permission of the owner. However, genetic material goes above and beyond the information found in a medical record, it has to ability to positively identify an individual's future risks. Because of the unique features of genomes, the genetic material extracted from an individual should follow a new set of laws.

Lawmakers should focus on affording special privacy laws to both the sequence information as well as the sample that is extracted from the individual. It is important to include the sample since once a physician or researcher extracts a genetic sample, they will have the ability to conduct tests on the sample in the individual's absence. The individual will be powerless and cannot stop what they do not know. Currently, in the U.S., genetic tissue samples of about twenty million people is being collected and stored each year in collections ranging from two hundred to ninety-two million samples.[29] The ease and proliferation of genome databases make them a gold mine for researchers who are focused on solving which genetic factors contribute to what diseases but at the same time the mass quantity places thousand if not millions of individuals at risk. The genetic sequences could be tied to individuals in the real world and be used to potentially harm them. Not only are the samples a risk but the large genome databases are a huge privacy concern for individuals.

Researchers need to focus on what it means to have a large central repository of genetic material. The data should be set to be off limits to users while allowing trusted and verified researchers blanket permission to use the dataset. One such method is to only allow trusted users would be to encrypt the genome data before it is placed into the database and only allowing those who poses the decryption key to work with it freely.[30] Additionally, instead of presuming that a breach will never happen, it is best to be proactive and safeguard against them. All metadata that contains identifying characteristics such as age, location, or year of extraction should be removed from the database. The power to malign individuals with the genomic sequence itself is very powerful; hackers should not have the ability to take it one step further. Lastly, researchers and scientists should be subject to the same codes of conducts, ones with enforceable penalties, which lawyers and doctors are subject to.[31] Individuals trust the confidential relationships they have with these professional because they take an oath to protect privacy and have penalties for breaching it.[32] With the advent of cloud-based genome databases such as the one Google recently launched, these safeguards will help minimize the risk individuals take to help further humanity.

It is the age-old battle between privacy and social good. Researchers contend that there is always some amount of privacy that individuals are willing to give up in order to further national security.[33] In the internet age, this translates to genomic privacy and the social good of providing individuals with better healthcare. However, with a few simple policies and regulations, individuals will not have to give up all their privacy rights in order to help their fellow community members. Laws and policies should recognize individual genetic rights such as the right to determine who has access to their genetic information and the right to determine who has access to their genetic samples. They should also prohibit the unauthorized use of genetic samples to solve crimes or determine paternity. Furthermore, these laws should be enforced and instituted with severe penalties in order to deter violators. With these simple actions, the world will be one step closer to establishing a standard for genetic privacy.

---

1 U.S. National Library of Medicine, "What Is a Genome?" *Genetics Home Reference.* 24 Nov. 2014. Accessed Dec. 2014 <http://ghr.nlm.nih.gov>.

2 Baase, Sara. *A Gift of Fire: Social, Legal, and Ethical Issues for Computing Technology.* Pearson Education Limited. Sep. 2012.

3 Collins, Francis S. "The HeLa Genome: An Agreement on Privacy and Access," *The NIH Director.* 7 Aug. 2013. Accessed Dec. 2014 <http://www.nih.gov>.

4 Hayden, Erika Check. "Privacy Protections: The Genome Hacker." *Nature.* 8 May 2013. Accessed Dec. 2014 <www.nature.com>.

5 Skloot, Rebecca. "The Immortal Life of Henrietta Lacks, the Sequel," *The New York Times.* 23 Mar. 2013. Accessed Dec. 2014 <www.nytimes.com>.

6 Ibid.

7 Ahmed, Abdul-Kareem. "Unhidden Traits: Genomic Data Privacy Debates Heat Up." *Scientific American.* 14 Aug. 2013. Accessed Dec. 2014 <www.scientificamerican.com>.

8 Ferguson, William. "A Hacked Database Prompts Debate about Genetic Privacy," *Scientific American.* 5 Feb. 2013. Accessed Dec. 2014 </www.scientificamerican.com>.

9 Ibid.

10 Hayden, Erika Check. "Technology: The $1,000 Genome," *Nature*. 19 Mar. 2014. Accessed Dec. 2014 <www.nature.com>.

11 Ibid.

12 Reardon, Sara. "Fast Genetic Sequencing Saves Newborn Lives." *Nature*. 30 Sep. 2014. Accessed Dec. 2014 <www.nature.com>.

13 Ibid.

14 Nerko, Charles J. "Assessing Fourth Amendment Challenges to DNA Extraction Statutes after Samson v. California." *Fordham Law Review / Edited by Fordham Law Students*. Nov. 2008.

15 Curley, Robert A. Jr. & Lisa M. Caperna. "The Brave New World Is Here: Privacy Issues and the Human Genome Project" *Defense Counsel Journal*. Jan. 2003.

16 Basse.

17 Curley and Caperna.

18 "Privacy and Progress in Whole Genome Sequencing." Presidential Commission for the Study of Bioethical Issues. Oct. 2014 Accessed Dec. 2014 <bioethics.gov>.

19 "Summary of the HIPAA Privacy Rule." *Health Information Privacy*, U.S. Department of Health & Human Services. Accessed Dec. 2014 <www.hhs.gov>.

20 Ferguson.

21 Curley and Caperna.

22 Ahmed.

23 Collins, Francis S. Collins & Margaret A. Hamburg. "First FDA Authorization for Next-Generation Sequencer," *New England Journal of Medicine*. 19 Dec. 2013.

24 Haynes, Allyson W. "Online Privacy Policies: Contracting Away Control Over Personal Information?" *Penn State Law Review*. 2011.

25 Collins and Hamburg, "First FDA Authorization for Next-Generation Sequencer."

26 Hayden, "Privacy Protections.

27 Ferguson.

28 Roche, Patricia A. & George J. Annas. "Protecting Genetic Privacy." *Nature*. May 2001. Accessed Dec. 2014 <www.nature.com>.

29 Ibid.

30 Ibid.

31 Church, George et al., "Public Access to Genome-Wide Data: Five Views on Balancing Research with Privacy and Protection," *PLoS Genet* 2 Oct. 2009.

32 Ibid.

33 Ahmed.

The Conflict of Privacy and Disclosure Law
The Criticality of Minimizing Collateral Data

Matthew Christian
January 2015

Abstract: This research note discusses the complex issues surrounding data collection and subsequent privacy issues. In particular, the paper explores the issues surrounding data collection by government agencies and public disclosure laws.

Privacy

"A person's "right to privacy," "right of privacy," "privacy," or "personal privacy," as these terms are used in this chapter, is invaded or violated only if disclosure of information about the person: (1) Would be highly offensive to a reasonable person, and (2) is not of legitimate concern to the public." RCW 42.56.050

Privacy is a complex topic. Privacy is one of those words where it is difficult to define without using it in its own definition. What is considered private changes with time and circumstance, and even more from person to person and from culture to culture. Privacy is often considered an inalienable right along with life, liberty, and the pursuit of happiness, though it is not explicitly defined in the Constitution. It can be traded away willingly or taken away as a consequence without issue, but if it is taken without being asked is treated in the same regard as basic human rights.

Privacy in the Information Age is a seemingly fleeting thing. Technology has enabled advanced communications and services that have made us better connected and informed, but as the saying goes, there is no free lunch. The same systems that connect us and inform us track our behavior and goings-on. Fortunately, market pressure has encouraged private companies to disclose what information consumers are changing and to offer and opt-out option if so desired, leaving consumers with a degree of control enabled by informed consent. This same degree of control does not hold true when examining image data held by government entities, especially with recent advances facial recognition software.

The single unifying element in all definitions of privacy is *informed consent*. In the context of information, informed consent is involved with making a person aware of what information is going to be collected and how it will be used.[1] Without informed consent, an individual has no opportunity to protect his privacy, even if the data being collected is seemingly innocuous. It is in informed consent that the Washington State law fails and exposes its citizens to privacy violations granted through image and video captured for other purposes. The majority of the following discussion is focused on how public disclosure laws allow citizens to gain access to much more information about each other than historically available due to public disclosure law.

Public Disclosure Law

In the U.S., the Freedom of Information Act[i] grants citizens access to federal records, and each state also maintains local public disclosure laws, which can vary from state to state. Liberal public disclosure policies are an essential cornerstone to a healthy democracy. Public disclosure laws not only inherently improve the behavior of public agents simply by the knowledge that most records are accessible to the average citizen, but also provide the means for a democratic society to govern itself in the manner that it chooses to be governed. The introduction of video recording technology and the rapid improvements in video hardware and software has opened a new frontier for monitoring public agents. However, as with any new powerful technology, the benefits may not always offset the cost.[ii]

---

[i] More information on the Freedom of Information Act can be found at http://www.foia.gov/

[ii] All references to "law" in the rest of this paper will be in reference to Washington State Law unless otherwise noted

"The people of this state do not yield their sovereignty to the agencies that serve them. The people, in delegating authority, do not give their public servants the right to decide what is good for the people to know and what is not good for them to know. The people insist on remaining informed so that they may maintain control over the instruments that they have created..."[iii]... RCW 42.56.030, Washington State

The principle of public record disclosure law in Washington State is stated in very clear terms; that the government put in place by the people is subject to monitoring by the people. This is supported by RCW 42.56.010, which defines public records in such a way that essentially all content generated by a public agent is subject to public disclosure law. RCW 42.56.040 further supports this principle by requiring all public state agencies to make the process of requesting public records easily accessible and understandable.

The state does grant a few exceptions to a select population of records. RCWs 42.56.230 and 42.56.240 outline specific parties and situations that are exempt from the public disclosure laws. These groups include minors in public schools, patients in public health

---

[iii] Remaining text of RCW 42.56.030 goes on to explain how the policy was written.

agencies, victims of crime, undercover police officers, and other groups. These statutes also restrict the disclosure of state-issued identification records that could be used in combination with other records to determine the identity of a protected group.

Now that the foundations of public disclosure laws have been explained at a high level, we can start to examine how image data complicates the issue. The scope of public data is very wide. It encompasses every record generated in every public office across the state. Some examples at the state level include the Liquor Control Board, Department of Natural Resources, and the State Board of Education. Each department, at both the city and state level, requires certain types of data in order to carry out its intended function. These departments are given the authority and resources to collect said data, and by default, are required to disclose that data to the public with the exception of exempt records.

Collecting data to support public agencies empowers public agents to make fact-based decisions that better the lives of the general public. Critical utilities, such as transportation and power, and public services, such as libraries and education services, function largely in part to the data that each agency is able to collect. Data collection is also essential to the public maintaining a watchful eye on the conduct of government agents. The concern at hand is not with agencies gathering essential data, but on the imprecise nature of image data[iv] that is being used at larger and larger scales and how it compromises the identity of protected citizens as well as the privacy and well-being of the general public.

Collateral Data

Technology can only be as smart as it is programmed to be. No matter how sophisticated the machine learning algorithm or coding, technology is still reliant on a person for guidance. Image capturing devices are no different. A camera captures all data in its lens regardless of the intent of the photographer. To the information scientist this additional contextual information is classified as *metadata*, or as Darin Stewart describes it in his book *Building Enterprise Taxonomies*, reference information not indicated explicitly in the content itself, but rather is supplementary to it. In other words, metadata is information "about" the data element that is not necessarily a part of the data element itself.[2] Metadata is what powers search algorithms, indexing functions, and data mining; it is the thing that makes information work.

[iv] Image data includes video and photograph media

Images are intrinsically rich with metadata. The phrase "a picture is worth a thousand words" is an excellent representation of the amount metadata that can be derived from a single image. Herein lies the problem. The imprecise nature of a camera and metadata-rich characteristic of an image generates large amounts of *collateral data,* data elements that, through intentional or unintentional means, are collected in addition to the specific data element being pursued that are not relevant to the purpose of the data collection process. The types of images being recorded vary widely by public office or department, yet the issue persists throughout. Each image will often include data that is outside of the scope of the purpose of collecting the data in the first place.

Metadata is only useful to a computer if it is coded in such a way that a software program can read it. This has, historically, been the primary challenge for managing metadata sourced from images because each image needed to have metadata entered manually. Modern technology is quickly negating that roadblock, most vividly exhibited in facial recognition software. The social media giant Facebook is able to automatically "tag" a person in a picture with 97.25 percent accuracy, only 0.28 percent lower precision than humans.[3] The capability to mass-analyze images has significant implications to protecting personal privacy for both the public and for specially protected groups.

As an example, look at Seattle parking police' practice of capturing images of cars parked in public places on a daily basis. This data is used primarily to track automobile movements throughout the city and to track parking utilization. A typical Seattle resident might agree that having the parking police take picture of the public parking spots where she parks on a daily basis is not offensive and that it would probably be of general interest to the public transportation system. However, if that same person were to find out that her abusive ex-boyfriend was able to use those same images to find where she worked and her daily schedule, her opinion might change.

Police brutality has been the subject of many headline releases in recent years,[4] spearheading additional efforts to monitor behavior in police departments across the state using body-mounted cameras. An incident on August 30, 2010 in Seattle highlights where a body-mounted camera may have been useful in determining what actually happened in a tragic event. John T. Williams, a Native American woodcarver, was shot and killed by a police officer in Seattle, Washington. Williams was walking down a sidewalk in downtown Seattle working on a wood carving with a small knife when he was approached by officer Ian Birk. Williams reportedly refused to put his knife away after being instructed to do so by Officer Birk. After a short but tragic series of events, John Williams was shot to death, and Officer Birk resigned immediately.[v5] The only video record of the event was the dashboard camera in Officer Birk's police vehicle. The video was able to capture some audio, mostly from Officer Birk, and was only able to show Williams walking across the street with the knife in his hand and Officer Birk exiting the vehicle and following Williams down the sidewalk.[vi]

This tragic incident, and others such as the August 9th, 2014 shooting of Michael Brown in Ferguson, Missouri has ignited support for increased deployment of body-mounted cameras in police forces across the country. Private companies like Taser[vii] seem to be ready to fill the need with a well-designed product, and there only seems to be support in the local communities for monitoring police activity. In fact, a pilot program in Rialto, CA saw a 60 percent reduction in use-of-force and 88 percent reduction in complaints against officers.[6] At the

---

[v] More details on the John T. Williams shooting can be found by searching on <www.seattletimes.com>

[vi] The dashboard camera video was posted on YouTube.

[vii] More information on Taser products can be found by searching on <www.taser.com>.

surface, this program seems to work extremely well and conceptually makes sense. A police officer is a highly visible, highly impactful government agent who is constantly placed in tenuous situations, so what harm could there be in monitoring police officer activities with video cameras?

The answer has two conflicting sides. The community benefits from monitoring police officer behavior through video. Both citizens and officers behavior is modified in knowing that each is on video and cases are resolved much more rapidly. This practice is fully supported by Washington State law and by the principles that citizens should monitor their government. What is *not* beneficial, however, is posting uncensored video of the citizens' interactions with police officers. As an example, the police department in Bellingham, Washington has also started to pilot body-mounted cameras for its police force. An unidentified citizen has started requesting every second of footage from the officer-mounted cameras in Bellingham and is posting those videos to YouTube. One such video contains footage of a bust of a prostitution ring, including a half hour interview with what appears to be a victim of the prostitution ring. This person's name and details of her life story, details that she may not have wanted to share with the public, are now on YouTube for everyone to see.

Another minor problem with body-mounted video is that recording a conversation requires the consent of both parties.[viii] Officers can accommodate the legal requirement by stating that the interaction is being recorded, but that may not always be feasible. Consider an on-foot pursuit of a convenience store robber. Should the officer notify the suspect that their conversation would be recorded while in pursuit through alleys and backyards?

Legal Conflict

This exact scenario will be played out for every single interaction between citizens and police officers, which raises conflicts in at least two statues. The first direct conflict is with RCW 42.56.240, which exempts information revealing the identity of victims of crime and minors that are victims of sexual assault from disclosure laws. Posting uncensored videos of crime victims is a direct violation of that statute, and violates the first condition of RCW 42.56.050, where this information would likely be highly offensive to a reasonable person. This also holds true for witnesses and undercover police officers, where the disclosure of a person's identity could place that individual in danger of serious harm. Citizens may request that the record be sealed, but the speed of disclosure has a strong chance of overtaking the speed of the request,

---

[viii] See Washington State RCW 9.73.030

which also assumes that the citizen is aware of the process.

Another area of significant concern stems from security footage recorded in classrooms, school campuses, and public transportation facilities. It can only record video images and not sound due to state law prohibiting recording conversations, but by definition, this video content is public record. While there may be additional factors such as FERPA regulations that prevent a school security video from being released,[7] the fact of the matter is that minors and other protected groups are being recorded, and the images are available to the public.

Permanence of the Internet

Before the widespread use of the Internet, the life of a record was based on the medium that it was held in. Electronic and paper records and other mediums last until destroyed or degraded. The same phenomenon holds true for modern public records, even if stored electronically. The possible expiration of data granted a degree of control over the information over time, creating advantages and disadvantages for both personal privacy and government transparency.

The Internet has fundamentally changed this principle. Once a data element has been published to the Internet, all control over the data disappears.

Links can be removed and search algorithms modified, but the content is permanently released. The data science industry has created (and will continue to create) mechanisms for finding, indexing, and analyzing data at ever-increasing magnitudes, which, true to the nature of technology,[8] only magnifies the privacy problems presented with collecting public image data.

"...highly offensive to a reasonable person..."

As discussed before, collecting data is a good thing. An image taken for a publicly oriented data-driven purpose is generally unobtrusive. It is not the single element that is the problem. It is the presence and cataloguing of many elements in relation to each other that create a whole greater than the sum of its parts. Public image data is enabling private and public sector agents to reach further than intended and approved.

Re-use of image data by government agencies is perhaps a greater cause for concern than how citizens or the private sector might use the same data. Baase raises the question of what government security forces may do with facial recognition software and the host of images available for analysis.[9] As Baase mentions, uncensored access to raw image data allows for easy monitoring of journalists, political dissidents, and to reflect a recent issue, suspected radical

Moslems. While citizens have a legal claim to request information on these activities, the public may not be aware that these activities are occurring in the first place. Regardless of what the data is being used for, the fact remains that collateral data is usable by whoever holds it. As far as Washington State is concerned, there seems to be a distinct lack of legislation guiding the use or re-use of image data, except for traffic camera images that have distinct usage guidelines.[ix]

Public image data also has significant implications to the private sector. Most agencies have restrictions on private sector companies requesting public data[x] to protect privacy. The ability to safeguard public data from being used by private entities stops when the data is published to the Internet. Google has made its mark on mapping applications but has had to do so by driving around and taking pictures of public spaces. Should a citizen request image data and post it online, there is nothing preventing Google from using the image and its metadata since it is now in a public space.

[ix] See Washington State RCW 46.63 for more information

[x] A specific statute in Washington State law regarding this issue was not found.

"…of general interest"

The presumption of innocence[xi] is a cornerstone of the American justice system, yet posting the uncensored footage of an arrest will do less to uphold that principle with the general public. What would happen if a man were arrested under suspicion child molestation? Even if he was acquitted later, how likely is it that he would have no negative repercussions in his community or in his career? In this situation, the suspect could easily be outraged by the release of the video footage, but what is the definition of what is "of interest" and "not of interest" to the general public? We can argue that, since communities approve both the laws that govern behavior and empower government agents to uphold those laws, that there is a justifiable interest in knowing about those that violate those laws.

We have seen with such incidents such as "tippergate" in Seattle of October 2011[10] that the general public can react quickly, negatively, and in some cases, violently to incidents not only between public agents and citizens but also between citizen and citizen. In the case of police video, there can be any number of situations where mass public reaction does more damage than the incident itself. Granted, a large-scale

---

[xi] Definition of the presumption of innocence can be found at
    http://www.law.cornell.edu/wex/presumption_of_innocence

public reaction is unlikely to occur for every arrest, but damage done by one individual is still damage and it can still be just as devastating. Juvenile criminals also face an additional complication. Uncensored video would prevent a record from ever being completely sealed and discloses the identity of a minor that falls into the "of interest" category to society, even though society has chosen to protect this class of citizen.

The records mentioned in this section have always been available, and the problems discussed have not happened at a nationally recognized scale. The key difference is that these records are now being posted to the Internet, and once the data is there, it can never be retracted. An argument could easily be made that an extreme criminals such as murderer or rapist has forfeited all rights to have information about his case controlled. The argument starts to weaken as the severity of the crime is lessened and as cases become more complex. Is it just for a person with a DUI from twenty years ago to have his image posted along with recent DUI offenders? What about the person who was given a traffic ticket for going 10 miles per hour over the speed limit? Does the position of a death row inmate change from criminal to victim if he is acquitted of his crime?

The measure of justice must be equitable to the measure of the crime. Posting uncensored video of every criminal incident to the Internet inhibits a sentence from ending, inhibiting a former criminal's ability to engage in the common occupations of life[11] once his dues to society have been paid. Uncensored image and video generates a higher cost to privacy and the wellbeing of our communities than the benefit gained for transparency.

Policy Alternatives

The fact that current policy does not address current privacy issues is a tired subject, but little actual progress has been made to date. President Obama's Consumer Privacy Bill of Rights[xii] is the most significant legislation designed to protect privacy, but the legislation is focused on private companies collecting consumer information. In order for the legislation to be effective, it needs to have explicit mandates for government to manage data is the same way as private companies. Even so, this particular legislative piece is still just a proposal to Congress, and the problem of disclosing public data and the risks it poses to privacy is a problem *today.*

[xii] The full text of the Consumer Privacy Bill of Rights is available at the following link:
http://www.whitehouse.gov/sites/default/files/privacy-final.pdf

The first critical policy change that must be made is to informed consent. Informed consent requires that the use and re-use of the data being gathered be disclosed and to allow the option to opt out. Informed consent will not be necessary for gathering publicly available data gathered in a public place

Part of the policy issue stems from two different problems being assessed in isolation. The first problem is that of collecting data; public agencies have a need to collect data in order to maintain and improve society. The second problem is that of privacy; citizens have a right to know what information the government collects and to keep sensitive information contained. If addressed in isolation, the best solution for each of these problems is the worst outcome for the other. If the problems were to be combined, the requirements of each issue may be re-stated as constraints for the solution. Rather than relying solely on image data, as it exists today, policies could be supplemented with the condition that the method of collecting data must be designed to optimize the collection of the target data and to minimize to collection of collateral data to the fullest extent that technology allows. Changing the assumption that images and video are the only medium for collecting data can open up a world of possibilities.

Images may not be necessary at all in the case of utilities data such as traffic flow and parking utilization. When I was younger, I worked for the City of Everett transportation department. One of the common traffic data collection devices were simple rubber tubes stretched across a road. These tubes were connected to a small box that would record the air pressure when a car or truck drove over the tubes. By analyzing the velocity of air and timing between airbursts, the engineers could determine the gross weight, axle count and dimensions, and speed of a vehicle along with the total count of vehicles that passed that spot throughout a period of time. Such a simple device collected highly usable data without compromising privacy. What innovations might spring up if the focus shifts to collecting the greatest amount of data on traffic movement and parking utilization *without* collecting personally identifiable information?

The same principle applies to body-mounted police video. The intent of the technology is to monitor the behavior of the police officer, not to broadcast sensitive information about citizens. To be fair, video appears to be the most effective method given current technology, but how the data is both recorded and disclosed to the public could be improved in light of a new policy. As an active agent of the government a police officer's conduct is subject to scrutiny, so none of the current situation would need to change; video of an officer's conduct should still be uncensored to the public. However, the citizens in the video have a right to privacy unless the video content is deemed to be of interest to the public. As such, the video content should be anonymized upon recording, to be de-anonymized upon the receipt of a court order during the investigation of a complaint or criminal case. The result would be publicly available video of interactions between police officers and citizens, (possibly with the badge number or police officer's name on the video along with a time and date stamp) without risking the identity of the involved citizen.

A similar concept is loosely captured in section 6, *Focused Collection*, of the Consumer Protection Bill of Rights, but the wording still leaves organizations open to the most convenient data collection method. Policies should focus on encouraging alternative methods of collecting data that minimize or altogether avoid collateral data. For smaller government offices, the issue of research and development resources comes to the forefront against this argument, but this can be avoided by providing funding for citizens or companies to invent solutions. What would happen if student loans were forgiven or there were new tax credits issued in exchange for coming up with a solution to a data-collection problem that did not create a privacy issue?

Content considered "of general interest" to the public also must be more clearly defined. Video and images of citizens involved in legal issues, either as victims or as criminals, have far-reaching consequences for those involved when released to the Internet. The permanent nature of online content should move policy to more robust informed consent procedures or re-structuring the way that data is disclosed.

Closing

In the Information Age, informed consent is the keystone around which privacy protection is built and is essential to protecting society's sense of privacy. The issue is not with government agents collecting public images. Taking pictures or video (not audio) of things going on in a public place is legal. In fact, it is a core tenant of the First Amendment.[xiii] The issue is that the use of images and video to collect information on traffic patterns, police officer behavior, school security cameras, and other elements generates *collateral data* that can be re-used by government agents, private sector businesses, and individual citizens for purposes outside of its original

---

[xiii] More information on the first amendment
     http://www.firstamendmentcenter.org/

intent. Informed consent is sorely missing in the management of government image data, and as such is creating multiple avenues for privacy violations. Significant policy changes are needed immediately, before major harm can be done.

What should *not* change, however, is public disclosure policy. The disclosure of public records is critical to a healthy democratic society. Washington State in particular has done what appears to be a good job defining legislation in favor of government transparency. The change in policy should be aimed at minimizing collateral data and optimizing the collection of target. Funding or incentives should support these new policies such that the cause of the problem is involved in creating the solution.

1 Baase, Sara. "Chapter 2: Privacy." *A Gift of Fire: Social, Legal, and Ethical Issues for Computing and the Internet.* 3rd ed. Upper Saddle River, NJ: Pearson Prentice Hall, 2008.

2 Stewart, Darin L. *Building Enterprise Taxonomies.* United States: Mokita, 2008. Print.

3 Anthony, Sebastian. "Facebook's Facial Recognition Software Is Now as Accurate as the Human Brain, but What Now?" *ExtremeTech.* 19 Mar. 2014. Accessed Nov. 2014 <www.extremetech.com>.

4 Elinson, Zusha. "Punishment of Police Under Scrutiny." *The Wall Street Journal.* 28 Nov. 2014. Accessed Nov. 2014 <http://online.wsj.com>.

5 Mapes, Lynda. "Police-shooting Victim 'Struggled with a Lot of Things'" *The Seattle Times.* 1 Sept. 2010. Accessed Nov. 2014 <http://seattletimes.com>.

6 Mims, Christopher. "What Happens When Police Officers Wear Body Cameras." *The Wall Street Journal.* 18 Aug. 2014. Accessed Nov. 2014 <http://online.wsj.com>.

7 Steketee, Amy. "The Legal Implications of Surveillance Cameras." *District Administration Magazine.* 1 Feb. 2012. Accessed Nov. 2014 <http://www.districtadministration.com>.

8 Toyama, Kentaro. "Can Technology End Poverty?" *Boston Review.* 1 Nov. 2010. Accessed Nov. 2014 <http://www.bostonreview.net>.

9 Baase, Sara.

10 Kindelan, Katie. "Seattle Waitress Exposes Rude Tipper Online, Nabs Wrong Guy." *ABC News.*13 Oct. 2011. Accessed Nov. 2014 <http://abcnews.go.com>.

11 "The Right of Privacy: Is It Protected by the Constitution?" Exploring Constitutional Conflicts. Project of the University of Missouri-Kansas City School of Law. Accessed Nov. 2014 <http://law2.umkc.edu>.

Chapter IV
Government Oversight

With a Nod and a Shrug

A Flawed Switch and Failures at General Motors and the NHTSA

Kristine Tomasovic Nelson
June 2015

Abstract: A faulty ignition switch designed into General Motors' vehicles led to thirteen deaths and dozens of accidents. It is well understood that these tragedies resulted from a series of systemic failures at General Motors. However, a complete analysis also takes into account risk factors contributed by GM's regulating agency, the National Highway Traffic and Safety Administration.

In 2002, a General Motors (GM) engineer named Ray DeGiorgio made a decision with catastrophic results. He included in the design of certain GM automobiles an ignition switch that was below GM's own specifications for torque. In other words, the switch turned with too little force. This allowed the engine to be turned off inadvertently, even with the bump of a knee or the swing of a heavy key chain. Cars containing the part, such as the Chevrolet Cobalt, were prone to shut off even while in motion; something called a "moving stall."[1]

This small decision ballooned to catastrophic impact. By the time the problem of the moving stalls was traced to its source, eleven years had passed, at least 54 accidents occurred, and more than 13 people had lost their lives. GM incurred tremendous reputational and financial damage. In 2014, the company was forced to recall 29mm vehicles worldwide, pay a $35 million fine (the maximum allowable) to the National Highway Traffic and Safety Administration (NHTSA), and send its CEO to testify in front of Congress, where senators accused the company of "criminal" behavior and of fostering a "culture of cover-up."[2]

How did one employee's design decision cause such damage? Not surprisingly, there were multiple contributing factors and events. Numerous people and process control failures occurred both internal and external to the GM organization. GM had no plan in place to prevent, identify, and mitigate its own operational errors, and the NHTSA, the regulating agency for auto industry safety, was cited in a congressional investigation for shortfalls and failures. Each organization's role will be considered in turn, but neither one demonstrated a strong control of operational risk. In fact, the ignition switch tragedy falls across five of the seven operational risk categories as defined by Basel II.[3] These include:

- **Internal fraud** - Committed by DeGiorgio
- **Clients, Products, and Business Practices** – Employees within both organizations failed to meet professional duties.
- **Damage to Physical Assets** – Flawed vehicles, subsequent recall, and maintenance requirements.
- **Execution, Delivery, and Process Management** - Lack of processes to identify the cause and repercussions of the faulty part.

It is somewhat reassuring that in hindsight GM has a clear picture of and has taken responsibility for its shortcomings. Shortly after initiating its first round of recalls, GM's CEO Mary Barra and its Board of Directors commissioned former U.S. Attorney Anton Valukas to conduct a thorough independent investigation in order to present "the unvarnished truth about what happened, why it happened, and what GM should do to ensure that it never happens again."[4] The investigation cleared top management of wrongdoing and found no sign of a cover-up. However, Valukas and his team found "a lack of urgency, lack of ownership, lack of oversight, and lack of understanding of the consequences of the problem." The report revealed that GM even had a name for this: the "GM nod", meaning that everyone nods in agreement to a plan of action but no one makes sure it gets done.

Indeed, GM had multiple opportunities to identify and fix the problem, but in every instance, the organization - more exactly, its people and processes - failed. Customers began complaining about the issue and reporting moving stalls as early as 2004, but more than one committee assembled to size and address the problem from the years 2004-2013 deemed it a convenience issue, not a safety issue. They failed to recognize that in the case of a moving stall, the airbags would shut off shortly after power from the engine was cut, leaving the airbags un-operational at precisely the moment when the safety feature was most crucial. As accident reports involving fatalities began to trickle in, GM engineers and even in-house counsel still failed to see the connection between the switch and the airbags. Investigators were in part misled by GM engineer DeGiorgio who had replaced the part for the 2007 model year car but did not renumber it, as protocol would require. Because investigators did not discover that the part had changed, they could not figure out why some (early) model year switches were failing while other (later) model years' were not. (Later DeGiorgio claimed he did not remember the change.) However, as early as 2007 a state trooper investigating a fatal accident figured out the switch/airbag connection. Similarly, outside investigators employed by plaintiffs' lawyers did the same in 2013 simply by comparing the "same" part from two different cars. The company lacked either the investigative process or willpower to do what others did relatively easily.

The Valukas report also found that while critical information passed through numerous hands within the company, no one brought it to the highest levels of the company. In addition, information crucial to decisions at multiple levels was often found lacking. For example, the trooper's report was found in GM's files as early as 2007, but not one GM engineer admitted to seeing it before the year 2014. And in late 2013, GM's recall committee deferred their decision on whether to recall vehicles with the switch for six weeks because the presentation given to them failed to contain information about fatalities.[5] Clearly, GM's processes and culture were inadequately configured to prevent and mitigate the risks that occurred.

There is no single, obvious explanation for why these inadequacies came to be, but one former employee, William J. McAleer, raised alarm bells about GM's culture (and its failures) more than fifteen years ago. In 2014 in light of the ignition switch recalls, he presented his theories to the media. McAleer was an auditor who ran a program at GM from 1985 to 1998

called Global Delivery Survey. This program sent
teams of GM personnel, including managers, to
conduct checks on finished vehicles delivered from
GM's assembly plants. The teams conducted "root-
cause analysis," assigning fault and responsibility for
any identified defects. McAleer says the program
discovered and mitigated many production problems
early, but he believes that when Congress began
requiring auto manufacturers to report more details
about possible vehicle defects to the government in
late 2000, GM stopped looking for the defects and
cancelled its program. McAleer is quoted as saying, "It
was no longer acceptable to have a problem at
General Motors, whether it was a safety problem or
any kind of problem, problems were not acceptable."
In response to McAleer's claims, GM countered that
the audit function was moved and conducted under a
program handled by the plants.[6] But an audit
program run by the same employees who produced
the cars could easily be less rigorous than one run by
an external team.

Another potential cause of the culture and process
inadequacies has been offered by GM expert Maryann
Keller, who wrote two books on the company. She has
attributed the problems to cost cutting. She asserts
that modern GM was dominated by "bean counters"

who had only one objective: to make the numbers, sometimes by sacrificing quality.

In hindsight, it is abundantly clear that GM lacked the controls and risk management processes needed to prevent this disaster. During the course of the growing crisis, GM failed to accomplish any of the five key operational risk management tasks as identified by risk expert Philippa Girling. These tasks include: 1) identifying operational risks, 2) assessing the size of operational risks, 3) monitoring and controlling operational risks, 4) mitigating operational risk, and 5) calculating capital to protect against operational risk losses.[7] Evidence suggests that the organization lacked or cancelled programs like McAleer's that identified risks. It is also clear that its committees and teams were unable or unwilling to connect the dots on the faulty switch, the airbag failures, and fatalities. Moreover, GM's people were neither motivated nor required to take responsibility for fixing or mitigating problems. Finally, no processes ensured that GM's senior leaders received the information needed to calculate the impact of operational risk losses.

However, the responsibility for the ignition switch crisis was not GM's alone. While the NHTSA accused GM of hiding information and being "slow to act" and "slow to communicate", frustrating the NHTSA's efforts to investigate and resolve the switch issues (Bunkley, 2014), a House of Representatives' report issued in the fall of 2014 also found that the NHTSA made critical mistakes in its investigation of the company and the switch problems.[8] The NHTSA's shortcomings – like GM's – were both procedural and cultural. For example, the House Report determined that the NHTSA also had access to and reviewed the trooper's 2007 accident report but failed to understand the implications. The NHTSA's failures, spread across several years, were at least three-part: 1) as early as 2008 the agency declined to explore the link between the switches and the airbags despite receiving several reports suggesting a connection. 2) The agency failed to track similarities in three independent investigations it conducted into non-deploying airbags in the Chevy Cobalt. And, 3) the NHTSA representatives appeared to lack crucial understanding of how the airbags worked – that the airbags would lose power if the engine were turned off. The report further pointed to the root causes of these dysfunctions: inadequate training, information silos, and the NHTSA "shrug." The report's wording on the "shrug" is scathing: "The agency does not hold itself to the same standard of accountability as those it regulates. There is a tendency to deflect blame and point the finger at others rather than accept responsibility and learn from its own failures. It is no different than the 'GM salute.'" (The GM salute is a reference to a gesture where its employees crossed their arms and pointed fingers at others – a sign of deflecting responsibility[9]).

To move forward, each organization, the auto manufacturer and its regulating agency, must change. These fixes are already underway. GM's CEO has vowed to correct the culture of "incompetence and neglect." She pledged to overhaul GM product-development organization and legal department to make sure that information about safety problems is communicated. Moreover, the company has fired 15 employees and created a new position, Vice President of Global Vehicle Safety.[10] The Valukas report contains nearly 20 pages of recommendations ranging from the organizational structure to individual accountability to investigation processes to the role of lawyers. To prevent a recurrence, GM will need to address all of the recommendations and more. Meanwhile, at the NHTSA, a newly appointed head has pledged to improve the agency's defect analysis and recall processes in part by requesting additional resources and authority from Congress.[11] Industry watchers and members of Congress have also suggested raising the maximum fine allowable from $35 million to as much as ten times that amount.

Each of these proposed solutions seem reasonable and appropriate. However, it is clear that both organizations must also change their cultures. To do so, both should thoroughly evaluate and develop or improve processes that identify and mitigate risks. Perhaps more importantly, each must create a culture were accountability and responsibility are highly valued. The Valukas report recommendations certainly encompass this goal. Other sources validate the importance of culture and conduct in preventing problems such as the ignition switch crisis. Risk expert Annie Searle has written about several practical steps that both GM and the NHTSA could employ to generate the necessary transformation. Three stand out as particularly applicable here. First, ask senior leaders to verbally and physically reinforce ethical conduct. The leaders of GM and NHTSA are saying the right things and taking the right steps. All layers of management must do so. Second, incent employees to do the right thing. Stories of accountability and responsibility should be shared and celebrated. Third, build a fraud misconduct plan, identify weaknesses and programs to identify and report fraud.[12] It cannot be ignored that one engineer's misleading – if not fraudulent – actions were left unchecked and allowed to destroy the credibility of not one, but two institutions.

We can hope that the increased oversight and scrutiny resulting from the ignition switch tragedies will have a positive effect. However, a cynic could point out that this is not the first auto industry safety cover up. For example, in 1978 Ford recalled nearly 15 million vehicles based on studies which showed the gas tanks were prone to exploding during collisions, and in 2010 Toyota recalled 9 million cars at a cost of billions due to gas pedals that got stuck in the down-mode, causing acceleration and fatalities. In fact, since the National Traffic and Motor Vehicle Safety Act was enacted in 1966 giving the government the power to recall unsafe cars, more than 425 million vehicles have been recalled[13] - GM's ignition switch recall is just one unfortunate example among many. While it may seem pessimistic to say so, the only way to prevent future tragedy is to assume that history is doomed to repeat itself.

---

1 Valukas, Anton. *Report to Board of Directors of General Motors Company Regarding Ignition Switch Recalls.* Jenner & Block. 29 May 2014. Accessed Feb. 2015 <www.beasleyallen.com>.

2 Klayman, Ben and Eric Beech. "U.S. Senator Accuses GM of 'Culture of Cover-Up' In Recalls." *Reuters.* 2 Apr. 2014. Accessed Feb. 2015 <www.reuters.com>.

3 Girling, Philippa. *The Operational Risk Framework.* Oct. 2013.

4 Valukas, 2014.

5 Ibid.

6 Gutierrez, Gabe. and Rich. Gardella. "'Willful Ignorance': Ex-Auditor Blasts GM for Cutting Safety Program." *NBC News.* 11 Jul. 2014. Accessed Feb. 205 <www.nbcnews.com>

7 Girling, 2013.

8 *Staff Report on the GM Ignition Switch Recall: Review of NHTSA.* Energy and
   Commerce Committee, U.S. House of Representatives. 15 Sep. 2014.
   Accessed Feb. 2015 <www.energycommerce.house.gov>.
9 Vlasic, Bill. "G.M. Inquiry Cites Years of Neglect Over Fatal Defect." *The New
   York Times.* 5 Jun. 2014. Accessed Feb. 2015 <www.nytimes.com>.
10 Bennett, Jeff and Mike Ramsey. "GM Fires 15 Employees Over Recall
   Failures." *The Wall Street Journal.* 5 Jun. 2014. Accessed Feb. 2015
   <www.wsj.com>.
11 Beene, Ryan. "Rosekind Says NHTSA Must Improve Defect Analysis System."
   Automotive News. 6 Jan. 2015. Accessed Feb. 2015 <www.autonews.com>.
12 Searle, Annie. "Ethical Misconduct: Is It Your Biggest Risk?" *Risk Universe.*
   Nov. 2012. Accessed Feb. 2015 <www.riskuniverse.com>.
13 "The 8 Most Infamous Car Recalls in History." *Bankrate.* 1 Aug. 2011.
   Accessed Feb. 2015 <www.bankrate.com>.

Risk Themes for America's Defense Industrial Base Sector

Casey Rogers

September 2013

Abstract: The Defense Industrial Base sector is a key source of American national security technology and a major driver of the American economy. The sector faces a multitude of risks across a variety of categorical groupings. This research note outlines three major categorical risk themes with an adjoining risk assessment of a specific risk source followed by treatment suggestions for each category. Topics such as intellectual property theft, contractor safety and economic espionage with a focus towards increasing public-private sector coordination in the Defense Industrial Base sector are also examined.

Introduction

The Defense Industrial Base (DIB) sector describes the global industrial complex that supplies the world's governments and militaries with defense technologies, research, support, logistics and many other vital services.1 The DIB sector is an enormously important American asset, not only for national security and defense but also as a powerful economic engine. The sector is truly worldwide with 100,000 component companies and contractors employing millions of highly skilled technical and mechanical workers.2 The sector's integral position in the U.S.' national security and economic strategy makes the sector an enticing target for other companies, militaries, terrorists and foreign governments.

The DIB has to manage a myriad of risks within a highly competitive business environment while meeting the contractual and legal obligations stipulated by their patrons. This research note will begin with a brief description of the current risk management framework being employed by the sector including a description of the structure, participants and stakeholder needs. After which, a broad risk identification process will be discussed, while singling out key risks for more detailed assessment, including historical anecdotes and terminating with treatment suggestions for each categorical risk source.

Sector Description

The many U.S. Critical Infrastructure and Key Resource (CIKR) sectors are managed under a very large bureaucratic umbrella that incorporates both public and private sector partners. The current bureaucratic framework and its executive backing is buttressed by the Homeland Security Presidential Directive-7 (HSPD-7), written by the Bush

Administration in 2003.3 The directive replaced President Bill Clinton's earlier directives with expanded attention given to the prevention and response to acts of terrorism that would affect the U.S. critical infrastructure. The directive forges a coherent national policy for the identification and protection of the systems that permit and maintain basic functioning of the U.S. economy and society.

Additionally, the HSPD-7 seeks to limit the impact of attacks on key resources and build cooperative systems between all the levels of government and private industry working within critical infrastructure sectors.4

The strategic imperatives of HSPD-7 are tactically addressed in the National Infrastructure Protection Plan (NIPP) which contains a sector-specific plan for the Defense Industrial Base sector. The Department of Defense (DOD) serves as the Sector-Specific Agency (SSA) charged with building, managing and updating the DIB's portion of the NIPP and works closely with other related executive branch agencies to manage the sector.

These agencies make up the Government Coordinating Council (GCC), which collaborates with its private counterpart the Sector Coordinating Council (SCC). The SCC is made up of private industry owners and operators in the DIB eco-system and the two councils share a forum as the Critical Infrastructure Partnership Advisory Council among other bureaucratic relationships and acronyms. Together the councils have worked to implement an "all-hazards" risk management approach with goals to improve information sharing, cyber-security and sector resilience.5

Risk Themes, Key Issues and Treatment Recommendations

The following sections identify the broader risk themes and the challenges that they pose to the sector's growth, security and economic viability. The broader themes will be treated as categorical supersets of similar risk sources and exposures. The purpose is to illustrate the sheer number of risks, the strategic goals they imperil and to offer anecdotal evidence on threats and vulnerabilities. Within each risk category a single risk issue is highlighted for a more detailed qualitative assessment and offer broad treatment recommendations for each category.

Risks to Competitive Advantage

This category contains risks that impact the DIB sector's ability to not only meet mission-critical security goals, but also risks to the sector's ability to meaningfully contribute to U.S. economic prosperity and stability. The private companies comprising the Defense Industrial Base sector are some of the most successful and unique organizations in the modern U.S. economy. The top five U.S. based defense contracting firms are all ranked within the Fortune 100, and combined these companies generated over a quarter-trillion USD in revenue last year.6 The defense industry and the larger Military Industrial Complex is a major employer of skilled labor, scientists and engineers. Again, the top five defense firms employ over 730,000 workers, many of which provide skilled mechanical and scientific labor.7 These workers are a national resource in dwindling supply and they meaningfully contribute to the nation's security and economy through their relative rarity and unique skill sets.

The single highest risk source in this category is Intellectual Property (IP) theft. The organized theft of defense industry IP erodes the sector's ability to compete for contracts and deters investment in expensive capitol research and development projects. The exfiltration and illegal utilization of intellectual property is performed by many different actors in pursuit of varied end goals. The competitive advantage of the U.S. DIB sector is attacked through traditional, industrial and economic espionage carried out by both friendly and adversarial nation states as well as other firms. The IP shakedown is performed in multitudinous ways ranging from cyber-intrusion, to simple bribes and breeches in physical security, to foreign intelligence agency penetration, and so on.8

The sector itself is a competitive high-stakes market space and there have been numerous cases of industrial espionage carried out by defense contracting firms against inter-sector competitors in pursuit of high-dollar government projects. For example, in 1998 the Boeing Company was successfully awarded a number of lucrative launch vehicle contracts over its chief competitor Lockheed Martin, only to have them revoked when officials realized that Boeing had procured confidential bidding documents from insiders within Lockheed Martin. The espionage effort resulted in considerable Justice Department scrutiny and later snowballed into a massive $615 million settlement between Boeing and the federal government.9 Additionally, foreign intelligence agencies routinely attempt to penetrate the DIB sector through employment and human intelligence assets in an effort to steal intellectual property and gain insight into U.S. military strategies and systems.

Examining the risk category at large we see that there exists enormous loss potential in dollars, security and innovation. The loss potential combined with the many different attackers clearly demonstrating both the capability; as well the intent to target the DIB sector's competitive advantage brings the risk profile into better view.

Key Risk – State Sponsored Economic Espionage

The defense industry is a potentially rich source of economic intelligence for a foreign nation state actor. The enormous costs associated with doing groundbreaking research and development is a major barrier for countries looking to modernize their economic and military strength. Put frankly, it is generally cheaper to simply steal someone else's research than to attempt to develop the knowledge organically. The scale and overall cost of economic espionage to the U.S. economy is shocking. Exact figures are difficult to produce but a recent report undertaken by the Commission on the Theft of American Intellectual Property states that annual impact to the U.S. economy exceeds $300 billion.10 To put this amount in perspective, the annual losses of IP to theft and espionage at least equal the value of all U.S. exports to Asia.11 If similar legal standards were applied to IP theft abroad like the ones used here in the U.S. it would translate to millions of American jobs.12

The IP commission generally agrees with a quote made by NSA Director General Keith Alexander that the current levels of Intellectual Property theft amount to "the greatest transfer of wealth in history."13 That said, when assessing our nation's and the DIB sector's risk exposure we can state that both the significance and the likelihood are high that a current economic espionage threat is exploiting the many vulnerable aspects of the Defense Industrial Base sector. Complicating the problem further is the rapid development of IP theft methodologies that now include the use of sophisticated malware, cyber-intrusion for the purpose of data exfiltration and even the infiltration of companies by intelligence agents.14 In essence, not only the Defense Industrial Base sector but the outright viability of the American economy and national security apparatus is being eroded year over year with little hope for cessation without major changes that span the public and private sector divide.

Treatment Recommendations

The situation is relatively dire yet there are some steps that can be taken in the short term to hopefully work towards managing our nation's key resource risks. Firstly, strengthen supply chain oversight and accountability to allow for the speedier and more accurate identification of Intellectual Property loss and make possible the tracking of goods that were manufactured using stolen intellectual property.

Second, allow provisions for the Treasury Department to sanction and exclude companies engaging in IP theft from participation in the U.S. banking and financial markets. This would provide some consequences in the short term for proven offenders and hopefully help to deter future thefts.15 Finally, address the human intellectual capital issues that arise from educating foreign students in American university system and not granting them the immigration status to work, reside, or eventually gain citizenship in the U.S.. Our higher education system is a source and focal dissemination point of valuable IP and if we do not provide foreign students the opportunity to work here then they will take those skills to competing companies abroad.16

Physical Risk Theme

Defense Industrial Base partners have to consider the risks to the physical safety and personal wellbeing of people as well as their electronic devices, paper documents and other media when traveling and working abroad. Of paramount consideration is the historical precedent of targeting contractors for kidnapping, detainment, or even outright violence. The defense industry must travel to serve its distributed client base and often must move through or operate within active conflict zones or locations where the rule of law has effectively broken down.

The sector has a moral and pragmatic mandate to provide adequate protection to its employees when required to work in areas where physical violence or martial conflict is common. Sector members must also analyze and treat the risks endemic to electronic devices that handle, store or transmit sensitive material like design drawings, financial figures or strategic company goals. The amount of proprietary information capable of being stored on your average Blackberry is really quite incredible let alone the quantities routinely handled by external storage devices, laptops, or tablet computers. These devices present a significant source of potential risk exposure when not properly configured, secured or operated. Contractors moving through high- traffic areas where people and items are scrutinized can expose valuable trade secrets to foreign intelligence actors and industry competitors if preventative measures are not employed. There are innumerable anecdotes that show the relative danger to devices and documents when simply transiting an airport or mass transportation facility. Abundant stores of personally identifiable information or other meaningful data are lost by unwitting travelers that lose bags or have their luggage stolen while traveling. Failure to implement basic information security risk mitigation steps like full disk encryption, device locking and password complexity can leave vital information highly vulnerable to interception.

Key Risk – Personnel Security in Warzones

Sadly, contractors are a "soft-target" when they have to work in warzones or conflict areas. Attacking American contractors offers terrorists the same opportunity to inflict psychic harm as attacking U.S. soldiers without many of the mortal risks. Participation in the defense industry is often interpreted by extremists as open support for the oppression of occupied peoples and thus terrorists have and will likely continue to kill, kidnap and maim foreign contractors. The images from the 2004 Fallujah ambush of four American private military contractors are still fresh in the minds of many, and show that there are losses greater than dollars or nebulous abstractions like competitive advantage and intellectual property.17

Assessment for this is simple. There is no higher impact than the loss of human life and thus the significance rating is being given the label "extreme" to denote its potential effect on life and limb. The likelihood determination is more difficult. We can assume that the overall percentage of contractors that are attacked while working abroad is quite low but it does happen in nearly every major armed conflict. Despite a lower probability, the potential significance is so costly that the risk exposure rating for personnel in warzones is still high.

Treatment Recommendations

To counteract threats to personnel working abroad, there needs to be an effort to increase information sharing, threat intelligence, training and collaboration between the Pentagon and contractors operating in areas where the U.S. military is active. The DIB sector should create a best practices plan to outline the preparations and security precautions that companies must provide when sending employees into dangerous areas. The plan could emphasize the baseline level of security required to show that companies and public agencies are very seriously considering the risk exposures endured by foreign deployed workers. The sector must go where they are required in pursuit of national defense and military support, but those travels must be made in a way that protects human life above all else. The sector can achieve greater alignment through collaborative threat sharing and analysis that will seek to determine when the risk exposure to non-military personnel is inordinately high.

Functional Risk Themes

The functional risk category contains risks that imperil the Defense Industrial Base sector's ability to function in a desired or acceptable state. This umbrella group of potential risk exposures imperils the sector's ability to deliver down-stream goods with the requisite level of quality in a timely and compliant fashion. Our modern global economy has created new modes of production and collaboration that are presently stretching the sector's ability to meet the contractual demands of its clientele. The degree to which the defense industrial base relies on sub-contractors and other producers of component parts is quite astonishing and makes quality assurance, regulatory compliance and vendor management extremely difficult.

Currently, the lack of oversight and standardization within the defense industry's global supply chain creates conditions in which the integrity of the production process is called into question. There is no agreed upon standard or even a best practices guide for insuring accountability and traceability within the supply chain and thus each link in the chain assumes that their sub-contractors are performing their due diligence. The lack of cohesion and auditability of the entire end-to-end system creates risk exposure that is inherently difficult to treat since its causation and attribution is distributed across a number of regulatory areas and geographical regions.

The Defense Industrial Base faces future hardships with the prospect of lowered military expenditures, budget cuts and the looming prospect of sequestration.18 The sector has profited immensely during the long period of uninterrupted military expenditure growth that came with the Cold War and extended through the War on Terror, but things are likely to change after a decade of continuous warfare.

During the years of elevated military spending the private sector companies have become over-reliant on the U.S. Federal Government and Department of Defense for contracts. Of great concern is the relative lack of commercial applicability that much of the defense sector's products have. As much as any private citizen would like to be the owner of a brand new M1A1 Abrams Tank, most consumers can't swing the $4,350,000 sticker price and thus in the face of sequester the industry needs to retool its offerings to have broader market appeal.19 In order for the DIB sector to continue innovation efforts and costly research and development initiatives the sector must have a stable revenue stream, else it is likely we might see a degradation in capability and future unwillingness to take on expensive capital investment projects.

Key Risk – Extended Supply Chains and Counterfeit Components

The intricacies of the military industrial complex make supply chain management, monitoring and security extremely difficult. The number of component systems and technologies required to design, build and maintain a modern weapons system is huge. The fidelity and integrity of U.S. military technology is jeopardized when supply chains become unwieldy and over-extended.20

Enormous supply chains are vulnerable to the insertion of counterfeit goods that are made using stolen intellectual property and manufactured in facilities that do not engage in proper quality assurance strategies. The threat here is that the unnoticed supply chain absorption of counterfeit components might cause critical systems to fail or be vulnerable to compromise. There is already evidence that the defense industry's supply chain has lost integrity.21 A 2010 study funded by the Naval Air Systems Command found that nearly 40 percent of survey respondents reported finding counterfeit electronics within their supply chain at all levels.22 Worse yet, the study displays the near total lack of standardization for record keeping, auditing and traceability within the industry and supply chain.23

Assessing DIB sector risk exposure here is inherently difficult. The global supply chain is sufficiently lacking in transparency and reporting mechanisms. The significance of vulnerable supply chain management procedures being exploited by unscrupulous or even outright malicious sub-contractors is potentially enormous but it likely ranges widely depending on the circumstances. Judging the earlier mentioned study, we can see that counterfeit items are routinely making it into the defense industry's supply chain at many different points.

Our risk exposure here is largely indeterminate without greater reporting data on the consequences that counterfeit items can have on complex military systems. Ultimately, the issues are going to require cooperation between the sector's private companies and their vendors to agree upon compliance standard and oversight controls. The public sector can offer assistance by drafting an enforceable legislative framework to empower any agreed upon standards.

Treatment Recommendations

Defense firms and especially the Pentagon, with its role as the most likely end consumer of defense products, must engage in a more rigorous and well documented testing procedure for parts as they move through the global supply chain. Performing testing will allow the sector to generate a list of trusted suppliers and isolate other suppliers that are failing to maintain a requisite level of quality assurance.

The sector needs to lean on legislators to mandate that upstream defense suppliers adopt a standardized system for recording the detection of counterfeit items that will provide traceability during auditing procedures.24 The risk treatment plan here cannot wholly account for the nature of globalized business but steps should be taken to increase the system's overall transparency, monitoring and quality.

Conclusion

In brief, performing a risk assessment on an entire critical infrastructure sector is an immense undertaking. The challenges that exist in this sector alone are taxonomically diverse, geographically distributed and extremely complex. The successful navigation of the challenges discussed in this research note will require experts from nearly every functional area of the modern economy (law, finance, science and engineering, information technology, etc.). Enacting some of the treatment suggestions made in this note will simultaneously improve America's homeland defense efforts and address certain threats to the sector's competitiveness and profitability. The sector must embrace these rare opportunities that offer mutual benefit to both the public and the private sector participants operating in a shared critical infrastructure space.

---

1 *National Infrastructure Protection Plan Defense Industrial Base Snapshot*. U.S. Department of Homeland Security. 2007. Accessed 2013 <www.dhs.gov>.

2 Ibid.

3 *Homeland Security Presidential Directive 7: Critical Infrastructure Identification, Prioritization, and Protection*. U.S. Department of Homeland Security. 17 Dec. 2003. Accessed 2013 <www.dhs.gov>.

4 Ibid.

5 *National Infrastructure Protection Plan Defense Industrial Base Snapshot*.

6 "Fortune 500 2013." *Fortune*. N.D. Accessed 2013 <www.fortune.com>.

7 Ibid.

8 *The IP Commission Report*. The Commission on the Theft of American Intellectual Property. May 2013. Accessed 2013 <www.ipcommission.org>.

9 Merle, Renae. "Boeing Agrees to Pay $615 Million Settlement." *The Washington Post*. 16 May 2004. Accessed 2013 <www.washingtonpost.com>.

10 *The IP Commission Report*, 2013.

11 Ibid.

12 Ibid.

13 Ibid.

14 Ibid.

15 Ibid.

16 Ibid.

17 Gettlemen, Jeffrey. "Enraged Mob in Falluja Kills Four American Contractors." *The New York Times*. 31 Mar. 2004. Accessed 2013 <www.nytimes.com>.

18 Botwin, Brad. "Defense Industrial Base Assessment Opportunities for Expanded Cooperation." National Defense Industrial Association. 28 Nov. 2011. Accessed 2013 <www.ndia.org>.

19 "M1 Abrams Main Battle Tank (MBT) (1980)." *Military Factory*. N.D. Accessed 2013 <www.militaryfactory.com>.

20 *The IP Commission Report*.

21 Botwin, 2011.

22 Ibid.

23 Ibid.

24 Ibid.

Quis Custodiet Ipsos Custodes?
Operational Risk within the GAO

Andrew Magnuson
May 2015

Abstract: The Government Accountability Office (GAO) has the heavy burden of auditing all use of government funds, that is to say, the entire U.S. Federal Government. But its unique position within the legislative branch leads to some specific, and hard-to-address, operational risks. How can the government both preserve the GAO's independence and ensure its accuracy and reliability?

About the GAO

The Budget and Accounting Act of 1921 established the General Accounting Office (GAO),[1] with an original mission to provide financial oversight over the Treasury Department. The GAO is independent of the executive branch and serves as an investigative arm of the legislative branch of the U.S. Government. Over the last 94 years, the GAO purview has expanded to provide a critical audit and oversight function to all government expenditures, and in 2004 its name was updated to the Government Accountability Office to reflect this expanded mandate. In practice, the GAO serves as an independent auditor for all government agencies through a combination of regular reports and specific investigations undertaken at the behest of Congress or particular Congressional committees.[2] The GAO is headed up by the U.S. Comptroller General, who is selected for a one-time 15-year term by the President from a list of candidates assembled by a 'bipartisan, bicameral congressional commission'. The eighth and current Comptroller General, Eugene L. Dodaro, took office in 2010 after his selection by President Obama.

The GAO and the Sixteen Critical Infrastructure Sectors

Because of its unique oversight role in the U.S. Government, the GAO is directly responsible for none of the sixteen critical infrastructure sectors[i] as laid out by the Department of Homeland Security (DHS),[3] but indirectly responsible for all of them. The DHS calls out eight specific agencies as responsible for one or more of the sectors, as follows: the DHS is responsible for ten sectors; the Environmental Protection Agency (EPA) is responsible for one

---

[i] Chemical; Commercial Facilities; Communications; Critical Manufacturing; Dams; Defense Industrial Base; Emergency Services; Energy; Financial Services; Food and Agriculture; Government Facilities; Healthcare and Public Health; Information Technology; Nuclear Reactors, Materials, and Waste; Transportation Systems; Water and Wastewater

(Water and Wastewater); the Department of Transportation (DOT) is responsible for one along with DHS (Transportation); the Department of Health and Human Services (HHS) is responsible for two; the Department of Agriculture (USDA) is responsible, with HHS, for the Food and Agriculture Sector; the Department of Defense (DOD) is responsible for the Defense Industrial Base Sector; the Department of Energy (DOE) is responsible for the Energy Sector; the Department of the Treasury (Treasury) is responsible for the Financial Services Sector.

The GAO, as the congressional watchdog for all government spending and efficiency auditing, effectively serves as oversight for the government agencies overseeing all sixteen critical infrastructure sectors. As such, it occupies a unique position in the U.S. Government. Taking its marching orders from its standing mandate and specific Congressional requests, the GAO has broad investigative and audit powers over the entirety of the federal government. On the other hand, it does not have the authority to act on any risks or inconsistencies that it discovers; rather, it must report on them and rely on the legislative branch to act on its findings.

While the GAO produces more than 900 reports per year, a good summary of the major risk findings in various government agencies can be found in the periodic High Risk Report.[4] The latest report as of this research note, published in February 2015, details risk findings in all but one (the exception is the DOE) of the government agencies responsible for the sixteen critical infrastructure sectors.

By way of example, the GAO provided two specific DHS-related risk reports in the latest High Risk Report. The first is a series of recommendations regarding improving the management functions at DHS:

"DHS's efforts to strengthen and integrate its acquisition, IT, financial and human capital management functions have resulted in progress addressing our criteria for removal from the high-risk list. In particular, DHS has met two criteria (leadership commitment and a corrective action plan) and partially met the remaining three criteria (capacity; a framework to monitor progress; and demonstrated, sustained progress)."[5]

The second looks at risks around the management of terrorism-related data, concluding that the DHS has met two of five long-term goals in this category as well, while still needing improvement in a proper action plan, demonstrated progress and proper monitoring of these initiatives.[6] Both of these high-level overviews, in turn, rely upon multiple in-depth research reports that monitor and track DHS progress in meeting these defined goals.

Similarly, detailed reports exist for the remaining agencies covered in the High Risk Report. By regularly researching and compiling these and other risk factors, the GAO is able to provide a valuable auditing function, as well as follow the risk trends over time.

Who Audits the Auditors?

However, this leads to a simple, but difficult to answer, question: if the GAO monitors the federal government, who monitors the GAO? The answer appears to be: nobody, at least not directly. As described above, the GAO depends for its funding and its authority on the Budget and Accounting Act of 1921, as well as the more recent GAO Human Capital Reform Act of 2004. The Comptroller General, once appointed, can only be removed by impeachment or a joint resolution of Congress, leaving him or her entirely independent of the appointing President. In the 94-year history of the GAO, no Comptroller General has been removed from office. However, should Congress choose to do so, it could remove the Comptroller General or even cut funding entirely to the GAO.

However, budgetary control is not the same as effective oversight. While there is certainly oversight within the GAO, there is no independent unit that can police the analysis and reporting of the GAO. Should the GAO, or high-ranking GAO officials, release inaccurate audit or efficiency reports, there is no clear mechanism for this situation to come to light. While this would appear to be an unlikely scenario, it becomes less outlandish when one considers the vast sums of money, and of political power, involved in the operations of the large government agencies mentioned above. It is conceivable that GAO officials could conspire with officials of one of the agencies that the GAO audits and analyzes, in order to conceal incompetence or malfeasance at the agency level. This, in turn, would serve to weaken or disrupt control over one or more critical infrastructure sectors.

Audit without Authority

Beyond the potential for a corrupt or simply incompetent GAO, consider the reverse case. If the GAO describes irregularities in financial or operational procedures and reporting, it is only able to report these issues but is unable to actually compel the relevant government departments to improve their processes. Instead, it is up to the U.S. Congress to take action on the GAO's findings. What would happen if, after a scathing report, Congress chose not to act? This is a rhetorical question, since this situation has in fact continuously been the case since 1996. Starting in that year, the federal government began producing consolidated fiscal statements, and from the beginning the GAO has refused to approve these statements on several grounds:

(1) Serious financial management problems at the Department of Defense (DOD), (2) the federal government's inability to adequately account for and reconcile intra-governmental activity and balances between federal entities, and (3) the federal government's ineffective process for preparing the consolidated financial statements. Efforts are under way to resolve these issues, but strong and sustained commitment by the DOD and other federal entities as well as continued leadership by the Department of the Treasury (Treasury) and the Office of Management and Budget (OMB) are necessary to implement needed improvements.[7]

Notwithstanding that the GAO has regularly called out these issues since 1996, Congress has taken no action to remediate any of them and, as the GAO notes, significant further commitments are needed, from the highest levels. Considering this fact, there is a serious risk that, should the GAO uncover serious malfeasance or poor resource management in any government agency, Congress might very easily choose to ignore the GAO report if it is not politically rewarding to act. This inaction could, as above, result in the weakening or disruption of control over one or more critical infrastructure sectors.[ii]

Effectiveness of Controls

By design, the GAO is effectively out of reach of any traditional oversight. It is led by a Comptroller General who is selected by a President, but only from a pre-selected list determined by a bipartisan, bicameral congressional committee. Once the Comptroller General is selected, he or she serves one fifteen-year term, and is not eligible for re-appointment. While it is possible for Congress to impeach or legislatively remove the Comptroller General, this has never happened in the 94-year history of the office. This insulates the Comptroller General almost completely from political pressure.

As alluded to previously, the one control Congress does have over the Comptroller General, and the GAO as a whole, is budgetary authority. Should Congress choose to withhold or limit funding to the GAO, this would put pressure on its operations and possibly lead to a restructuring or complete

---

[ii] A closely related risk is that of Congress using the GAO as a political tool, to investigate enemies of (members of) Congress that are subject to GAO scrutiny.

disbanding of the GAO structure. However, as also described above, this control can only be brought to bear on issues that Congress knows (and cares) about. If a GAO report is inaccurate, it is unlikely that Congress will realize this immediately. However, a GAO report that is politically dangerous or unwelcome will be noticed immediately. The combination of these facts means that if Congress does exert budgetary control over the GAO, it is much more likely to be for political reasons rather than concerns over the accuracy or integrity of the reports themselves. And even if this situation presents itself, it is much more likely that Congress will demand the resignation of the Comptroller General than attempt to restructure or replace the GAO as a whole.

A third control, and one that is not immediately apparent, is external to both Congress and the GAO. Media attention on Congress, and on the reports produced by the GAO, serves as a strong check against both risks outlined above. Were the GAO to provide clearly misleading or inaccurate reports, media scrutiny of the published report would be likely to turn up the inaccuracy, particularly if a whistleblower at the GAO or the audited agency tipped off relevant media outlets. On the other hand, were Congress or one of its committees to deliberately bury a politically inconvenient GAO report, this would provide a juicy story for any reporter lucky enough to discover (or be tipped off to) the situation. But while the media can shine a spotlight on both of these major risks, its reach only extends so far. Consider the example described above: the GAO has refused to endorse the federal budget since 1996. Media attention, strong at the start, faded quickly as the same situation continued year over year, and the standoff has not yet been resolved.

Finally, let us consider internal GAO controls. The GAO serves a model – deliberately – for audit organizations through the Generally Accepted Government Auditing Standards (GAGAS), or the Yellow Book.[8] This set of auditing standards, created in 1972 and regularly updated (most recently in 2011) is designed for use in auditing government organizations, and is used by the GAO itself in its audits. Though they do not state so explicitly, it is reasonable to surmise that these or similarly comprehensive rules are used in internal review of GAO-sponsored research. Were an individual researcher to misstate audit results, accidentally or deliberately, standard review processes would almost certainly catch the issue. Therefore, the most likely case of inaccurate or dishonest reports would be via high-level GAO incompetence or corruption.

Recommendations

As was previously mentioned, the GAO is independent of legislative or executive oversight. This is deliberate; if the GAO were accountable to Congress or to the President, this would raise questions as to its independence and to the accuracy of its reports and analyses. While Congress holds the purse strings and can reduce or cut GAO funding, budgetary control is too blunt an instrument to provide oversight of GAO operations, accuracy, and efficiency. The GAO is therefore in the unique position of providing oversight and audit functionality to the U.S. Government while being itself effectively immune to operational scrutiny. This unique situation leads to two specific risks, as detailed above. The first is the risk of the GAO itself, in the person of high-ranking GAO officials or the Comptroller General, colluding with officials of another government agency to conceal evidence of incompetence or malfeasance. The second risk is in many ways the mirror image of the first: because the GAO has the responsibility to audit government agencies, but lacks the authority to compel them to comply with audit findings, it is possible that Congress, which does have that authority, might fail to act on GAO recommendations.

The obvious recommendation, to create a new agency responsible for overseeing the GAO and ensuring that it is accurately and honestly auditing the remainder of the government, merely pushes the problem one step back. If this new agency (A) audits the GAO, then who will audit A? The same problem remains, and cannot be addressed by creating another new agency (B), which would need to be audited by C, and so on infinitely. Similarly, new legislation to make an existing agency responsible for auditing the GAO would lead to a related problem, since that agency would both audit the GAO and be audited by the GAO, as a recipient of government funds. A circular auditing relationship of this nature would also be unsatisfactory, because in the case of a discrepancy, there would be no overarching authority to determine the truth.

And that is the crux of the issue: in auditing, there must be a final authority to determine what is, and is not, an accurate accounting of a given project, or agency, or government. The GAO, in the current U.S. Government, is that authority, and any effort to subject them to outside oversight is doomed to failure for the philosophical and practical reasons outlined above. But this does not mean that the current situation is hopeless. If the GAO is compromised at a high level, the complex web of interdependencies among agencies means that an effective cover-up is only one whistleblower away from public outrage. The GAO in particular, and the federal government in general, should enforce and strengthen whistleblower protection statutes to ensure that malfeasance of this nature does not remain hidden through a culture of silence or retribution.

Regarding Congressional inaction, on the other hand, the most effective control that already exists is that of outside interest – media and public attention to GAO reports and their conclusions. As long as GAO reports are not private, there is certain to be a good deal of scrutiny on the GAO, its operations, and the congressional mandates guiding these operations. The GAO is already very good about publishing all of their reports in a timely manner on their website; beyond this it is the responsibility of the public, and the media, to read and understand the reams of information available. However, as we have already seen in the case of the GAO's continued refusal to endorse the federal government's annual financial statement, information, even when known, does not guarantee action. Instead, only sustained interest and public pressure can lead to action on GAO findings that Congress has chosen not to address.

While there is no way to force this kind of pressure, the GAO can make its case to the U.S. public more directly. While they already produce hundreds of reports annually, there is little welcoming, public-facing information available on the GAO website. Articles summarizing the conclusions of the GAO technical reports, written for a popular audience, might go a long way to reaching a wider audience and helping the public understand the work that the GAO does and the findings that it has produced.

The GAO occupies a unique and complex place within the U.S. Government. Though there is little chance of significant changes in GAO practices – and little likelihood that such changes would be beneficial – the foregoing recommendations will strengthen the GAO's effectiveness and authority.

---

1 "The History of GAO - GAO's Start." U.S. Government Accountability Office. n.d. Accessed Mar. 2015 <www.gao.gov>.

2 "About GAO." U.S. Government Accountability Office. n.d. Accessed Mar. 2015 <www.gao.gov>.

3 "Critical Infrastructure Sectors." Department of Homeland Security. n.d. Accessed Mar. 2015 <www.dhs.gov>.

4 "High Risk Report 2015." U.S. Government Accountability Office. 11 Feb. 2015. Accessed Mar. 2015 <www.gao.gov>.

5 "Strengthening Department of Homeland Security Management Functions." U.S. Government Accountability Office. 2015. Accessed Mar. 2015 <www.gao.gov>.

6 "Establishing Effective Mechanisms for Sharing and Managing Terrorism-Related Information to Protect the Homeland." U.S. Government Accountability Office. 2015. Accessed Mar. 2015 <www.gao.gov>.

7 "U.S. Government's Fiscal Years 2014 and 2013 Consolidated Financial Statements." U.S. Government Accountability Office. 26 Feb. 2015. Accessed Mar. 2015 <www.gao.gov>.

8 "The Yellow Book." U.S. Government Accountability Office. 1 Dec. 2011.
  Accessed Mar. 2015 <www.gao.gov>.

Chapter V
Innovation

Patient Lives In Our [Robotic] Hands

Risks and Implications of Robotic Surgery

Brooke R. Brisbois

November 2014

Abstract: This research note explores the risks associated with robotic surgery, as faced by both public and private sector organizations, including patient harm, legal liability and technical challenges.

Introduction

Technological innovations in healthcare have led to breakthroughs in the treatment of and care for patients. Conversely, these same innovations are hotly debated on the overall effectiveness, safety, and risks to patients. A recent healthcare technology under debate is robotic surgery, which involves a surgeon performing a procedure with the assistance of a robot. These surgeries have seen a steep rise in popularity during the last ten years; as of 2012, nearly one out of every four hospitals in the U.S. had at least one robotic surgery system.[1] However, popularity alone cannot vouch for the safety or reliability of these technologies; complications arise and even deaths occur.[2] This is a problem for everyone involved, from the patients, to the manufacturers of robotic surgery systems, to the hospitals that perform the surgeries, and even for the federal agencies responsible for healthcare regulations. However, new technologies should not be abandoned in the face of difficulties, especially when there are clear benefits; a balance must be struck somewhere.

The U.S. Food and Drug Administration (FDA) highlights this idea of balance on the webpage that introduces the *Food and Drug Administration Safety and Innovation Act (FDASIA) Health IT Report: Proposed Strategy and Recommendations for a Risk-Based Framework*. It leads with this statement:

> "Health information technology (HIT) presents tremendous benefits to the American public, including greater prevention of medical errors, improved efficiency and health care quality, reduced costs, and increased consumer engagement. However, if HIT is not designed, developed, implemented, maintained, or used properly, it can pose risks to patients."[3]

This statement perfectly illuminates the need to evaluate the risks in the case of robotic surgery: technological innovation must be in balance with patient safety.

The Current Robotic Surgery Landscape

Before the risks of robotic surgery can be explored further, we must have a clear picture of what the current robotic surgery landscape looks like, as well as view of the actual system. But first, a preparatory discussion of *what* exactly a surgical robot is must be conducted. In *A Consensus Document on Robotic Surgery*, robotic surgery is defined as "a surgical procedure or technology that adds a computer technology enhanced device to the interaction between a surgeon and a patient during a surgical operation and assumes some degree of control heretofore completely reserved for the surgeon."[4] However, this definition is lacking in specific reference to the *physicality* of the robotic system, which is an important factor when considering the risks and implications of this technology. In his book, *Robot Futures,* Illah Reza Nourbakhsh alludes to the physical nature and action-oriented role of robots, calling them "a new form of living glue between our physical world and the digital universe we have created."[5] Ryan Calo takes this a step further in *Open Robotics*, in which he explains the robotic field's "potential for crippling legal liability" due to the fact that "robots are in a position to cause physical damage and injury directly."[6]

All three of these characterizations of robots can be combined to form a cohesive definition of what a surgical robot is: a computer technology enhanced device that physically aids the surgeon in performing the surgery. However, it is interesting to note that the FDA's web page about "Computer-Assisted (Robotic) Surgical Systems" states that the computer-assisted surgical system "is not actually a robot because it cannot perform surgery without direct human control."[7] This is a somewhat misleading statement, because it depends on the definition of "robot," which Nourbakhsh concludes that it changes too rapidly to be fixed or standardized.[8] The rest of the FDA's definition is fairly consistent, if not slightly more detailed than the definition given in the *Consensus Document*. It describes more specifically what the device does, stating that not only is it a device that uses computer technology, but also one that is designed to "control and move surgical instruments through one or more tiny incisions in the patient's body (minimally invasive) for a variety of surgical procedures."[9]

Now that a clearer definition has been given, the robotic system and its components can be better understood. The only commercially available, FDA-approved system in the U.S. currently is the da Vinci Surgical System, created and sold by Intuitive Surgical, Inc.[10] As detailed on the da Vinci Surgery Online Community website, the system is composed of four distinct parts:[11]

1. *Surgeon Console*: Where the surgeon performs surgery using the master controls while viewing the patient's insides as a high-definition, 3D image.

2. *Patient-Side Cart*: The part of the system that is attached to the patient. Three or four robotic arms connect to instruments that are inside the patient's body, which carry out the surgeon's commands.

3. *EndoWrist Instruments*: Surgical instruments designed to fit onto the robotic arms, enhanced with a range of motion greater than that of the human wrist.

4. *Vision System*: Consists of a high-definition, 3D endoscope that provides the view inside the patient's body, as well as the accompanying high-definition monitors that provide the operating room team with the same view as the operating surgeon.

All of these elements come together in the operating room (see Figure 1), where the surgeon performs the surgery in the surgeon console, at a distance from the patient (in the room, but outside of the sterile field), while the robot carries out the movements, directly inside the patient, that the surgeon inputs.[12]

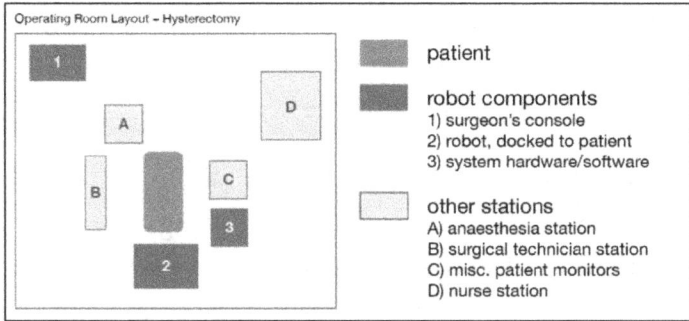

Figure 1: Potential Operating Room Layout For Robotic Surgery[i]

The FDA has approved the da Vinci surgical system for "laparoscopic surgical procedures in general surgery cardiac, colorectal, gynecologic, head and neck, thoracic and urologic surgical procedures."[13]

Robotic Surgery Risks

From the beginning of its commercial implementation, robotic surgery has continuously received both criticism and praise. It is criticized due to the harm it has caused patients, the costs it incurs, and the hype it receives.[14] This is tempered by the praise from doctors and patients alike, both of which extoll the benefits of robotic surgery over existing alternatives.[15] These opposing attitudes create a push-pull dynamic, which is unsurprisingly encapsulated in the risks presented by this new technology. First, the

---

[i] I designed this graphic after observing a robotic laparoscopic hysterectomy surgery. To protect the identity of those involved, the names of the patient, hospital staff, and hospital are withheld for confidentiality purposes.

risk of patient harm or death; and second, the risk of abandoning an emerging technology before the potential benefits are fully assessed.

Of these two overarching risks, it is easy to see the risk of patient harm or death as being the most threatening. If robotic surgery is harming, or even killing patients, why should it be allowed to continue at all? This is a fair question, and it can be answered first by saying that if there was a significant amount of harm and deaths resulting from robotic surgery, as opposed to regular surgery, it would not be allowed to continue. In 2013, the Medical Product Safety Network (MedSun), a program that was started in 2002 by the FDA designed to conduct studies on the use of medical devices, investigated this issue.[16] They conducted a small sample survey, in which eleven surgeons (who have used the da Vinci surgical system to perform 70 to 600 surgeries over the last three years) were asked about their training, patient outcomes, and any difficulties experienced with the device.[17] Overall, the responses indicated a strong consideration for patient safety, as opposed to a blind enthusiasm for the new technology.[18] Additionally, the surgeons reported the benefits posed to patients as well as the problems; in all cases, the number of benefits outweighed the number of problems.[19] Even though the novelty of the device is one of its draws, this report demonstrates that surgeons do not elect to use it on anyone that may be harmed by it. On the contrary, surgeons appear to treat it as any other surgical option and embrace the risk for patient harm or death as they would with other more traditional options.

The results from the MedSun report seem to suggest a positive reaction to robotic surgery within the medical community, as well as a conclusion that the robot is safe to use on patients. However, this is not the only reaction – there is plenty of criticism present as well. Some of this criticism comes from the American Congress of Obstetricians and Gynecologists, which denounced the use of robotic surgery for hysterectomies in March 2013. The professional association said that "robotic surgery is not the only or the best minimally invasive approach for hysterectomy. Nor is it the most cost-efficient."[20] Additionally, the organization criticized Intuitive Surgical, Inc. for their aggressive marketing campaigns, and argued that there is a lack of data to support robotic surgery over other types that have "*proven* track records for outstanding patient outcomes and cost efficiencies."[21] Other members of the medical community also do not accept the risk of patient harm or death presented by robotic surgery as any other risk associated with surgery. Instead, they see a volatile new technology, with an as-yet unproven track record, and therefore see it as untrustworthy.

Aside from the novelty and lack of proven success, others blame the manufacturers for the risk of patient harm, due to the difficulties associated with the robots themselves. Intuitive claims that the robotic movements are safe, stating that "repeated safety checks prevent any independent movement of the instruments or robotic arms."[22] However, in January 2014 an incident was reported of a robotic arm not letting go of tissue that was being grasped during a colorectal surgery, and another where a robotic arm hit a patient in the face.[23] Whether the robot was moving of its own volition or not, it is true that the physical components of the robotic system are capable of harm. Similarly, several malfunctions were catalogued in the MedSun report.[24] These included an arm missing its mark by a 0.5 to 1 centimeter at times, arm articulation (EndoWrist) lock, 1-second delay from the console, and a failure of memory function, all of which can result in serious problems.[25] Not only do difficulties arise from technical malfunctions, but from user error as well. This is also reflected in the report, which states, "All respondents report that learning how to use the da Vinci Surgical System is the biggest challenge because of the device's complex user-interface."[26]

Others believe that the risk of patient harm comes from not only the procedures or robots themselves, but the fact that patients are often not fully informed of the risks, and that the complications associated with robotic surgery are underreported. With regard to informing patients, Lee Char et al. argue "while the introduction of new drugs and medical devices is strictly regulated, the vast majority of patients undergoing innovative surgery do so outside the protections of clinical trials, which require institutional review board approval and detailed, comprehensive informed consent. Outside the context of clinical trials, patients still must consent to surgery, but there is no legal requirement to inform them of its innovative nature."[27] There have also been several papers published on the underreporting of complications due to robotic surgery. Cooper et al. cross-referenced search results from a database of legal judgments and events that contained the terms "Intuitive" or "da Vinci" with the FDA adverse events databases.[28] They found that over the twelve-year period they had investigated, there were eight cases where the FDA reports were inaccurate, filed late, or not filed at all.[29] Arguably, correct reporting contributes to the correct informing of patients, which in turn is critical to patient safety. The risk of patient harm is therefore increased by misinformation and underreporting.

The last factor associated with the risk of patient harm is due not to the newness of the technology, but instead to the *connectivity* of the technology. The da Vinci surgical system has computer components that run software, which is periodically updated.[30] Additionally, the hospital can choose to use da Vinci OnSite remote monitoring of the system, which entails real-time diagnostic feedback, issue identification and resolution, and minimization of technical issues.[31] Both of these system enhancements require remote connectivity, which makes the system vulnerable to cyberattacks. This is especially troubling, given that hospitals are a main target for cybercriminals since healthcare data can be sold for high prices on the black market, as noted in the article by Dune Lawrence.[32] What is worse is that healthcare companies do not have very good cybersecurity; in an analysis conducted by BitSight Technologies, healthcare was ranked lowest overall amongst the other industry groups, which included finance, utilities, and retail.[33] Specifically, the health sector sees the most security problems and takes the longest to fix those problems, about five days on average.[34] Though this problem extends throughout all technologies associated with healthcare, surgical robots are not immune; this is yet another way to cause patient harm.

After hearing about all of the factors associated with the risk of patient harm, it could be easy to dismiss robotic surgery as an endeavor too perilous to pursue. However, it must be remembered that the risk of patient harm is offset by the risk of abandoning the benefits of this technology. In their article, "Robotic surgery: applications and cost effectiveness," Leddy et al. highlight the many benefits of robotic surgery, which include decreases in blood loss, post-operative pain, narcotic use, and length of hospital stay.[35] Though many of these benefits are also associated with laparoscopic surgeries, robotic surgery offers improvements over traditional laparoscopy, specifically: "three-dimensional visualization, mitigation of surgeon tremor, ergonomic and intuitive hand movements, a magnified view and a range of motion approximating the human wrist."[36] Furthermore, the robot eliminates the confusing counter-intuitive fulcrum effect seen in laparoscopic surgery, in which the surgeon must move in the opposite direction of the target.[37] All of these improvements enhance the surgeon's ability to perform surgery, but if the technology is abandoned patients will not see these benefits.

The development of new technology is also at risk due
to regulations enforced by U.S. government entities.
Intuitive Surgical, Inc. cites this in their 2013 *Annual
Report* in the "Risks" section, which articulates the
impact of their regulation by the FDA. The report
further elucidates these risk factors, first by stating
that their products "are subject to a lengthy and
uncertain domestic regulatory review process...the
FDA regulates the development, bench and clinical
testing, manufacturing, labeling, storage, record
keeping, promotion, sales, distribution and
postmarket support and reporting of medical
devices."[38] While this is understandable, the FDA also
has a policy that dictates that new devices may be
cleared if it is "substantially equivalent to another
device" with preexisting clearance.[39] This stance
increases the threat to the improvement of existing
technology because it creates an easier, less innovative
path for companies to take. Another risk to the
regulatory environment is the Health Insurance
Portability and Accountability Act of 1996 (HIPAA).
Like many other healthcare technologies, robotic
surgery systems make use of patient information,
which according to HIPAA's Privacy Rule must be
"properly protected while allowing the flow of health
information needed to provide and promote high
quality health care and to protect the public's health
and wellbeing."[40] Compliance with this rule also

requires compliance with HIPAA's Security Rule, which "establishes national standards to protect individuals' electronic personal health information" and "requires appropriate administrative, physical, and technical safeguards to ensure the confidentiality, integrity, and security of electronic protected health information."[41] Given these considerations, compliance with HIPAA can therefore be costly, time-consuming, difficult, and above all another threat to technological advancement.

An additional reason to mitigate the risk of abandoning this technology is because of the potential it has to continue to change surgery for the better. To see an existing surgical innovation that did just this, we can look to laparoscopic surgery. Lee et al. cite this as an example in their article on robotic surgery training, explaining that the *very first* laparoscopic nephrectomy (kidney removal) was successfully completed in 1990, then a very innovative surgery.[42] Now, 24 years later, this method has come to be considered the "gold standard" for use in this type of procedure.[43] As it continues to mature, robotic surgery could itself become a "gold standard," but only if we can objectively and intelligently weigh the risks that it presents.

Key Players On the Robotic Surgery Landscape

Just as the risk factors present in robotic surgery are very complex, so is the cast of characters. Entities from both the public and private sectors are involved, including regulators, vendors, and customers. The key players in the public sector are regulating bodies that are all located within the U.S. Department of Health and Human Services (HHS). These include the FDA, the Office for Civil Rights (OCR), and the Office of the National Coordinator for Health Information Technology (ONC). The FDA is the body that grants approval for the use of medical devices[44], while the OCR is the body that enforces HIPAA.[45] Finally, the ONC is the "principal federal entity charged with coordination of nationwide efforts to implement and use the most advanced health information technology and the electronic exchange of health information."[46] Between them, these three public organizations have the responsibility to regulate new, technologically advanced healthcare devices, such as surgical robots.

Those involved in the private sector are the vendors and the consumers. The vendors, at the moment, include only Intuitive Surgical, Titan Medical, and various educational institutions. As noted previously, the only FDA-approved device presently on the market belongs to Intuitive Surgical.[47] However, Titan Medical, a competing commercial surgical robot company, states on their website that their SPORT (Single Port Orifice Robotic Technology) Surgical System is expected to be available in 2015.[48] Aside from this pair of bigger corporate players, there are also a handful of educational institutions that are working on surgical robots, including the University of Washington and the University of California Santa Cruz, whose teams collaboratively developed a robot called the Raven.[49] The robot manufacturers, whether commercially- or research-driven, must factor the risk of patient harm into their system design considerations, so as not to be liable for injuries. This is an area that they are already facing consequences for, as evinced in Intuitive's *Annual Report,* which states that they are "currently named as a defendant in about 76 individual product liability lawsuits," by plaintiffs who allege that they were injured as a result of the da Vinci Surgical System.[50] Even though the company has a procedure in which they "model patient value as equal to *procedure efficacy/invasiveness,*" and apparently maximizing procedure efficacy, they are still dealing with the risks of both harming patients and losing their ability to innovate due to these lawsuits.[51]

There are two types of consumers included in the robotic surgery landscape: healthcare organizations and patients. Healthcare organizations can actually be part of either the public or private sectors, and are arguably owners of the most risk. This is due to the fact that not only are they absolutely required to be compliant with government regulations, but they must also implement their own safety standards and organizational guidelines according to their policies, culture, and overall goals.[52] Then they have to factor in an initial investment of $1-2 million for the robot and ongoing annual maintenance costs of around $340,000.[53] Finally, they must consider their primary customers, their patients, above all else; all of these risks come with a hefty price tag.

Patients are perhaps the most interesting players on the robotic surgery landscape. They are the bearers of the most immediate and critical risk (their own harm or death), yet they also hold all of the veto power, that is, the ultimate power to say yes or no to robotic surgery. The patient assumption of both life-threatening risk and economic power makes them a key factor for the other players to consider when they are weighing their own responses to risk.

Recommendations

Now that we know the risks, and where those risks lie, what can be done about them? In his book *COSO Enterprise Risk Management*, Robert R. Moeller outlines what organizations can do about risk. He gives four types of risks responses:[54]

1. *Avoidance*: Strategy of avoiding risk altogether.
2. *Reduction*: Strategy of reducing risk by taking action.
3. *Sharing*: Strategy of sharing risk with other players.
4. *Acceptance*: Strategy of no action.

Each of the players involved with robotic surgery has a reaction to the risks presented (see Figure 2). To begin, there are a few players that can neither avoid nor accept either risk; those are the regulators and the robot manufacturers. To reduce risk for themselves, the regulators must create rules and guidelines that allow them to share responsibility with entities such as robot manufacturers and health organizations. As noted previously, the FDA does this by enforcing specific standards and granting approval, while the OCR does this by creating and enforcing rules (HIPAA). Recently, the FDA, ONC, and Federal Communications Commission (FCC) created a report, as directed by FDASIA

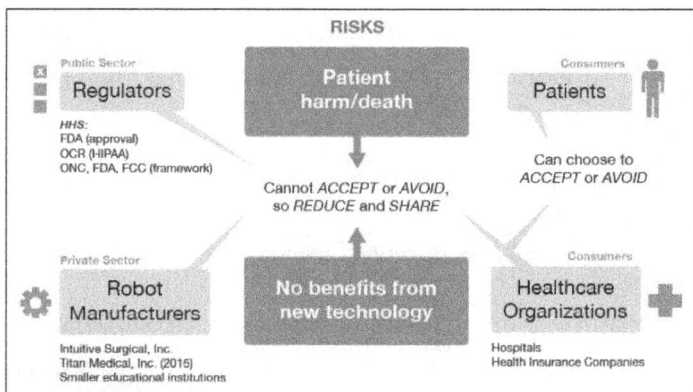

Figure 2: Robotic Surgery Risk Responses

(Public Law 122-144), that contains a recommendation for "an appropriate, risk-based regulatory framework pertaining to health information technology...that promotes innovation, protects patient safety, and avoids regulatory duplication."[55] Some of the principles included in the framework are very sound, such as the directive to "facilitate, rather than impede, innovation," and to "promote transparency of product performance and safety."[56] The promotion of transparency is echoed in current medical literature, specifically Lee Char et al.'s article, which reports that "over 70 percent of patients reported they could not decide whether to have robotic surgery without the following information: a general description of the procedure, known risks and benefits, acknowledgement of potentially unknown risks and benefits, whether the surgeon was doing the procedure for the first time, and the surgeon's special training for the procedure."[57] The framework also addresses the need to "build upon and improve the evidence-based foundation for health IT safety by analyzing the best available data."[58] Cooper et al. echo this recommendation, emphasizing the importance of proper capture, reporting, and evaluation of data.[59]

The FDASIA framework is a good start, but it does not cover all of the risk inherent to robotic surgery. Though there is reference in the document to "robotic surgical planning and control," the overall focus is very broad.[60] It does not make any reference to the hazards of robotic physicality, such as harm from robotic movement. This is why I would like to propose a more specific risk-based framework, exclusive to robotic surgery, made by regulators in conjunction with both robot manufacturers and healthcare organizations (Figure 3).

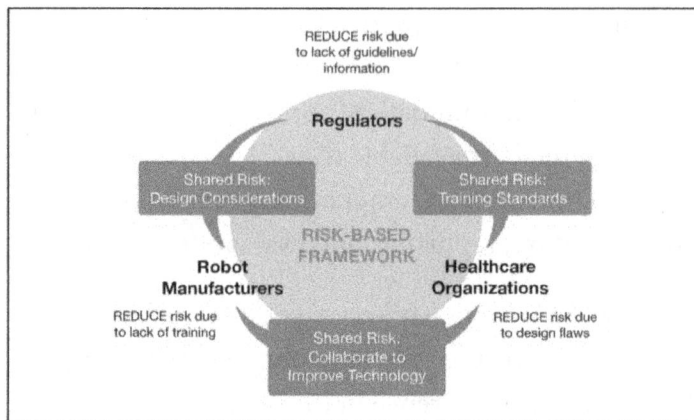

REDUCE risk due
to lack of guidelines/
information

Regulators

Shared Risk:
Design Considerations

Shared Risk:
Training Standards

RISK-BASED
FRAMEWORK

**Robot
Manufacturers**

**Healthcare
Organizations**

REDUCE risk due
to lack of training

REDUCE risk due
to design flaws

Shared Risk:
Collaborate to
Improve Technology

Figure 3: Proposed Robotic Surgery Risk Framework

The framework would cover the specific risk factors presented by robots, such as device design, surgeon training, and harm by robots. By doing so, regulatory bodies could not only reduce risk, but share it as well, creating an environment that could better foster collaboration and innovation. Robot manufacturers would benefit from this arrangement as well, since they would be able to reduce much of their risk by complying to design standards (especially those for ease of use), and collaborating with healthcare organizations in order to improve technology. Risks that could not be mitigated in that way would then be shared with healthcare organizations and regulators in the form of healthcare personnel training requirements. Right now there is no standardized training; though Intuitive offers training courses, it is ultimately left to the hospital and the surgeon to decide when a surgeon is ready to operate.[61] As Lee et al. conclude, a standardized robotic surgery credentialing process would be ideal.[62]

Though it would be beneficial to collaborate, healthcare organizations would not have to participate at all if they found the endeavor too risky. They have the most options regarding risk response: they can choose to avoid, accept, or reduce and share risk. Conversely, patients have the simplest option, though their decision about risk carries the most weight. They can choose to either accept the risks and have robotic surgery, or avoid the risks altogether and choose an alternative. Nevertheless, it would be the goal of the framework to make the decision of whether or not to have robotic surgery an easier one for the patient to decide than it is currently.

Conclusion

As with any new technology, the long-term consequences are not always immediately apparent. In response, caution should be used during the early stages of use. This is especially true when lives are at stake, and the consequences of mistakes are often irreparable and permanent. If anything, all of the key players must continue forward with patient safety at the front and center of concerns. This will help ensure continued growth in the field of robotic surgery.

1 Tanner, Lindsey. "FDA Takes Fresh Look At Robotic Surgery." *USA Today.* 9 Apr. 2013. Accessed Jun. 2014 <www.usatoday.com>.

2 Ibid.

3 "FDASIA Health IT Report." U.S. Food and Drug Administration. 21 Apr. 2014. Accessed Jun. 2014 <www.fda.gov>.

4 *A Consensus Document on Robotic Surgery.* SAGES-MIRA Robotic Surgery Consensus Group. Nov. 2007. Accessed Jun. 2014 <www.sages.org>.

5 Nourbakhsh, Illah Reza. *Robot Futures.* Cambridge, Massachusetts: MIT Press, 2013.

6 Calo, Ryan. *Open Robotics.* 70 Maryland Law Review, 571. 2011.

7 "Computer-Assisted (Robotic) Surgical Systems." U.S. Food and Drug Administration. 4 Jun. 2014. Accessed Jun. 2014 <www.fda.gov>.

8 Nourbakhsh.

9 "Computer-Assisted (Robotic) Surgical Systems."

10 Greenemeier, Larry. "Robotic Surgery Opens Up." *Scientific American.* 11 Feb. 2014. Accessed Jun. 2014 <www.scientificamerican.com>.

11 "Components of the *da Vinci* Surgical System." Intuitive Surgical, Inc. 2014. Accessed Jun. 2014 <www.davincisurgerycommunity.com>.

12 *A Consensus Document on Robotic Surgery.*

13 "Computer-Assisted (Robotic) Surgical Systems."

14 Tanner, Lindsey.

15 Ibid.

16 *MedSun Survey Report: da Vinci Surgical System.* U.S. Food and Drug Administration. Nov. 2013. Accessed Jun. 2014 <www.fda.gov>.

17 Ibid.

18 Ibid.

19 Ibid.

20 Breeden, James T. "Statement on Robotic Surgery." *The American Congress of Obstetricians and Gynecologists.* 14 Mar. 2013. Accessed Jun. 2014 <www.acog.org>.

21 Ibid.

22 "Components of the *da Vinci* Surgical System."

23 Tanner, Lindsey.

24 *MedSun Survey Report: da Vinci Surgical System.*

25 Ibid.

26 Ibid.

27 Lee Char, SJ et al. "Informed Consent for Innovative Surgery: A Survey Of Patients And Surgeons." *Surgery.* Apr. 2013; 153(4): 473-480.

28 Cooper, et al. "Underreporting of Robotic Surgery Complications." *Journal for Healthcare Quality.* 2013.

29 Ibid.

30 "Product Support and Service Features." Intuitive Surgical, Inc. 2014. Accessed Jun. 2014 <www.intuitivesurgical.com>.

31 Ibid.

32 Lawrence, Dune. "Health-Care Companies Have Worse Cybersecurity Than Retailers." *Bloomberg Businessweek.* 28 May 2014. Accessed Jun. 2014 <www.businessweek.com>.

33 Ibid.

34 Ibid.

35 Leddy, Laura Sigismund et al. "Robotic Surgery: Applications And Cost Effectiveness." *Open Access Surgery.* 2 Sep. 2010. Accessed Jun. 2014 <www.dovepress.com>.

36 Ibid.

37 Ibid.

38 *Annual Report 2013.* Intuitive Surgical, Inc. 2013. Accessed Jun. 2014 <www.intuitivesurgical.com>.

39 Ibid.

40 *Summary of the HIPAA Privacy Rule.* Office for Civil Rights, U.S. Department of Health and Human Services. May 2005. Accessed Jun. 2014 <www.hhs.gov>.

41 "The Security Rule." Office for Civil Rights, U.S. Department of Health and Human Services. n.d. Accessed Jun. 2014 <www.hhs.gov>.

42 Lee, Jason Y. et al. "Best Practices for Robotic Surgery Training and Credentialing." *The Journal of Urology.* Apr. 2011; 185: 1991-1197.

43 Ibid.

44 "What We Do." U.S. Food and Drug Administration. 19 Sep. 2013.
   Accessed Jun. 2014 <www.fda.gov>.

45 *Summary of the HIPAA Privacy Rule.*

46 "About ONC." HealthIT.gov. U.S. Food and Drug Administration.
   n.d. Accessed Jun. 2014 <www.healthit.gov>.

47 Greenemeier, Larry.

48 "Home." Titan Medical Inc. 2014. Accessed Jun. 2014
   <www.titanmedicalinc.com>.

49 Greenemeier, Larry.

50 *Annual Report 2013.*

51 Ibid.

52 Moeller, Robert R. *COSO Enterprise Risk Management.* John Wiley
   & Sons, Inc., 2011.

53 Leddy, Laura Sigismund et al.

54 Moeller, Robert R.

55 *FDASIA Health IT Report: Proposed Strategy and Recommendations
   for a Risk-Based Framework.* U.S. Food and Drug Administration,
   Office of the National Coordinator for Health Information
   Technology, and Federal Communications Commission. Apr. 2014.
   Accessed Jun. 2014 <www.fda.gov>.

56 Ibid.

57 Lee Char, SJ et al.

58 *FDASIA Health IT Report.*

59 Cooper, et al.

60 *FDASIA Health IT Report.*

61 Tanner, Lindsey.

62 Lee, Jason Y. et al.

3D Printing and the Future of Intellectual Property

Carolyn Tweedy

June 2014

Abstract: Provides a brief background of 3D printing, and contributes a focused discussion of the implications of 3D printing technologies in the world of information management and intellectual property, specifically copyright and patent laws and the development of policies to govern this burgeoning domain.

Introduction

Sometimes referred to as a "disruptive and transformative technology,"[1] 3D printing is a relatively new additive manufacturing process developed over the past few decades. At its essence, a 3D printer uses a digital model to create a three-dimensional solid object, typically by building up layers of liquid plastic on top of one another[2]. One can imagine the impact this technology would have on the manufacturing industry - enabling more rapid prototyping and increased flexibility in the design process[3], but as Michael Weinberg, a staff attorney at Public Knowledge[22] and author of several whitepapers on the subject states, "3D printing is a tool and, like

---

[22] Public Knowledge is a non-profit Washington, D.C.-based public interest group that is involved in intellectual property law.

any tool, can be used for productive and not-so-productive purposes."[4]

In recent months, 3D printing has been in the news for a variety of reasons, because of ethical concerns about printing biomedical implements,[5]its use in aerospace and defense technologies,[6] and questions about safety and regulations concerning 3D-printed weapons.[7] Also alarming, the burgeoning stock prices of 3D print companies potentially could indicate the growth of an economic bubble.[8] And finally, there are growing concerns about intellectual property and legal issues.[9,10] Clearly, it is a particularly salient time to discuss 3D printing, at the apparent dawn of its ubiquity in our society; a time when society can still influence policy and reexamine about the approach to this new technology. This research note briefly touches on each of these issues, but primarily focuses on the implications of 3D printing technologies in the world of information management.

Given the potential implications that this technology has on manufacturing processes, it is not surprising that one can barely get through reading the news without seeing some mention of 3D printing. Individuals and businesses are increasingly saving money by making customized designs at lower time and material costs. One designer for a motorsports technology company has been using 3D printing for non-functional prototypes in his company for the past five years, and claims that on one single project, "a total of £80,000 was saved using 3D printing."[11] There are countless success stories on the web about cost savings achieved by this emergent technology. Though the financial barrier to entry was high in the early days of development,[12] there are now desktop versions of 3D printers that can be obtained by individuals and small businesses. A low-end model on Amazon.com® can be purchased for less than $400.[13]

Canalys estimates that the global 3D printing industry – including printer sales, materials, and associated services – grew to $2.5 billion in 2013, and is set to rapidly grow 52.0 percent in 2014 to $3.8 billion.[14] And the market research firm forecasts that the pace of growth will continue to grow strongly, advancing at a compound annual growth rate of 45.7 percent from 2013 to 2018. Gartner has gone on record to predict, "That by 2015, seven of the 50 largest multinational retailers will sell 3D printers."[15] Clearly, the market is growing, and has not yet settled - *Forbes* expects that this will almost certainly bring peril upon some investors and companies, but it appears the public's appetite for 3D printing is here to stay.[16]

Aside from the commercial consumer market, 3D printing technologies have made significant inroads into the biomedical field, from custom-printed eyewear[17] to prosthetic limbs[18], to printing living organs and tissue[19]. Peter Basiliere, research director at Gartner, makes a good point that,

"These initiatives are well-intentioned, but raise a number of questions that remain unanswered. What happens when complex 'enhanced' organs involving nonhuman cells are made? Who will control the ability to produce them? Who will ensure the quality of the resulting organs?"

In the same way that small-scale manufacturers like the motorsports technology company mentioned above have created demand for 3D printers, there is a great need for this low-cost, accessible technology in geographic locations whose population has poor access to health care,[20] regardless of how global stakeholders choose to answer the "bioethical" questions posed by Basiliere.

Along with these relatively benevolent applications for 3D printing technology comes a darker side - or, what some might consider more morally troubling implications associated with the freedom to produce any object that can be dreamt up and designed in the privacy of one's home. There have been several recent successful attempts to duplicate and distribute "non-duplicatable" keys typically used by law enforcement personnel for handcuffs and prison doors.[21] Perhaps even more troubling is the case of "The Liberator"—a fully-functioning, plastic, 3D printed gun that was created by Cody Wilson in 2012 and posted to a 3D design file sharing site (more on this site later). Mr. Wilson's pattern for The Liberator was downloaded more than 100K times in two days before the U.S. State Department removed it from the website. Mr. Wilson was a twenty-something law student when he created the pattern and founded an organization called "Defense Distributed," which describes itself as "non-profit anti-monopolist digital publishing."[22] Aside from the thought that anyone with access to a 3D printer and an Internet connection could print off a gun, the plastic nature of The Liberator makes this scenario especially frightening. Plastic weapons are currently not caught by traditional security metal detectors, like those in airports or in other secure locations. Carole Cadwalladr, a reporter for *The Guardian*, stated:

> *"It is one thing to be pro-Edward Snowden, pro-internet privacy, pro-open source movement. And it is another to be pro-the freedom to print off your own assault weapon. And it is this discomfort that Cody Wilson is reveling in ... In fact, the issues that 3D guns raise are more complicated, sophisticated and ultimately unknowable than might first appear. Wilson and Defense Distributed are pushing at the*

margins of the Internet, the margins of freedom, of what the ramifications of this technology will mean. And it is impossible to know. Technology is changing our relationship with everything."[23]

The type of change that Cadwalladr describes is inherent to technology, and one might ask about the precedent of other, similar technological advancements in the past, like the copy machine, or the printing press. Weinberg suggests, "…computers were not the first time that incumbents welcomed new technologies by attempting to restrict them. The arrival of the printing press resulted in new censorship and licensing laws designed to slow the flow of the spread of information."[24]

Clearly, there are precedents in the realm of information management that we can call upon to guide our policy decisions when we consider how 3D printing impacts intellectual property and vice versa. What is slightly different between 3D printing and printing presses/copy machines of old is perhaps the level of proliferation that 3D printing has, and will have, with the public. As Baase suggests, "… earlier technologies were not nearly as serious a challenge as digital technology."[25] Therefore, it may be more appropriate to look at more recent historical examples for guidance, such as the case of Napster and other peer-to-peer file sharing sites in the 1990s and early

2000s. The distribution model used by Napster, Kazaa, and others is similar to 3D design distribution sites like Thingiverse.com (we will discuss this more later). The Recording Industry Association of America (RIAA) eventually was successful in serving a copyright infringement lawsuit to Napster,[26] but neither the result nor the rules may be as cut and dried for 3D printing. Regardless, there is some evidence that product makers are concerned about their intellectual property, and wonder if "3D printers might hurt the physical product market like digital media hurt the music industry."[27]

Before diving into the intricacies of intellectual property and 3D printing, it will be important to understand how 3D designs are created and distributed. As mentioned above, a file for the design of an object must be created or obtained before a system can print the object. This design file is typically one that is created on a computer with Computer Aided Design (CAD) software, much like the software that architects use to model buildings.[28] Once the CAD design file has been generated, it can be shared in the same way one might share any other document—through email or FTP, over a cloud server, on a portable USB drive, etc. Suppose that someone decided to use a 3D scanner to create a 3D model of a vase they own. If they know their friend

Jane loves the vase, they can send Jane a copy of the CAD file. Jane receives the file and prints out her an identical copy of the vase on her 3D printer. The original model owner might also choose to upload the CAD file of the vase to a website like *Thingiverse.com*. On a site like this, anyone can download CAD models to print, or make modifications to the original design, and repost it as their own creations. Is this breaking the law by creating a digital copy of a vase? Did Jane break the law by infringing upon any copyrights— either the original model designer, or that of the original vase designer? Is *Thingiverse.com* as guilty as Napster of distributing licensed-works? Perhaps not.

In order to answer these questions, let us first review the differences between copyrights, patents, and trademarks. All three are types of intellectual property.[29] As Michael Weinberg simply put it, "Generally speaking, copyright covers creative works, patent covers technical works, and trademark covers the ways in which goods are identified in the marketplace." Artists or content creators do not have to seek out obtaining a copyright on their work; it is received as soon as the work has been created, and it lasts for the creator's natural life and protects their work 70 years after their death.[30]

Patents are different from copyrights because a creator or inventor must apply for a patent, it is not granted automatically, as with copyright. Furthermore, the invention must be "new, useful, and non-obvious." Once a patent is obtained for an object, unauthorized reproduction is not allowed, even if the individual doing the reproduction is not aware of the original.[31] Patented works are only protected for 14 or 20 years (depending on whether it is a design patent or a utility or plant patent).[32] As stated in U.S. Patent Law (Title 35 U.S. Code, Section 101), "Whoever invents or discovers any new and useful process, machine, manufacture, or composition of matter, or any new and useful improvement thereof, may obtain a patent therefor, subject to the conditions and requirements of this title."[33]

So where does leave 3D printed works, you ask? The answer is, in a very gray area. Weinberg says that:

> *"the result of all of this is that only a small portion of the objects coming out of a 3D printer will actually be protected by intellectual property: those objects protected by copyright and some number of useful objects protected by an active patent. The rest – those objects that do something but are unprotected by patent – will be free to be used by anyone for any purpose."*[34]

It is possible, however, to protect a useful object with a copyright using the concept of severability. As defined in the legal dictionary, severable refers to, "a contract that can be divided and apportioned into two or more parts that are not necessarily dependent upon each other."[35]

Hence, the intellectual property for an object that has some useful parts as well as some artistic parts can still be protected under copyright. Consider modern video games: most game studios employ designers and artists that produce very distinct visual aesthetics—this intellectual property is copyrightable. The utilitarian aspects of a video game, like the algorithms and code on the back end, are not copyrightable. Weinberg suggests a few rules for finding severability in these cases:

1. Look to see if any potentially severable elements were driven by utilitarian needs,
2. Determine if there are creative elements that were designed without regard for functional requirements,
3. Determine if independent, artistic judgment drove the creation of the non-functional elements.[36]

That said, 3D CAD files are still within the realm of copyrightable work, but the law limits the protection to say, "The design of a useful article ... shall be considered [a work eligible for copyright protection] only if, and only to the extent that, such design incorporates pictorial, graphic, or sculptural features that can be identified separately from, and are capable of existing independently of, the utilitarian aspects of the article. 17 U.S.C. § 101."[37]

Now that it has been established that these designs can be copyrighted, the nature of 3D printing brings us back to questions about copyright infringement when 3D designs are printed, scanned, shared, and/or modified. Theft of intellectual property is a huge concern with this emerging technology. Along with the forecasts for financial gains within this industry, Gartner predicted that on a global scale, 3D printing will be responsible for a loss of "at least $100 billion per year" by 2018. [5] That doesn't give us much time for legal precedents (though there have been a few, like the case of Ulrich Schwanitz's Penrose triangle).[38]

In one of his whitepapers on 3D printing, Weinberg explains that it is legal for someone to use a 3D scanner to scan an object and create a CAD file, even if the object is protected by copyright. This CAD file would not be protected by copyright. If that person wanted to distribute the CAD file, they would need permission from the individual who controls the copyright of the original object. If an individual created a work in a CAD program (read: did not scan an object), that CAD file would be protected by copyright, and the creator would need to provide permission for any printing, copying, or distribution. He suggests that rights-holders distribute their work under something akin to a Creative Commons license:

"Attaching a Creative Commons license is a signal that the creator wants to include her work in an ever-expanding and evolving network of creativity. It gives the rest of the community confidence that they can build on the object … Every object on Thingiverse lists information about what it is derived from and what has been derived from it. This has created a rich ecosystem of creation, design and innovation."[39]

This sense of creative freedom and iterative improvement is deeply engrained within 3D printing; in fact, most 3D printers can print their own replacement parts. Jonathan Palecek, writer for Creative Commons, says,

"A large portion of why the RepRap (Replicating Rapid-prototyper, a low-end 3D printer) is so interesting is that the schematics are released under the GNU GPL copyleft license. This means that anyone can copy and improve the project as long as they share alike their modifications, just as one must with GPL'ed free and open source software."[40]

It seems that Richard Stallman, creator of the GNU movement, would agree. Baase writes, "[Stallman] points out that the primary purpose of copyright, as stated in the U.S. Constitution, is to promote progress in arts and sciences, not to compensate writers."[41]

Given Gartner's projections about monetary losses due to IP theft,[42] it is clear that this is the type of environment where thieves will likely thrive until there are clearer regulations in play. Brianna Ford, from American University's Washington College of Law *Intellectual Property Brief* surmises that,

"Although there will likely be issues with trade secret if a design is misappropriated, there is no special trade secret issue due to 3D printing that will change the law. However, 3D printing could change the way we view copyright, patent and trademark law because the technology covers all of these at the same time."[43]

Conclusion

Weinberg suggests that the future may include a kind of "quasi-patent system" where useful 3D printed objects may be protected differently than they are under today's current laws.[44]

As with other emerging information management issues, policy implications surrounding 3D printing are just breaching the surface of public attention, so it is particularly important to discuss them at this time. The development of new 3D printing policy will need to respond and adapt to issues that one might not be able to anticipate now, as this technology is still relatively new. 3D printing allows a reexamination of society's views on intellectual property in the age of modern technology, and provide an opportunity to make changes where existing systems are not fulfilling current and future needs. The next few years will be interesting to observe, as 3D printing units become less expensive, more widely available to the public, and as the technology improves to use more ubiquitous 3D printing in non-plastic materials (i.e. metal, glass, ceramic, etc.), allowing for expansion into new markets. As Michael Weinberg said, "Just as with the printing press, the copy machine, and the personal computer before it, some people will see 3D printing as a disruptive threat. Similarly ... [others] will see [it] as a groundbreaking tool to spread creativity and knowledge. It is critical that those who fear not stop those who are inspired."[45]

---

1 Hall, Kathleen. "How 3D Printing Impacts Manufacturing." *Computer Weekly*. Feb. 2013. Accessed Mar. 2014 <www.computerweekly.com>.

2 Rouse, Margaret. "3-D Printing (Additive Manufacturing)." *TechTarget*. May 2013. Accessed Mar. 2014 <www.whatis.techtarget.com>.

3 "3D Printing Opportunities & Challenges Symposium: January 28-29, 2013." Information Management Institute. Jan. 2013. Accessed Mar. 2014 <www.imiconf.com>.

4 Weinberg, Michael. "What's the Deal with Copyright and 3D Printing?" Institute for Emerging Innovation, Public Knowledge. Jan. 2013. Accessed Mar. 2014 <www.publicknowledge.org >.

5 Rivera, Janessa, and Rob Van Der Meulen. "Gartner Says Uses of 3D Printing Will Ignite Major Debate on Ethics and Regulation." Gartner. 29 Jan. 2014. Accessed Mar. 2014 <www.gartner.com>.

6 McGlaun, Shane. "NASA to Send 3-D Printer to the ISS in 2014." *DailyTech.com*. 1 Oct. 2013. Accessed Mar. 2014 <www.dailytech.com>.

7 Cadwalladr, Carole. "Meet The Man Who Created The 3D Printed Gun." *Business Insider*. Guardian.co.uk, 10 Feb. 2014. Accessed Mar. 2014 <www.businessinsider.com>.

8 McCue, TJ. "3D Printing Stock Bubble? $10.8 Billion by 2021." *Forbes*. Forbes Magazine, 30 Dec. 2013. Accessed Mar. 2014 <www.forbes.com>.

9 Weinberg, Michael. "It Will Be Awesome If They Don't Screw It Up: 3D Printing, Intellectual Property, and the Fight Over the Next Great Disruptive Technology." Institute for Emerging Innovation, Public Knowledge. Nov. 2010. Accessed Mar. 2014 <www.publicknowledge.org>.

10 Weinberg, Michael. "What's the Deal with Copyright and 3D Printing?"

11 Hall, Kathleen.

12 Rouse, Margaret.

13 Amazon.com. *Amazon.com: 3D Printer*. Amazon. N.D. Accessed Mar. 2014 <www.amazon.com>.

14 "3D Printing Market To Grow To US$16.2 Billion In 2018." Canalys. 31 Mar. 2014. Accessed Mar. 2014 <www.canalys.com>.

15 Hall, Kathleen.

16 McCue, TJ.

17 "World's First Fully 3D Printed Glasses by LUXeXceL." *Royal Eyewear*. 19 Jun. 2013. Accessed Mar. 2014 <www.luxexcel.com>.

18 Gruber, Ben. "Bespoke Innovations' 3D-Printed Prosthetics: If Lizards Can Grow Tails, Humans Should Print Limbs." *Reuters*. Accessed Mar. 2014 <www.reuters.com>.

19 Williams, Rhiannon. "3D Printing Human Tissue and Organs to 'Spark Ethics Debate.'" *The Telegraph*. 27 Oct. 2014. Accessed Mar. 2014 <www.telegraph.co.uk>.

20 Rivera, Janessa, and Rob Van Der Meulen.

21 Molitch-Hou, Michael. "Do Not 3D-Print: MIT Hackers Duplicate 'Non-Duplicatable' High-Security Keys." 3D Printing Industry. 9 Aug. 2013. Accessed Mar. 2014 <www.3dprintingindustry.com>.

22 "Makers of the Liberator Pistol." *Defense Distributed*. Accessed Mar. 2014 <www.defdist.org>.

23 Cadwalladr, Carole.

24 Weingberg, Michael. "It Will Be Awesome If They Don't Screw It Up."

25 Baase, Sara. "Chapter 4: Intellectual Property." A Gift of Fire: Social, Legal, and
   Ethical Issues for Computing Technology. 2012.

26 King, Brad. "The Day the Napster Died." *Wired.* 15 May 2002. Accessed Mar.
   2014 <www.wired.com>.

27 Ford, Brianna. "3D Printing and Intellectual Property: Copyright." *Intellectual
   Property Brief,* American University Washington College of Law. 22 May
   2013. Accessed Mar. 2014 <www.ipbrief.net>.

28 Weinberg, Michael. "It Will Be Awesome If They Don't Screw it Up."

29 Baase, Sara.

30 Weinberg, Michael. "What the Deal with Copyright and 3D Printing?"

31 Weinberg, Michael. "It Will Be Awesome If They Don't Screw It Up."

32 Moore, Adam. "Intellectual Property." The Stanford Encyclopedia of
   Philosophy. 8 Mar. 2011. Accessed Mar. 2014 <plato.stanford.edu>.

33 Baase, Sara.

34 Weinberg, Michael. "What the Deal with Copyright and 3D Printing?"

35 "Severability." The Free Dictionary, Farlex. Accessed Mar. 2014 <www.legal-
   dictionary.thefreedictionary.com>.

36 Weinberg, Michael. "What the Deal with Copyright and 3D Printing?"

37 Ibid.

38 Ibid.

39 Ibid.

40 Palecek, Jonathan. "CC and the 3D Printing Community." Creative
   Commons. 4 Jan. 2012. Accessed Mar. 2014 <www.creativecommons.org>.

41 Baase, Sara.

42 Rivera, Janessa, and Rob Van Der Meulen.

43 Ford, Brianna.

44 Weinberg, Michael. "It Will Be Awesome If They Don't Screw it Up."

45 Ibid.

Technology Risk and Business Impact

Divya   **Yadav**

October 2013

Abstract: The Patient Protection and Affordable Health Care Act (PPAHC) launch was in the news for all the wrong reasons. One of the most striking parts of this entire showdown has been how the healthcare.gov website failed to take off. Millions of people tried to register but were unable to do so but the IT infrastructure was not stable enough to balance out this load. Website management is important for any type of business to sustain not only customers but their web presence as well. An important part of this strategy is to be able to anticipate spikes in web traffic and have a plan in place to divert this traffic or load balance it out to make the website accessible.

Introduction

The Patient Protection and Affordable Health Care Act (PPAHC) launch on October 1, 2013 drew a lot of media attention. Most Americans woke up to the news that the website for the PPAHC was down due to heavy traffic. As a result, many were unable to register for a health insurance plan, let alone explore their options. Technical glitches slowed down and partially disabled the website, making it ultimately inaccessible to many prospective registers. The

Department of Health and Human Services determined that 2.8 million people visited the federal HealthCare.gov since the midnight of its launch.[1] It is also been widely perceived that federal government had to spend an enormous amount of money, around $300 million, to offer its healthcare plan online.[2] One would hope that, if such magnitude of money is being spent, it would ensure a fast website that is able to sustain the number of visitors it projected. While it does indicate the desperate need for such coverage of millions of uninsured Americans, it on the other hand indicates the risks involved when business is dependent upon IT. Setting up services online is definitely convenient and enables businesses such as healthcare and banking to reach to a wider audience, but a robust IT infrastructure needs to been in place to manage web traffic and provide availability of services at all times.

Healthcare.gov – More Expectations and What Went Wrong?

The Obama administration is known for being tech savvy, as indicated with the 2012 presidential elections when they showed their technical prowess and superiority in reaching out to people through social media, applications for mobile phones, and so on. So it came as a huge shock to many when the Obama administration was not able to deliver on the healthcare site. While many will argue that "orchestrating a website of this magnitude that needs to be compliant and align with many systems such as Federal systems, insurance companies, can be challenging"[3] expectations were nonetheless very high, and the bottom line is they weren't remotely met. It is also being argued that the U.S. is home to major Internet companies that have revolutionized Web 2.0 but still the administration failed to build a functionally competent site that had the potential to withstand traffic of such magnitude.[4]

Some experts say the site was never stress tested and any developer can tell you how important load testing is whenever a website is being launched.[5] The people responsible for the design of the website spend too much time designing a pretty UI but the back end and server side transaction was not handled well enough that prevented people from registration process. Another reason for the front end and back end mismatch for the site seems to be that it was built by two different contractors and there appeared to be a problem with integration testing before the site was launched.[6]

The federal government awards contracts to agencies that have some federal experience. Experienced website developers without government experience probably did not qualify under terms of the contract.

This vastly limits the choice for government and can contribute to the fact that a standard and balanced website was not created.

It also looks like officials got the number of people logging to the website on the day of launch as vastly wrong. It highlights how important it is to anticipate the web traffic and design back end or have enough number of servers to balance out the load.

What Can be Done to Prevent Such Failures?

The basic architecture for a website is very simple and it can be used for building from simple to complex websites. The system is divided into three layers and each layer has servers, routers, and network connections that take care of the web traffic by load balancing, retrieve results, save information and so on. Well in reality servers, connections, routers will fail but if the design of the system is right it at best can mitigate the impact of these failures.[7]

Testing is extremely important for launching any website. It is the key to the gate of the website so as to speak of. There are different types of testing load testing, beta testing, QA testing and all of these techniques are in place for a reason so that websites do not fail. It is clear that healthcare.gov was not load tested and hence the site was inaccessible to many. There were "404 Errors" that indicate web server was requesting for a page that didn't exist.[8] These errors could have been easily discovered had proper testing techniques were in place.

Websites need to be at all times ready to provide for a spike in traffic. One work around for this according to Google webmaster is to prepare a lighter version of the website. The homepage is the most requested page and if there is a spike in traffic that traffic can always be directed to these lighter versions.[9]

A website maintenance plan from the start also ensures issues such as spike in traffic and load balance is taken care of. "For risk management, a business-continuity plan needs to be in place for any website as it ensures that the hosting service provider has a backup and maintenance plan that is in line with business service levels."[10]

Conclusion

In the end all the measures are only preventative but prevention is the essence of risk management. If these measures are taken care of within a reasonable time frame most likely businesses will remain unaffected. I will be watching out for how healthcare.gov rebounds from the failure it witnessed after its launch.

1 Morgan, David and Caroline Humer. "Web Traffic, Glitches Slow Obamacare
   Exchanges Launch." *Reuters*. 1 Oct. 2013. Accessed Oct. 2013
   <www.reuters.com>.

2 Couts, Andrew. "We Paid Over $500 Million For The Obamacare Sites And All
   We Got Was This Lousy 404." *Digital Trends*. 8 Oct. 2013. Accessed Oct. 2013
   <www.digitaltrends.com>.

http://www.digitaltrends.com/opinion/obamacare-healthcare-gov-website-cost/

3 Eilperin, Juliet. "Why Obama's Tech-Savvy Team Couldn't Make Obamacare
   Glitch-Free." *The Washington Post*. 9 Oct. 2013. Accessed Oct. 2013
   <www.washingtonpost.com>.

4 Ibid.

5 Turner, James. "What Developers Can Learn From healthcare.gov." *Forbes*. 9
   Oct. 2013. Accessed Oct. 2013 <www.forbes.com>.

6Auerbach, David. "Err Engine Down." *Slate*. 8 Oct. 2013. Accessed Oct. 2013
   <www.slate.com>.

7 Sharf, Joshua. "No Good Excuses Exist For The Failure Of Obamacare's
   Expensive Website." *PJ Media*. 11 Oct. 2013. Accessed Oct. 2013
   <www.pjmedia.com>

8 Sharf, 2013.

9 Moskwa, Susan. "Preparing Your Site For A Traffic Spike." *Google Webmaster
   Central Blog*. 9 Feb. 2012. Accessed Oct. 2013
   <www.googlewebmastercentral.blogspot.com>

10 Doe, Gissimee and Demand Media. "Why Is Website Maintenance
    Important?" *Chron*. 11 Oct. 2012. Accessed Oct. 2013

Innovation and Litigation
Uma Joshi
September 2014

Abstract: Provides an overview of intellectual property perspectives in literature, and contributes a focused discussion of the landmark Apple vs. Samsung patent trial of 2011. A discussion of the U.S. Patent system is also provided and gaps in this system are addressed as well as recommended solutions, which allow for continued innovation while curbing litigation.

The laws that govern intellectual property are intended to provide legal protection to the author or creator of an invention, intangible idea, or tangible creative work. The intent is to prevent others from reproducing, copying and distributing similar work and gaining a profit from the originality of others. In a fast paced society where every day equals time spent to deliver a bottom line, people cannot afford to work hard towards a product or idea without financial benefits. We no longer live in a time where creativity and innovation can exist merely for the purpose of personal satisfaction or joy. Even if that is the intended purpose of the work, as soon as it begins to turn a profit, the law begins to unravel itself to protect the creator and everyone wants a piece of the profit. "The stated objective of most intellectual property law is to promote progress. If some intellectual property is desirable because it encourages innovation, they reason, more is better. The thinking is that creators will not have sufficient incentive to invent unless they are legally entitled to capture the full social value of their inventions."[1] So when does the protection of the law in one's journey to creativity turn into the limitation of creativity? And why then, if intellectual property comes with such great risks, do people continue to create and innovate? To understand this, we will examine perspectives in literature and see if it is supported in history with a real world case.

The first groups of individuals are personality theorists who claim that individuals have moral claims to their own feelings, talents, and experiences.[2] They believe that intellectual property is an extension of one's own personality because by expanding beyond our own minds and mixing this with tangible and intangible items, we define ourselves and are able to take control over our goals and projects. If personality theorists are accurate then in their claims, then it means that any creative work or innovation made is tied to the personality and reputation of the creator. Intellectual property rights are then not only justified to cover the damages of economic loss that could be incurred if the work is damaged or stolen, but it is also protecting the reputation of the individual who created it, since it is merely a tangible extension of that person. That certainly feels to be a justifiable rationale for protection, and this can be seen in many forms of today's society through branding or trademarking. There is a reputation behind certain brands and faces, such as in the music industry, technology industry, and many others. There is also an argument against personality theorists, stating that there are times when there is no evidence of a creator's personality in intellectual innovations.[3] While this may be true, in today's society most authors, creators, and innovators want to stand by their reputation and brand, and want it to be a constant symbol of whom they are and what the consumer is to expect when seeing it. This is very different from a single person's personality attribute behind that brand, but in some cases, even large corporations strive to stand by their original founding member's values.

Another group of individuals makes the case for justifying intellectual property rights as incentive based and utilitarian. The theories behind utilitarian arguments for intellectual property are by granting limited rights of ownership; authors and creators can promote more intellectual works based on this incentive. Without it, they may not create any intellectual property, which will inevitably slow social progress.[2] If this were an entirely accurate argument, then copyleft movements and free, open source software sharing would not fall under this domain. Many software programmers believe that developing computer programs based on open source code will not be done for the pure joy of coding, and without the restrictions of intellectual property laws, they will not create or innovate new technological ideas based on this open source code. On the other hand, this is the premise for the majority of ideas, innovations, and creative works used in commerce today. Without a financial backing, both companies and individuals would not be able to function and generate goods and services. Most companies go to extreme lengths to protect their own intellectual property and can become the foundation for its very own existence. An example of this would be at The Boeing Company, where employees take quarterly training and sign annual Code of Conduct to ensure that privacy and security measures are in place day in and day out so that intellectual property of the company is not lost or stolen. Locks are placed on laptops and all engineering drawings and email is securely located on servers that cannot be accessed outside of the company firewall. Without these extreme measures, even large companies can falter in the face of intellectual property loss.

This then takes us to the Lockean justification of intellectual property, based on the theories of philosopher John Locke. Locke believed that individuals are entitled to the fruits of their labor, and since we each own our bodies and the labor that it produces, it is translated to the goods that are produced from ourselves. To counter this argument, since the skills, tools and inventions that are used in conducting this labor are social products, then there is no justification for the individual to make intellectual property claims on their ideas.[4] Locke's theories still generally hold true today in some forms, such as creative writing and entertainment industries. Books, movies, and music that are created are the labor that generates enormous fruits, and it should be the sole property of the artist.

Taking a step away for a moment from the perspectives of the holders of intellectual property rights, we now examine how this affects those consumers and individuals who benefit on a daily basis from the innovations and creations of these laborers. How do the copyright law, patent law, and other governances influence the average citizens who with or without knowledge infringe on these rights more often than they know? For simplicity reasons, we look to the U.S. Copyright Act, which was created in 1976, at a time when the Internet barely existed and computers primarily existed in businesses for industrial and corporate purposes, or were a luxury of the rich. Media during this time was only available to the consumer in hard format, and books, magazines, and newspapers were only available in print form. Fast forward to 2014, the digital age has allowed nearly every person who has access to the Internet, to be more likely to become a copyright owner of some type of work. The simplicity of the U.S. Copyright Act becomes ever so complex in the digital revolution. Similarly, U.S. Patent Law (Title 35 U.S. Code, Section 101) states: "Whoever invents or discovers any new and useful process, machine, manufacture, or composition of matter, or any new and useful improvement thereof, may obtain a patent therefor, subject to the conditions and requirements of this title." Patents protect inventions by giving the inventor a monopoly for a specified period of time. Patents differ from copyrights in that they protect the invention, not just a particular expression or implementation of it.[5] With the digital revolution then, does the U.S. Patent Law still hold true then, or is it in need of updating just as the U.S. Copyright Act is? To understand this, we will examine closely a case scenario that highlights whether intellectual property laws are supporting or hindering innovation.

In the spring of 2011, Apple Inc. (herein referred to as 'Apple') began filing patent lawsuits against their industry rival and business collaborate, Samsung Electronics Co., Ltd. (herein referred to as 'Samsung'). Following the release of Apple's iconic iPhone as well as their many other laptop and tablet products, Samsung released similar smartphones and tablets that utilized many of the innovative features of the Apple products. Apple subsequently filed over 50 lawsuits against Samsung over a span of ten countries, with over a billion dollars in litigation claims between them. Samsung then counter-sued Apple in four countries, alleging that Apple infringed Samsung's patents for mobile communications technologies. The lawsuits that Apple filed against Samsung are claims of breaches of seven of their patents as well as other trade dress violations. Many of the Apple patents were undoubtedly infringed upon and were considered epic in terms of smartphone touchscreen capabilities, such as several touchscreen interactions, tap-to-zoom and navigation features. There were also many trade-dress and ornamental design patents that indicate what the Apple products generally looks like from a distance, and if a consumer would be confused seeing the Apple and Samsung products side-by-side based on general visual appearance. This claim about the ornamental design of the phone was held by an Apple patent and was at the heart of the dispute; it was depicted in court by various figures showing a thin rectangle with rounded corners. Ultimately, the jury returned a verdict largely favorable to Apple based on patent infringement on Apple's design and dilution of Apple's trade dresses relative to the iPhone, and awarded Apple more than $1 billion in damages.[6]

While the outcome of this landmark patent case will conceivably raise questions, it highlights a new era of intellectual property rights and the ethical validity of them. How far is too far when not only infringing on patents, but granting them in the first place? Should Apple have gone to such extreme lengths to patent so wide and deep into their products, and then when there was no tangible product or innovative feature left to patent, they claimed patents on overall look and feel. A similarly criticized system of patenting is using patent trolls, which are companies that make all of their money by licensing patents and collecting fees for them, and then suing other companies for patent infringement. Patent trolls set up shell companies to hide their activities. Those who are facing litigation then do not know the full extent of the patent that is being held by their adversary. This in turn prevents innovators from being able to find each other, and undermines companies' understanding of the competition.[7] Critics of this type of patent system observe that when companies collect patents for the sole purpose of bringing lawsuits for infringement, the law does not serve the goal of encouraging innovation.[8] Following the jury verdict in the Apple/Samsung trial, Samsung made the following public statement which remained consistent with the critics perceptions of the patent system: "Today's verdict is a loss for the American consumer. It will lead to fewer choices, less innovation, and potentially higher prices. It is unfortunate that patent law can be manipulated to give one company a monopoly over rectangles with rounded corners, or technology that is being improved every day."[9]

Since there is a great dichotomy in the opinions for and against the verdict of this trial, we will take a deeper look to see if the intellectual property rights that were awarded to Apple stay true to the moral justification of these rights as held by the Personality, Utilitarian and Lockean theorists. Per the personality theorists, since they believe that the intellectual property is an extension of the creator and is tied to their physical selves in the form of a tangible product, they would likely agree with the verdict largely favorable to Apple. In the case of Apple's overwhelming comeback in the computing industry based on the iconic iPhone, this success is largely attributed to the visions and innovation of its creator,

Steve Jobs. Steve Jobs was then CEO of Apple, and it is agreed upon by industry professionals that he was the reason for the success of the products, and therefore the products would be very closely tied to his reputation and the reputation of the Apple brand. It can then be inferred that there is evidence of the creator's personality in the product, and therefore per personality theorists, property rights were justified in the verdict to cover the damages of economic loss that were incurred with the work being reproduced by Samsung, as well as to protect the reputation of Steve Jobs and Apple.

If the utilitarian theorists were to weigh in on this trial, they would believe that intellectual property rights are granted so that authors and creators can continue to promote more intellectual works based on gaining an economic incentive. Therefore, if Apple were not granted all of the property rights that they had, they would not continue to create more innovative products. The utilitarians may not agree with the verdict in this case, because gaining profit from the $1 billion in infringement damages was going to neither motivate nor hinder the future of the Apple Company and their evolving product line. It was merely a lawsuit that was intended to slow the progress of the rival companies, but in reality most consumers are well aware of the Apple products and know what they are purchasing whether they purchase Apple or Samsung. The Apple Company will continue to develop products and to innovate, and utilitarians would largely agree.

The last group of individuals are the Lockean theorists, and they would likely agree with the verdict of the trial. They believe in creators benefiting from the fruits of their labor, and thus they would agree that Apple should be the only company turning a profit based on the innovations that they created and implemented into their products. Locke would argue that it is unjust for people to misuse another's ideas. In the case of the trial, it would be a fair assumption that Samsung was out to profit from the success of Apple.

If there is a divide in opinions of the theorists of intellectual property moral justifications, then how as a society can we better understand and change the policies of intellectual property in the future to support both innovation and minimize unwarranted lawsuits? The premise should be to reward innovators for their creative work, and if the rights to this work are liberally protected, it offers others visions and encouragement to build upon their work without stealing it. If there are facets of the creator's work that must be used, then royalties must be paid and requested in a legal platform. There is the innovation that is epic and landmark, and then there is innovation that builds upon that and continuously improves. From the first ever automobiles, to flat screen televisions, until someone develops a new way of doing something, there will never be this evolution of products without reproduction and distribution to some level. The holder of the 1895 patent on an automobile sued Henry Ford;[10] does that mean then that Henry Ford never should have revolutionized the automobile industry by developing the first automobile that middle class Americans could afford? He did not invent the automobile nor the assembly line, but he was able to revolutionize transportation forever by developing a system to lower costs through mass production. When Apple first released its iPhone, it was at a selling price that most consumers could not afford, and it was contracted to only one service provider. This made the phone a very exclusive commodity, and created even more reasons for competitors to want to make a similar device at a more affordable rate. Without other companies doing this, just as Henry Ford did, it would make the consumer market very shallow and create a monopoly for the leading company. While the iPhone is not required for one's livelihood the way an automobile is, it can change the world and that type of power to a single company furthers into blanket patents, which then translate into unwarranted lawsuits, and billions of dollars at stake. "Regardless of the outcome of the trial, we might want to step back and consider whether society should be granting such powerful rights so easily. Are the [iPhone] features at issue really deserving of so much protection? On the whole, the trial is one more indication of a patent system that has lost its bearings, with litigation rather than innovation leading the way."[11]

The policies surrounding the patent system (in the U.S.) are governed by federal laws, and are executed by the U.S. Patent and Trademark Office. While patent attorneys do their best to identify what is and is not patentable, there are just not enough resources to dig deep to ensure that patents are innovative, not used in the past, and are non-conflicting. The Patent Office has a backlog of more than 600,000 patents and issues approximately 40,000 patents a year.[12] Decisions about granting patents are generally complex, and these decisions require knowledge of history of that related technology. In the fast-developing industries such as software, the Web, and smartphone technologies, this becomes even more complex and mistakes are inevitable. In an effort to improve patent reform, in 2013, President Obama and his administration began to pass landmark legislation through a series of initiatives designed to combat patent trolls, further innovation and

strengthen the patent system.[13] The basic premise of
the executive actions are first, to use crowdsourcing
techniques to find relevant prior art for the patent
that is being requested. The public, applicants, and
patent holders and examiners will have access to the
information and more data can be collected to
identify whether an invention is truly novel. Second,
there will be more robust technical training to help
patent examiners keep up with fast-changing
technologies. Third, the administration will appoint
Pro Bono legal representation to inventors who are
not able to maintain their own representation. The
presidential administration will also be working with
Congress to pass further laws to combat patent trolls
and curtail abusive patent litigation by improving
transparency in the patent system. Lastly, the
administration will continue to work to strengthen
the current patent system through making patents
clearer, and making educational tools, resources and
academic scholars to volunteer their time to make
available more robust technical training to patent
examiners. With these executive actions in play, it will
help to level the playing field for inventors and
litigators alike, ideally fostering innovation.
Ultimately, it will be up to the individuals who create
their art to strike a fine balance in protecting what is
rightfully theirs, but sharing it so that the world can
continually build upon it in the years to come.

1 Lemley, Mark A. "Property, Intellectual Property, and Free Riding." Stanford Law School. 6 Aug. 2006.

2 Moore, Adam. "Intellectual Property." Stanford Encyclopedia of Philosophy. 8 Mar. 2011. Accessed Feb. 2014 <www.plato.stanford.edu>.

3 Hughes, Justin. "The Philosophy of Intellectual Property." Georgetown Law Journal. Dec. 1988. Accessed Feb. 2014 <www.justinhughes.net>.

4 Moore, Adam.

5 Baase, Sara. A Gift of Fire. Aug. 2012.

6 Lowensohn, Josh. "Jury Awards Apple More than $1B, Finds Samsung Infringed." CNET. 24 Aug. 2012. Accessed Feb. 2014 <www.cnet.com>.

7 "Executive Actions: Answering the President's Call to Strengthen Our Patent System and Foster Innovation." Office of the Press Secretary, The White House. 20 Feb. 2014. Accessed Feb. 2014 <www.whitehouse.gov>.

8 Baase, Sara.

9 June, Laura. "Apple vs. Samsung: The Verdict." The Verge. 24 Aug. 2012. Accessed Feb. 2014 <www.theverge.com>.

10 Baase, Sara.

11 Feldman, Robin. "Tech Giants Gear Up for Patent Battle." Science Friday. 3 Aug. 2012. Accessed Feb. 2014 <www.sciencefriday.com>.

12 Baase, Sara.

13 "Executive Actions"

Chapter VI
Disasters

Disappearance of Malaysian Airlines Flight MII 370

Divya Yadav

April 2014

The disappearance of Malaysian Airlines Flight MH 370 captured the attention of the world, becoming a mystery that created more questions than answers. This research note, published the month after the flight disappeared, discusses some of the social and political issues surrounding the disappearance. Divya reports on key takeaways that can be gleaned from the tragedy for better understand during similar incidents in the future.

Introduction

The disappearance of Malaysian Airlines flight MH370 traveling from Kuala Lumpur to Beijing was not only tragic but also a baffling mystery that captured attention around the world. An intense search was launched, with resources from as many as twelve nations, but as this paper goes to publication not many promising clues or leads have been found.

What many people find surprising is the fact that a plane can disappear amidst all the satellite and communications technologies covering almost the entire earth. However, keep in mind that there is limited coverage in the remote southern part of the

Indian Ocean. This disappearance is first of its kind in a long time where authorities are finding it hard to locate the plane or any of its debris. When Air France flight 447 crashed into the Atlantic in 2009, authorities were able to locate the wreckage despite of not being able to find the black box for two more years.1 While the incidents are not comparable, the task of locating wreckage deep in the ocean with weak satellite and communication signals does seem to link the two incidents. Chances of aerial disappearances are low but not impossible, and given the sophistication of today's technology it seems it should be possible to have the general location of the plane, even if reaching the zone take time.

While the mystery surrounding the disappearance makes an interesting topic for public discussions, the families at the center of these tragedies are left helpless. At the least, what they want is to be able to locate their loved ones and find some closure. The information dissemination by the media and government in particular should be handled in a sensitive and respectful manner. This research note discusses the events surrounding the airplane's disappearance, and how to better prepare for dealing with other unforeseen tragedies going forward.

Complex Role and Stakes for Government

The search and rescue operation for the Malaysian airplane began as a more complex affair because while the airline is Malaysian, the majority of the passengers on board were from China. This changed the stakes for each nation involved. While both nations want the missing plane to be found, the involvement of both sides created a lot of confusion and infighting. The Malaysian government was accused of not being transparent and not sharing information while China ramped up its rescue efforts. The Malaysian government made the announcement that the plane had crashed into the South Indian Ocean without providing any evidence or satellite data, angering the Chinese government and creating a lot of mistrust and a diplomatic rift between the two governments. The fallout from this could potentially have long-term economic and political implications.2 Some travel agents in China have reported that bookings between China and Malaysia have already fallen and that Chinese citizens are cancelling trips "amid anger at the perceived lack of information provided by the Malaysian government to passengers' families."3

Unfortunately, this fallout is typical for an international aerial tragedy, since the origin and destination of an airplane are in different countries with many nationalities represented in the passenger manifest. Therefore multiple countries have interest and responsibilities in an incident, some by authority of operating the airline, others by having citizens onboard. Consequentially, it is important for governments to handle these types of incidents with transparency and clarity, not only for the sake of passengers' families but also to avoid a diplomatic divide and any resulting long-term consequences.

Cost of Search and International Cooperation

Experts already expect that the hunt for Malaysian Airlines Flight MH370 will be the most costly search in aviation history.4 A truly international search, some 26 countries have contributed resources, including planes, ships, submarines, and satellites to help in the rescue process. *Reuters* estimates that the search has already cost around $44 million just accounting for funds spent by the U.S., China, Australia, and Vietnam. The news agency expects that by the time the search is over - and once the money from the other 22 countries is counted - the total cost may reach hundreds of millions of dollars.5

Countries are invested in this operation; not only for the families seeking answers and closure, but also for trying to answer the question how a high-tech Boeing 777 airplane can vanish into seemingly thin air amid all the satellite tracking. The peculiarity of this incident has made the story resonate with people across the world, and everyone wants answers as soon as possible. Racing against the clock, authorities must locate the plane's black box before the batteries run out. The black box is likely the only source for finding answers to questions that will otherwise never be known - particularly for learning why the plane flew off course. The bottom line is that the cost of the search operation is immensely high, but it is important from all perspectives to know what happened to MH 370 to help prevent such tragedies in the future.

Despite the diplomatic tensions between Malaysia and China over information sharing, the event has resulted in countries with long history of disputes to set aside differences for aiding in the rescue effort. China and Japan, for example, have sparred for months over the occupation of islands in East China Sea but are now working jointly with the U.S. and New Zealand. India and China have a long historic rivalry going back to the 1960s but are now sharing a military base to conduct searches in the Indian Ocean. In all there have been 26 countries taking part in the search, working against the clock and facing the unpredictable and sometimes severe weather in the Southern Indian Ocean. The harsh weather conditions not only undermine the operation's efforts, but also can put the lives of rescue crews in severe danger. According to John Blaxland, an expert on Asia-Pacific defense and security issues at Australian National University, "we're seeing a level of collaboration that's pretty much unprecedented."6

Role of Media

The crash has highlighted the growing role of social media as a global platform where people generate and share theories about possible causes for incidents like the missing plane. Information from official sources has been scarce, and many feel disappointed by perceived and real lack of government transparency. People around the world have created and speculated on a wide range of theories, some bordering, and then crossing the line into the ridiculous. Speculative theories about the cause of the disappearance have ranged from terrorism and meteors to black holes and aliens. While this kind of speculation is the norm on social media sites, some mainstream news media sources have also participated in propagating wildly speculative theories, showing a lack of apathy for affected families and the victims of the crash. The 24/7 content model and the rising demand for instant updates online has created a fixation on bolstering ratings around the clock, but in particular mainstream news media outlets should be careful coverage does not come at the expense of personal lives and grief. Reuters reports that some in Malaysia have been offended about the rampant coverage of conspiracy theories, which they say have only aggravated the pain and suffering of the affected families.7

Other Takeaways

The peculiar disappearance of MH 370 has generated many theories, and the answers are greatly outnumbered by the number of questions that have arisen. While this particular international incident will not necessarily trigger any changes for U.S. airlines or the American aviation industry, there are still a few takeaways that can be gleaned from this tragedy to keep in mind during future incidents.

When the news of the disappearance first surfaced many news outlets were quick to jump to the conclusion it might be a hijacking or terrorist attack. However, statistically these are not the most likely cause of fatal crashes. According to a database complied at PlaneCrashInfo.com8 that collects and examines data on airplane crashes, between 2000 and 2010 all types of pilot error accounted for 54 percent of 1,085 fatal accidents involving commercial aircraft worldwide. The second most common cause of these crashes was mechanical failures (24 percent), then sabotage (9 percent), and finally weather (8 percent). Keeping this data in mind, investigations must remain open to all possibilities, while fact-less speculation is kept to a minimum.

The job of an airline pilot is undoubtedly a stressful job, owing to the irregular time schedules, long hours, and extended time away from their families. During the MH 370 investigation, the Flight Captain's role has been heavily assessed and many discussions have arisen about his state of mind. Speculation has included dissecting his personality, professional life, and personal life – wondering if he was under a lot of stress or fatigued. News agencies and experts alike have tried to determine whether his behavior in the preceding weeks was abnormal or questionable, and if there were other possible reasons that that may have led him to deliberately divert the airplane's flight path.

While the world may never know the answers about the MH370 pilot, it is important for the aviation industry to continue to support the regular evaluation of airline pilots to assess if they are fit for flying. Pilots should be well rested and in a positive frame of mind when on board; they are often the only ones on board with the skills required for flying, and are charged with the safe transportation of the passengers on board. Since pilot error causes the largest number of fatal airline crashes, the value of these evaluations cannot be underestimated.

Another important facet during international incidents such as the MH 370 flight search is determining who is in charge of the situation. There is a lot depending on aviation authorities and governments cooperating between different countries. Guidelines from the International Civil Aviation Organization, a United Nations agency, recommend that during incidents the airplane's manufacturer's country participate in the operations.9 Therefore, since the MH 370 airplane was an American-built Boeing 777, the U.S.-based National Transportation Safety Board (NTSB) has been involved in the search. Additionally, the country from where the airline took off also needs a lot of information from NTSB to make informed decisions and provide information. Miscommunications or a lack in information between agencies can create a lot of confusion and inefficiencies. Therefore, in wake of such disasters it is critical for investigations to have accurate and timely information flow between all involved parties, a difficult undertaking particularly in an international setting.

The disappearance of MH 370 also raises the question of whether or not there is too much dependency on the recovery of an airplane's "black box" after a crash. The "black box" - which in reality consists of two orange boxes containing the cockpit voice recorder

and digital flight data recorder - is designed to
survived catastrophic conditions. While often
recovered, these devices are not always found,
sometimes because of severe damage or due to the
batteries dying after the average 30 days. Moreover,
even if it is found, the data recorded may not provide
all the answers to the many complex questions that
arise during and after an investigation. These
limitations have prompted industry observers like the
NTSB to propose upgrading the technologies required
in airplanes, including a "crash-protected image
recorders in cockpits to give investigators more
information to solve complex accidents."10 Others
have suggested replacing the "black box" with systems
that can transmit data continuously and in real time,
but like many technological improvements that would
aid in investigations, cost is a factor.

Conclusion

Tragedies like the disappearance of flight MH 370 are
a painful reminder that no matter how much
technology is developed, such incidents can occur
anytime and anywhere. Therefore, lessons from these
tragedies should be extracted and changes
implemented in order to mitigate future risks, no
matter how small or insignificant the change seems to
be. There are times when the incentive to change
might not seem significant enough but for the sake of

human lives, nothing should be taken for granted. With this, we hope the families of the passengers on Malaysian Airlines MH 370 receive closure about their loved ones.

---

1 Interim Report on the Accident On 1st June 2009 to the Airbus A330-203 Registered F-GZCP Operated by Air France Flight AF 447 Rio De Janeiro – Paris. Bureau d'Enquêtes et d'Analyses. Jun. 2009. Accessed Apr. 2014 <www.bea.aero>.

2 Jamieson, Alastair and Constance Cheng. "Missing MH370: China, Malaysia Mistrust Becomes War of Words." NBC News. 25 Mar. 2014. Accessed Apr. 2014 <www.nbcnews.com>.

3 Ibid.

4 Wardell, Jane. "Search for MH370 to be Most Expensive in Aviation History." Reuters. 8 Apr. 2014. Accessed Apr. 2014 <www.reuters.com>.

5 Ibid.

6 Lee, Don. "Chinese Plane Spots Object In Malaysia Jet Search Area." LA Times. 23 Mar. 2014. Accessed Apr. 2014 <www.latimes.com>.

7 Blanchard, Ben, and Brian Leonal. "Wild Theroies Fill Void Left by Missing Malaysian Plane." Reuters. 11 Mar. 2014. Accessed Apr. 2014 <www.reuters.com>.

8 McGee, William J. "8 Lessons We Need To Learn From Malaysia Airlines Tragedy." Yahoo News. 25 Mar. 2014. Accessed Apr. 2014 <www.news.yahoo.com>.

9 Ibid.

10 Ibid.

Pandemic Risk Assessment

Katherine Hagan

August 2013

Abstract: Influenza is more than simple flu-like symptoms. Influenza comes in multiple strains, the most serious being type A. This subtype of virus has been responsible for large-scale death and the global spread of disease. Risk assessment is difficult due to the constantly mutating nature of influenza virus. In order to assess potential risk, organizations must constantly monitor patient data on local, state, national, and worldwide levels. Compilation of data and coordinated responses are necessary to prevent spread of the virus and develop vaccines.

What is Influenza?

Influenza comes in three basic types: A, B, and C. Influenza C is the weakest. Influenza A and B can be equally as strong, but type B has never caused a worldwide pandemic. Influenza A is often distinguished by H's and N's. H stands for Hemagglutinin and has 16 different versions. N stands for Neuraminidase and only has nine versions. Each strain is assigned a letter H and a letter N, such as H9N7. While all flus can be carried in birds – technically making all flus a form of the bird flu – some cross over into other animals.[1]

H1N1 is commonly called the swine flu, but can actually be found in birds, pigs, horses, and people.[2] It is not simply the ability for a virus to be contracted by multiple species that causes danger, but the ability of the virus to mutate upon encountering additional viruses. If a virus formerly only contagious to birds mixes with a cross-species virus such as swine flu, the new virus can be transmitted to the additional species, yet we have no previous immunities as humans to this virus. This new virus is referred to as a novel virus. Mutations such as these were considered the causes for the 1957 Asian flu pandemic and 1968 Hong Kong flu pandemic; killing over 100,000 Americans combined.[3]

Epidemics, Pandemics, Pandemonium

A disease outbreak is the term used when the number of reported disease cases exceeds the number of expected disease cases.[4] An outbreak itself has no specific geographic area, and no specific number. The term outbreak can actually refer to as few as one person or incident, if the disease is either new or thought to be absent from the population for a long time. An epidemic involves the rapid transmission of disease among many people, i.e. SARS 2003. A pandemic is a global disease outbreak such as HIV/AIDS. Occurrence of a pandemic is marked by: an unknown virus strain where humans have little immunity, much like the mutated influenza mentioned above, easy transmission of the virus such as through sneezing, and the global spread of serious illness. The World Health Organization (WHO) marks pandemics in six phases. Phase 1 denotes a virus in animals with no known human transmission. Phase 6 and the most serious marks human contagion in multiple countries and regions.[5]

Risk Assessment

Risk assessment begins with four primary steps. These steps include identification, assessment, prioritization of response, and continued monitoring.[6] Identification is difficult to do properly and must be managed across all organization levels, not simply the easiest areas to identify and fix. Questions should be asked regarding both the greatest risk and the consequences of the unknown. In assessing risk it is important to understand both the probability and the magnitude of the threat.[7] For example, an influenza virus in birds would be highly likely with little to no impact on the human sector. A mutated influenza virus would be far less probable, but have a much greater magnitude of consequence, with the possibility of a disease outbreak.

Figure 1: GRC Risk Management Processes [8]

Assessments are often done using computer simulations to map out possible consequences, however those same risks rarely following predictable models. Prioritization of response is often based off of these models to try and mitigate the threat. Constant monitoring must be conducted throughout to provide the most timely response possible.[9]

Monitoring of a Pandemic

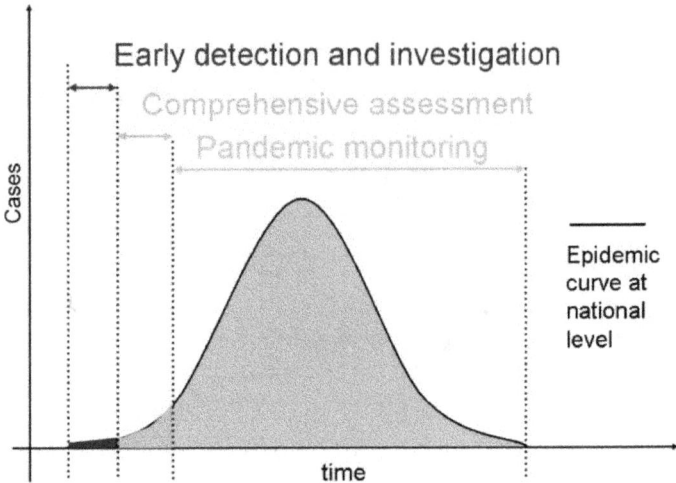

Figure 2: Overview of the Three Surveillance Companies at National Level[10]

The World Health Organization demonstrates how pandemics need a different level of monitoring over different periods of time.[11] The first step includes early detection and investigation. At a national level, health providers are expected to detect, assess, investigate, control, and report all disease incidents above expected levels. If initial investigation shows sustained human-to-human transmission, then the first 100 cases are the most important. These cases will be used to help non-affected countries prepare for upcoming infection. The data is also used to help derive the necessary components of a future vaccine. The monitoring phase is mostly a data gathering phase, which can vary from country to country, however many countries are starting to standardize procedures for data reporting of respiratory illness. Monitoring by country allows data to be compiled and monitored at a global level.[12]

Diseases Outbreak News

The World Health Organization monitors and reports all recent outbreaks. From June 2013 through May 2013, three different diseases are listed on their report. While the poliovirus has been reported in Somalia, the Horn of Africa, and Israel one time each. H7N9, an avian Influenza A has been reported 132 times with 37 deaths, but no confirmed cases of human-to-human transmission. The Middle Eastern respiratory coronavirus (MERS-CoV) has reported 50 confirmed cases and 30 deaths, with limited local patient transmission.[13] With these issues being current considerations, different groups conduct monitoring and response in different manners before reporting to the WHO.

US Government Planning – Federal Level

The Department of Homeland Security has taken measures to plan for the pandemic risks identified with influenza. In 2005 President Bush announced a *National Strategy for Pandemic Influenza* based on three pillars: preparedness and communication, surveillance and detection, and response and containment.[14] Addressed in this strategy is the acknowledgement that full preparation for a pandemic can take years. Every segment of society must prepare and will be part of the response. The Federal Government is expected to provide clear criteria to inform State, local, and private sector responses. Federal Government response goals are the following: stop, slow, or limit the spread of disease in the U.S.; mitigate death, suffering, and disease; and sustain infrastructure and mitigate economic impact. The Federal Government will bear primary responsibility for containment of overseas infection and preventing spread of this infection to US soil. Additionally the guidance of how to take protective measures and changes in any needed regulations will fall under this jurisdiction. Further responsibility includes Modification to monetary policies to mitigate economic impacts, distribution of vaccines, and acceleration of disease research.[15]

Center for Disease Control and Prevention – Risk Assessment

As a Federal agency that will take a leading role in the case of a pandemic, the Center for Disease Control and Prevention, better known as the CDC has developed an Influenza Risk Assessment Tool (IRAT).[16] The risk assessment tool focuses on two different scenarios. "Emergence" refers to a bird influenza virus acquiring the ability to spread easily to people. "Public Health Impact" refers to the potential severity of human disease and burden on society (missed work, hospital capacity, public services). The tool evaluates all new viruses based on the ten primary criteria which can be grouped into three categories: properties of the virus, attributes of the population, and ecology and epidemiology of the virus.[17]

The tool cannot predict a pandemic, but is meant to be a reliable tool for planning. IRAT allows for the prioritization and maximization of preparedness efforts by defining which risk factors are strongest. Updating of data is standardized and can help keep the information process transparent when informing management decisions. The ten criteria allow for different methods to weigh data and also designate key gaps in knowledge that may need further study. The IRAT should not be confused with other risk tools that provide quantitative measures about likelihood or exposure or disease risk. The tool focuses on specific existing strains of virus, currently only found in birds, and assesses the future pandemic potential.[18]

Private Sector Mitigation and Planning

Unlike other natural disasters such as earthquakes or floods, basic physical infrastructures will remain intact. Power lines will not fall down and computer networks will not go dark. The danger to the private sector is from a lack of personnel. At the height of a pandemic it is expected that up to 40 percent of employees could be out of work for a period of at least two weeks. Lesser levels of absence would also occur near the beginning and the end of the outbreak.[19]

Continuity in the private sector is of utmost importance in those areas considered to be critical infrastructure. The Federal Government defines, "Critical infrastructure encompasses those systems and assets that are so vital to the U.S. that the incapacity or destruction of such systems and assets would have a debilitating impact on security, national economic security, and national public health or safety."[20] The safeguarding of these infrastructures is considered indispensable, and 85 percent of this critical mass falls within the private sector. Key measures that need to be taken to prevent infrastructure loss include plans for maintaining a workable level of staff and preventative measures to ensure the continued health of necessary workers.

Washington State

Washington State releases weekly reports on the status of influenza A within the state. For the week of May 12- May 18th, 2013, considered CDC week 20 there were a total of 154 tests performed and 0 were positive for influenza A.[21] No specimens tested have been determined novel, or avian, in origin. No specimens tested were considered antiviral resistant. Less than one percent of emergency room visits in week 20 were for influenza related symptoms throughout the state. Death statistics for the week show 5.4 percent of mortalities caused by pneumonia or influenza, and 54 total influenza related deaths in the entire 2012-2013 period.[22] The combined total data, along with seasonal flu knowledge would put Washington state at low risk overall for an influenza outbreak. Other factors such as population size by city, and the act of being a travel hub towards Asia may act to increase this risk, but it is not likely to be a drastic increase at this point.

Additional data can found on national, international, and county levels through the following sources:

- International Influenza Data: <www.who.int>
- National Influenza Surveillance Report <www.cdc.gov>

- Washington Local Health Department Influenza Surveillance Reports
  - ○ Clark County <www.clark.wa.gov>
  - ○ King County <www.kingcounty.gov>
  - ○ Pierce County <www.tpchd.org>
  - ○ Whatcom County
    <www.whatcomcounty.us>

Researchers

The University of Washington is one of the local organizations that are working to understand existing data and help create predictive models for future planning and assessment. Researches collaborate across media and sharing of studies with organizations such as the CDC to better predict future consequences of a novel virus. Studying data from past outbreaks in the U.S. helped researchers develop a framework for the potential effects of a novel virus.[23] Epidemics were studied at both the beginning of an outbreak and during the end as more data becomes readily available. The process of combining the limited data from outbreak beginnings with the detailed data on full-blown epidemics is hoped to inform an evidence based assessment and guide decision-making.[24]

Summary

Understanding the risks of influenza A is important to comprehend the risks involved. A constantly mutating virus that causes severe symptoms is difficult to combat. The disease outbreak can quickly multiply and become an epidemic or pandemic. The key to proper planning and risk mitigation lies in data gathering and cross collaboration. The World Health Organization acts as a team leader in assess potential threats and compiling data. In the U.S., the Center for Disease Control and Prevention works with Homeland Security and the Federal Government to monitor and assess influenza data. Additionally the Federal Government works to mitigate additional damage such as consequences in the economy and risk the private sector. The private sector operates 85 percent of the nation's critical infrastructure, which magnifies the importance of local data and response. Washington State releases weekly data on current influenza statistics allowing for timely response and assessment by employers. Additional resources are available at county and national levels to supplement this information. Finally, researches are regularly working to develop new and more accurate assessment tools, helping to guide efforts and decision making when preparing for a pandemic.

1 Doucleff, Michaeleen. "What's in a Flu Name? H's and N's Tell the Tale." *NPR Health News.* 7 May 2013. Accessed Jun. 2013 <www.npr.org>.

2 Ibid.

3 Ibid.

4 Karriem-Norwood, Varnada, MD. "What Are Epidemics, Pandemics, and Outbreaks?" *WebMD.* 12 May 2012. Accessed Jun. 2013 <www.webmd.com>.

5 Ibid.

6 Searle, Annie. "IMT 589: Operational Risk Management in the Public and Private Sectors." University of Washington Lecture, Spring 2013.

7 Ibid.

8 Moeller, Robert R. *COSO Enterprise Risk Management, Second Edition.* 2011.

9 Searle, Annie.

10 *Global Surveillance During an Influenza Pandemic.* Apr. 2011. World Health Organization. Accessed Jun. 2013 <www.who.int>.

11 Ibid.

12 Ibid.

13 "Global Alert and Response." World Health Organization. 2013. Accessed Jun. 2013 <www.who.int>.

14 *National Strategy for Pandemic Influenza Implementation Plan.* U.S. Department of Homeland Security. May 2006. Accessed Jun. 2013 <www.flu.gov>.

15 Ibid.

16 "Influenza Risk Assessment Tool (IRAT)." Center for Disease Control and Protection. Jun. 2012. Accessed Jun. 2013 <www.cdc.gov>.

17 Ibid.

18 Ibid.

19 *National Strategy for Pandemic Influenza Implementation Plan*

20 Ibid.

21 "Communicable Disease Epidemiology." Washington State Department of Health. May 2013. Accessed Jun. 2013 <www.doh.wa.gov>.

22 Ibid

23 23

24 Reed, Carrie et. al. "Novel Framework for Assessing Epidemiologic Effect of Influenza Epidemics and Pandemics." *Emergency Infectious Diseases.* Jan. 2013. Accessed Jun. 2013 <www.blogs.uw.edu>.

Importance of Compliance, Regulations, and Ethics in the Wake of Korean Ferry Accident

Divya Yadav

May 2014

Abstract: The sinking of the Korean ship MV Sewol resulted in the deaths of nearly 300 people, a majority of them high school students. This tragic incident brings attention to lack of government enforcement of international maritime laws and the negligence of regulations and standards by the captain, crew, and shipping company. The sinking highlights loopholes in the very successful South Korea's shipping industry and this research note discusses these issues in detail in the context of this maritime disaster.

Introduction

The sinking of the Korean Ferry MV Sewol on 16 April 2014 is one of the most tragic incidents in the history of South Korea with reported deaths of 239 people and 35 still missing. What makes this incident more tragic is most of the passengers onboard were high school students going on a day trip from Incheon to the nearby island Jeju. There have been compliance failures of magnitude proportions and this incident highlights the importance of compliance and regulatory standards. The primary reason for the ferry capsizing has been attributed to the ferry being overloaded beyond capacity, which was in direct violation of the ship safety act. The more concerning fact remains that this was not the first time the ferry was carrying excessive cargo but had made 139 trips overburdened during the period of one year[1] highlighting a consistent lack of oversight and violation of rules. It has been reported that the parent company Cheonghaejin Marine earned an extra 62 million for carrying the cargo on April 16 accident and have earned almost 3 billion in extra profits for all of the excess cargo that the ferry carried since March 2013.[2] Timely inspections and more stringent maritime checks in place could have prevented this tragedy. Below, this paper examines various aspects related to the accident, including reviewing the role of crew and captains, the lack of compliance and regulatory standards, the role of governments, cultural issues, and the importance of risk management.

Role of Crew and Captain

The role of a ship's crew and captain is always scrutinized in wake of such disasters, since they are entrusted with the responsibility of effectively managing any crisis and ensuring the safety of passengers. The captain of the MV Sewol was one of the first people to abandon the sinking ship, leaving behind hundreds of passengers. Captains are obligated to see to the safety of passengers and are expected to stay on the ship until the ship is safely is evacuated, since "an international maritime convention on the safety of life at sea makes a captain responsible for the vessel and all the people on board."[3] While the convention does not necessarily require a captain to die with a sinking ship but the captain should try to make the best efforts and save as many passengers on board as possible. The most disturbing fact about this crisis remains that the captain was one of the first few to abandon the ship. Similar behavior was exhibited by the captain of the Italian cruise ship back in 2012 that left 32 people dead. This kind of behavior creates a leadership vacuum and increases the crisis on board that leads to an impossible recovery.[4] U.S. law does not require a captain to stay on the ship but it has been a long-standing tradition that a captain is the last person the ship in the wake of such crisis. What makes the role of captain in the Korean ship more appalling is he failed to communicate the right information to the passengers as the ship started floundering that delayed evacuation and could have possible saved many lives when in this case each second counts. It is important for a captain to communicate timely and accurate information to passengers. Hence the importance of the role of captains and crew should be stressed, since they know the insides and out of the vessel and must act with prudence and judgment when carrying out the evacuation efforts.

Importance of Risk Management

The ferry sank because of being both overcrowded and carrying excessive cargo, but also because there was a communication failure between the passengers and the crew. Had it been avoided, it could have potentially saved more lives. This highlights a lack of effective risk management and the gaps in any existing disaster planning strategy. A risk management plan should be in place that includes physical maintenance of the vessel, crew selection, crew qualification and experience, and a disaster plan.[5] All countries should follow international maritime rules, since they consist of a comprehensive plan that includes best practices for operating vessels and can help avert such disasters. In addition to these rules, every country has conditions that are specific to them; these should be clearly evaluated and taken into context.

Cultural Issues

The Korean ferry accident resonates with so people around the world because of the number young high school students, people at an age who had so much of life ahead of them. South Korea is a developed nation with a strong economy, leading in many critical infrastructure sectors. However, there have been far too many accidents in the last two decades that point towards to a society that has overlooked and traded safety standards for rising economic growth. Many believe taking shortcuts has enabled the rapid rise to the economic growth, and over time, it appears citizens are suffering the consequences.[6] This incident has unfortunately reiterated the fact that South Koreans have a tendency to overlook safety standards, based on previous incidents. Owing to a culture that values high-end technology, government jobs in field of security and public safety is not ranked very highly.[7] Also pervasive seems to be the sentiment that a competitive edge comes from being able to complete work quickly and cheaply with the least resources, time and money, even if it requires overlooking compliance and standards.[8]

Investigation so far into the tragedy also points to the fact that the ship had many contract workers that were not as aware of the ship as a regular crew would have been. This compounded the problem of failing to enforce other global safety norms. The ship was carrying three times the recommended cargo and the audit report on the company shows how it was dependent on that extra cargo for generating profits, compensating for declining passenger revenues. The ship's designed was changed to add more sleeping cabins that undermined its ability to regain balance after tilting. While the design was approved the Korea Register of Shipping with some guidelines to make up for the lost balance, these were clearly overlooked by the company.[9]

This penchant for negligence has cost the Koreans dearly and this tragedy will serve as a reminder for enforcing stricter rules governing any form of infrastructure within the country and providing highest form of public safety.

Lack of Compliance and Regulatory standards

The lack of safety standards is the focus of the ongoing investigation into the sinking of the Korean Ferry MV Sewol. Questions regarding the ethical conduct of the company owners have told the story of a business that compromised the safety of the vessel and route in an effort to make up profit, including compromising cargo stowing procedures, emergency exit planning, and the training of the crew. The world continues to wait for more answers about what happened on the day of April 16, whenever the full report is released. While the companies that provide transportation services obviously want to be able to make a profit by providing services as economically as possible, this mindset might sometimes lead to cutting costs of administration and compliance as far as possible.[10] Unfortunately, minimizing costs by reducing regulations seems the most lucrative and public safety can take a back seat.

Governments can play a stronger role in enforcing existing rules and regulations across all businesses and industries and make sure no cuts are made at the expense of regulatory boards and departments. This will help prevent the loss of human lives and provide a better environment for the future.

Conclusion

While there is no scale of rating tragedies, the sinking of the MV Sewol is especially painful because of the number (and age) of innocent lives lost. It will take some time for the country to come to terms with dealing with this loss and make changes to what seem like a very lax system in terms of governance and public safety, which is in complete contrast to its stellar economic and technological growth. South Korea has progressed a lot and has come far from the days of Korean War, which shows this country has the strength, determination, and ability to make the best out of any adverse situation. Its character is being put to test and people are hopeful the country will show resiliency and move forward by making changes for the welfare of its citizens.

1 Kim, Stella." Prosecutor: CEO Arrested, Charged in South Korea Ferry
   Disaster". CNN World. 8 May 2014. Accessed May 2014 <www.cnn.com>.
2 lbid.
3 Mullen, Jethro. "Abandon Ship? In Recent Maritime Disasters, Captains Don't
   Hang Around." CNN World. 23 Apr. 2014. Accessed May 2014
   <www.cnn.com>.
4 lbid.
5 Akomah, Chinkwe. "Risk Management A Failure In Ferry Disaster, With
   Aussie Impacts Minimal." 2 May 2014. Insurance Business Online. Accessed
   May 2014 <www.insurancebusinessonline.com.au>.
6 Song-Hun, Choe. "Korea Confronts Tendency to Overlook Safety as Toll in
   Ferry Sinking Grows." New York Times. 22 Apr. 2014. Accessed May 2014
   <www.nytimes.com>.
7 lbid.
8 lbid.
9 lbid.
10 Hamilton, Andrew. "Workplace Safety Issues In South Korean Ferry
   Disaster." Eureka Street. 28 Apr. 2014. Accessed May 2014
   <www.eurekastreet.com.au>.

Typhoon Haiyan and Disaster Preparedness
Divya Yadav
December 2013

Abstract: *Typhoon Haiyan has impacted the Philippines in a way that is sure to change its course of history. In this paper we look at some of the reasons and understand why the impact of such disasters is felt more in remote areas and what can be done to ensure that locals and governments are better prepared and equipped to administer and take charge of these situations by building mitigation, preparedness, response and recovery strategies as disasters can't be prevented, but can be effectively managed.*

Introduction

Typhoon Haiyan – known as Typhoon Yolanda in the Philippines - has been one of the most devastating and deadliest storms to have hit in recent times. In early 2013, the Typhoon caused massive destruction and affected around 11 million people in South East Asia, unofficially making it the fourth strongest storm ever recorded. While the Philippines government issued evacuation alerts, it still was not enough and around 5,600 lives were lost. In the aftermath of the storm there has been severe criticism to the government's response in slow relief efforts, search and rescue program, and its inability to control looting and provide protection to women who were especially vulnerable during this time.

The *2010 Asia Pacific Disaster Report* released last week says that people in the Asia Pacific region are four times more likely to be affected by natural catastrophes than those in Africa and 25 times more likely than those in North America or Europe.[1] Despite these reports that clearly indicate that the region is at a high risk, not many disaster preparedness or crisis management initiatives have been set up that address building resiliency and control the impact of such disasters. The measures are especially lacking in early warning and evacuation systems, disaster risk awareness and local disaster management capacities.[2]

It is essential to note that developing countries suffer more than 95 per cent of all deaths caused by natural disasters as their high population densities and poor infrastructure, coupled with unstable landforms and exposure to severe weather events, makes them particularly vulnerable.[3]

In order to identify systemic gaps and understand precisely what went wrong and how it can be fixed we will look into some important aspects that if met can help develop an effective disaster management cycle.

Technical Equipment Too Difficult to Acquire

Remote sensing equipment is expensive and costly to implement. Governments in developing countries have to often rely on international support and reporting to equip themselves with preparedness measures which sometimes can cause delay in evacuation procedures and accumulation of relief goods. This equipment provides long term climate modelling and early learning that can help countries monitor and evaluate and develop response strategies such as identifying escape routes, crisis mapping, cyclone monitoring, and storm surge predictions.[4]

But equal access to these technologies is still an issue and cost is huge barrier. The UN Economic Commission for Africa (UN ECA) argues that having timely access to remote sensing data is a powerful tool for regional sustainable development.[5] Several initiatives have been formed to overcome this barrier. Authorized users can call the International Charter on Space or Major Disaster to request information and acquire imagery over the affected area.[6]

Inefficient Operations due to lack of training

Lack of training in disaster and crisis management is one of the main causes that Typhoon Haiyan was able to wreak havoc of such magnitude. While first responders and relief workers are deployed to take control of situation in wake of such disaster, government could also provide training programs to locals who live in storm susceptible areas. What people do before a disaster can make a dramatic difference in their ability to cope with and recover from a disaster, as well as their ability to protect other household members and family possessions from avoidable losses[7]. Ability to decipher warning signs, following evacuation orders, and stocking up with necessary food supplies are some of the preventative measures citizens can take to protect themselves from such disasters.

Typhoon Haiyan demonstrated how locals distrust in the government made them repeatedly ignore evacuations orders. It is the responsibility of citizens to follow procedures and take warning signs seriously and this trust and knowledge can only be entrusted by government officials.

Coping with Disasters without International Support Preparedness

International support is extremely important in coping up with disasters, in terms of additional funding, relief supplies and emergency responders and medical camps. But by the time this support arrives, it is sometimes too late and the damage is already been done. Therefore it is the responsibility of the local administration such as rural hospitals, providers and emergency medical services who will be critical first responders in the event of natural disasters, and they should be equipped with the supplies, training and infrastructure alternatives to protect and safeguard evacuees. Coping without international support can be challenging and requires advance planning and strategy to build a sustainable framework. Being able to mount relief operations and begin disaster recovery is all the more important after the storm has caused devastation. Providing food, shelter, medications, water to victims is an ongoing operation and important in terms of limiting casualties. The Philippine government was slow to respond in its relief work and many casualties were witnessed as a result in the aftermath of Typhoon Haiyan.

Lack of Scientific Basis for Pre-Positioning

Prepositioning of goods before disaster strikes always helps in coping up with the situation and enhancing the relief work. It also saves a lot of money that is spent otherwise in logistics, transportation and personnel after the event has occurred. Pre-positioning relief items in areas vulnerable to natural disaster can save lives, particularly in remote areas. Buying and storing supplies locally brings economic benefits to communities, builds resilience, and means emergency assistance can be delivered at maximum

speed and minimum cost.[8] In the aftermath of the
crisis, having fewer supplies leads to cost spikes from
suppliers, with the government bargaining to procure
items. Governments need to allocate substantial
money for a crisis management plan that includes a
pre-positioning model to save goods and relief items.
Many non-profits agencies are participating in these
programs and governments of areas that are prone to
frequent disasters should consider collaborating with
them and build strategies around it to be better
prepared when a disaster strikes again.

**Previous   Disaster   Experience   and   Future
Preparedness**

Previous disaster experience is helpful in coping with
future disasters. A case in point is Hurricane Sandy
that struck the US East Coast in November 2012.
Authorities were well prepared in advance with
evacuations of the low-lying areas being mandatory
and coasts were secured with surge barriers and sea
gates. The government had learnt its lesson from
Hurricane Katrina back in 2006 and did not want to
see a repeat of it.

Cyclone Phailin that struck the eastern coast of India
in October 2013 was a Category Five tropical storm
that may have affected as many as 12 million people.[9]
This cyclone prompted India's biggest evacuation and
more than 900, 000 people were moved away from the

coastlines to cyclone shelters. Though it was a very severe storm, there were no major casualties reported and the cyclone exited in due course of time. The Indian government's preparedness and effectiveness in carrying out the evacuation and relief work was highly appreciated and averted what would otherwise have been a severe tragedy. But India has seen its fair share of natural disasters most recent being the North India Flash floods that left around 10,000 people trapped in the Himalayan valley. The government was ill-equipped and not prepared at all to deal with the crisis and as a result suffered lot of negative reactions from media and countrymen. This prompted them to take charge in advance and implement emergency procedures when Cyclone Phailin made landfall and the results are there for everyone to see.

These cases point to the fact that governments can and should leverage previous disaster experience to avert tragedies and build safety procedures. Governments can conduct root cause analysis of the actual events and use these experiences to understand lessons learnt, what needs to be done and what went wrong.

Conclusion

The saying that "prevention is better than cure" can't be truer in case of disasters that change our lives forever. While many disaster recovery strategies can be put in place to monitor the impact and prevent from such events, sometimes it is just not enough. Areas that are especially prone to disasters should consider whether it is worth re-building every time. Climate change definitely has had its impact on the frequency of disasters that are occurring every now and then. Keeping in mind these factors governments should seriously monitor these areas and prohibit construction to safeguard its citizens by relocating them and compensating them to build safer lives for themselves. While it is never easy to leave your house and very existence behind and probably easier said than done, it is important to live a safe life and reduce the risk associated with building unsafe places.

---

1 Kuntjoro, Irene and Sofiah Jamil. "Natural Disasters In Indonesia: Strengthening Disaster Preparedness." *East Asia Forum.* 17 Nov. 2013. Accessed Dec. 2013 <www.eastasiaforum.org>

2 Ibid.

3 Lewis, Sian. "Remote Sensing for Natural Disasters: Facts and Figures". *SciDevNet.* 11 Nov. 2009. Accessed Dec. 2013 <www.scidev.net>.

4 Ibid.

5 Ibid.

6 Ibid.

7 *A Citizen's Guide to Disaster Assistance.* Federal Emergency Management Agency. 7 Sep. 2013. Accessed Dec. 2013 <www.training.fema.gov>.

8 Roopanarine, Les. "How Pre-Positioning Can Make Emergency Relief More Effective". *The Guardian.* 17 Jan. 2013. Accessed Dec. 2013 <www.theguardian.co.uk>.

9 Bhalla, Nita. "Cyclone Phailin Threatens 12 Million, Says Disaster Authority." *Reuters.* 12 Oct. 2013. Accessed Dec. 2013 <www.reuters.com>.

www.ingramcontent.com/pod-product-compliance
Lightning Source LLC
Chambersburg PA
CBHW060541200326
41521CB00007B/436